SAS for Finance

Forecasting and data analysis techniques with real-world
examples to build powerful financial models

Harish Gulati

BIRMINGHAM - MUMBAI

SAS for Finance

Commissioning Editor: Amey Varangaonkar
Acquisition Editor: Divya Poojari
Content Development Editor: Amrita Noronha
Technical Editor: Nilesh Sawakhande
Copy Editor: Safis Editing
Project Coordinator: Shweta H Birwatkar
Proofreader: Safis Editing
Indexer: Aishwarya Gangawane
Graphics: Jisha Chirayil
Production Coordinator: Shantanu Zagade

First published: May 2018

Production reference: 1250518

Published by Packt Publishing Ltd.
Livery Place
35 Livery Street
Birmingham
B3 2PB, UK.

ISBN 978-1-78862-456-5

www.packtpub.com

`mapt.io`

Mapt is an online digital library that gives you full access to over 5,000 books and videos, as well as industry leading tools to help you plan your personal development and advance your career. For more information, please visit our website.

Why subscribe?

- Spend less time learning and more time coding with practical eBooks and Videos from over 4,000 industry professionals

- Improve your learning with Skill Plans built especially for you

- Get a free eBook or video every month

- Mapt is fully searchable

- Copy and paste, print, and bookmark content

PacktPub.com

Did you know that Packt offers eBook versions of every book published, with PDF and ePub files available? You can upgrade to the eBook version at `www.PacktPub.com` and as a print book customer, you are entitled to a discount on the eBook copy. Get in touch with us at `service@packtpub.com` for more details.

At `www.PacktPub.com`, you can also read a collection of free technical articles, sign up for a range of free newsletters, and receive exclusive discounts and offers on Packt books and eBooks.

Contributors

About the author

Harish Gulati is a consultant, analyst, modeler, and trainer based in London. He has 15 years' financial, consulting, and project management experience with leading banks, management consultancies, and media hubs. He enjoys demystifying his complex line of work in his spare time. This has led to him being an author and orator at analytical forums. He has also co-authored *Role of a Data Analyst*, published by the British Chartered Institute of IT (BCS). He has an MBA in brand communications and a degree in psychology and statistics.

About the reviewer

Rashmi Gupta is an entrepreneur and consultant for established media and financial brands in the field of marketing and digital analytics. She is currently the director of Agile Fintech Partners. Artificial intelligence is a subject area that interests her, and she is currently building her expertise in the area.

Packt is searching for authors like you

If you're interested in becoming an author for Packt, please visit `authors.packtpub.com` and apply today. We have worked with thousands of developers and tech professionals, just like you, to help them share their insight with the global tech community. You can make a general application, apply for a specific hot topic that we are recruiting an author for, or submit your own idea.

Table of Contents

Preface

SAS is the world's largest privately held software business that offers an integrated suite of software solutions to manage data, produce reports, and build statistical models.

Who this book is for

The book introduces statistical models in the finance industry in a simplified manner. It has real-world examples supported by data and code that reproduces the models. The chapters explain the relevance of the models to business problems, and the discussions about the diagnostics explains how the models can be implemented. The book uses various graphical illustrations, rather than having a focus on equations, to help the reader understand complex models. The book is designed to be a quick introduction to various modeling techniques by explaining their key concepts.

The intended reader is someone aspiring to work in the financial industry, or one of the many financial industry professionals who want to explore its various facets. The reader could also be a student curious to know how theoretical knowledge is applied in the industry, or a finance professional who wants to up-skill and move on to another role. The book's audience may also include any individual who works as a data analyst, data scientist, data architect, data engineer, analytics and insights professional, business analyst, or someone who integrates the outputs of models in business strategy but isn't aware of how problems are solved.

What this book covers

Chapter 1, *Time Series Modeling in the Financial Industry*, introduces time series modeling, and discusses its importance, the characteristics and challenges of data, and explains its use in the financial industry. The chapter also discusses the way forecasting is used across industries and what is meant by a good or bad forecast.

`Chapter` 2, *Forecasting Stock Prices and Portfolio Decisions using Time Series*, discusses the concept of portfolio forecasting and the decisions involved in managing portfolios. After exploring the forecasting process and the visualization of time series data, the chapter discusses modeling techniques and explains how to select the most suitable one based on real-world modeling examples.

`Chapter` 3, *Credit Risk Management*, provides context regarding the highly regulated nature of the industry. Basel norms and key terms such as PD, LGD, EAD, and EL are discussed. A PD model build methodology is briefly discussed.

`Chapter` 4, *Budget and Demand Forecasting*, helps create an understanding of the Markov model and showcases how to build a model. The chapter goes on to compare the Markov model forecast with ARIMA-generated forecasts. It also explains how Markov Chain Monte Carlo can be used for data imputation.

`Chapter` 5, *Inflation Forecasting for Financial Planning*, defines inflation, explores the reasons for inflation, and discusses its outcomes using the theory of the Phillips curve. The chapter also shows how to leverage various procedures for data quality checks. Univariate and multivariate modeling techniques are used for forecasting and a comparison of the results.

`Chapter` 6, *Managing Customer Loyalty using Time Series Data*, introduces survival modeling, data preparation techniques, and various methodologies, including parametric and semi-parametric methods. It does this in the context of solving a business problem related to customer loyalty.

`Chapter` 7, *Transforming Time Series – Market Basket and Clustering*, provides multiple business examples while discussing the background and methodology of these techniques.

To get the most out of this book

Basic knowledge of undergraduate-level mathematics is necessary. However, no advanced mathematical degree is required to decipher how the financial industry uses time series modeling to solve problems. Functional knowledge of SAS is desirable but isn't mandatory.

SAS University Edition is free software that is used throughout the book. Download details can be found at `https://www.sas.com/en_gb/software/university-edition.html`.

Download the example code files

You can download the example code files for this book from your account at www.packtpub.com. If you purchased this book elsewhere, you can visit www.packtpub.com/support and register to have the files emailed directly to you.

You can download the code files by following these steps:

1. Log in or register at www.packtpub.com.
2. Select the **SUPPORT** tab.
3. Click on **Code Downloads & Errata**.
4. Enter the name of the book in the **Search** box and follow the onscreen instructions.

Once the file is downloaded, please make sure that you unzip or extract the folder using the latest version of:

- WinRAR/7-Zip for Windows
- Zipeg/iZip/UnRarX for Mac
- 7-Zip/PeaZip for Linux

The code bundle for the book is also hosted on GitHub at https://github.com/ PacktPublishing/SAS-for-Finance. In case there's an update to the code, it will be updated on the existing GitHub repository.

We also have other code bundles from our rich catalog of books and videos available at https://github.com/PacktPublishing/. Check them out!

Download the color images

We also provide a PDF file that has color images of the screenshots/diagrams used in this book. You can download it here: http://www.packtpub.com/sites/default/files/ downloads/https://github.com/PacktPublishing/SASforFinance_ColorImages.pdf.

Conventions used

There are a number of text conventions used throughout this book.

`CodeInText`: Indicates code words in text, database table names, folder names, filenames, file extensions, pathnames, dummy URLs, user input, and Twitter handles. Here is an example: "The variables `tall` and `grade` have different values for height and scores in a test."

A block of code is set as follows:

```
data matrix (drop = lhand1 lhand2);
set stage2 (drop = id);
if product1 ne product2;
if product1 ne product3;
if product2 ne product3;
combo=compress(product1||product2||product3);
lhand1=scan(combo,1);
lhand2=scan(combo,2);
lhand=compress(lhand1||"|"||lhand2);
run;
```

 Warnings or important notes appear like this.

 Tips and tricks appear like this.

Get in touch

Feedback from our readers is always welcome.

General feedback: Email `feedback@packtpub.com` and mention the book title in the subject of your message. If you have questions about any aspect of this book, please email us at `questions@packtpub.com`.

Errata: Although we have taken every care to ensure the accuracy of our content, mistakes do happen. If you have found a mistake in this book, we would be grateful if you would report this to us. Please visit www.packtpub.com/submit-errata, selecting your book, clicking on the Errata Submission Form link, and entering the details.

Piracy: If you come across any illegal copies of our works in any form on the Internet, we would be grateful if you would provide us with the location address or website name. Please contact us at copyright@packtpub.com with a link to the material.

If you are interested in becoming an author: If there is a topic that you have expertise in and you are interested in either writing or contributing to a book, please visit authors.packtpub.com.

Reviews

Please leave a review. Once you have read and used this book, why not leave a review on the site that you purchased it from? Potential readers can then see and use your unbiased opinion to make purchase decisions, we at Packt can understand what you think about our products, and our authors can see your feedback on their book. Thank you!

For more information about Packt, please visit packtpub.com.

Disclaimer

SAS Institute Inc. hereby grants the author permission to use screenshots of SAS output using SAS® University Edition software. It is with the understanding that the data produced will be customized/provided by the author.

Created with SAS® University Edition software. Copyright 2014, SAS Institute Inc., Cary, NC, USA. All Rights Reserved. Reproduced with permission of SAS Institute Inc., Cary,NC

1
Time Series Modeling in the Financial Industry

A space center is monitoring the weather pattern to schedule a departure time for its latest Martian explorer. An economist is readying his **gross domestic product (GDP)** forecasts to be used by equity traders, who are eager to know if we had a quarter of growth or another economic contraction. In both cases, they are relying on time series data. In the former instance to forecast a weather event, and in the latter to determine which direction GDP forecasts are headed. So, what do we mean by time series?

A series can be defined as a number of events, objects, or people of a similar or related kind coming one after another; if we add the dimension of time, we get a time series. A time series can be defined as a series of data points in time order. For example, the space center will use data from the last few years to predict the weather pattern. The data collection would have started a few years ago and subsequent data points would have given rise to an order in which data was been collected. Another aspect of the data that we usually observe is periodicity. For example, weather data would usually be collected daily, if not hourly. The periodicity of time series data is a slow-moving dimension as it seldom changes. The periodicity of recording observations is broadly driven by three factors, which are relevance, behavior driven, and purpose. In the case of weather patterns, we probably need to know how the weather will change over the course of the day. The **point of sales (POS)** data from debit card transactions of an individual will be recorded every time there is usage. GDP data, however, is usually aggregated in a time series format every quarter, as these numbers are usually reported on a quarterly basis by central banks or related institutions.

In this chapter, we will explore the following topics:

- Time series illustration
- The importance of time series
- Forecasting across industries

- Characteristics of time series data
- Challenges in data
- Good versus bad forecasts
- The use of time series in the financial industry

Time series illustration

The following graph shows the quarterly GDP growth of one of Europe's leading economies. The series has been compiled at a quarterly level, and all data points from 2005 to Q3 in 2017 have been used to plot the graph. We can see that there was a decline in GDP between Q3 in 2006 and Q1 in 2009, but GDP has primarily seen an upward trajectory since then, as follows:

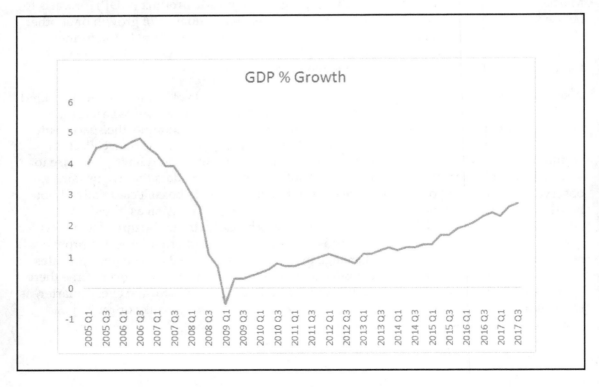

Figure 1.1: GDP quarterly growth of a leading European economy

The importance of time series

What importance, if any, does time series have and how will it be relevant in the future? These are just a couple of fundamental questions that any user should find answers to before delving further into the subject. Let's try to answer this by posing a question. Have you heard the terms big data, **artificial intelligence (AI)**, and **machine learning (ML)**?

These three terms make learning time series analysis relevant. Big data is primarily about a large amount of data that may be analyzed computationally to reveal patterns, trends, and associations, especially relating to human behavior and interaction. AI is a kind of technology that is being developed by data scientists, computational experts, and others to enable processes to become more intelligent, while ML is an enabler that is helping to implement AI. All three of these terms are interlinked with the data they use, and a lot of this data is time series in its nature. This could be either financial transaction data, the behavior pattern of individuals during various parts of the day, or related to life events that we might experience. An effective mechanism that enables us to capture the data, store it, analyze it, and then build algorithms to predict transactions, behavior (and life events, in this instance) will depend on how big data is utilized and how AI and MI are leveraged.

A common perception in the industry is that time series data is used for forecasting only. In practice, time series data is used for:

- Pattern recognition
- Forecasting
- Benchmarking
- Evaluating the influence of a single factor on the time series
- Quality control

For example, a retailer may identify a pattern in clothing sales every time it gets a celebrity endorsement, or an analyst may decide to use car sales volume data from 2012 to 2017 to set a selling benchmark in units. An analyst might also build a model to quantify the effect of Lehman's crash at the height of the 2008 financial crisis in pushing up the price of gold. Variance in the success of treatments across time periods can also be used to highlight a problem, the tracking of which may enable a hospital to take remedial measures. These are just some of the examples that showcase how time series analysis isn't limited to just forecasting. In this chapter, we will review how the financial industry and others use forecasting, discuss what a good and a bad forecast is, and hope to understand the characteristics of time series data and its associated problems.

Forecasting across industries

Since one of the primary uses of time series data is forecasting, it's wise that we learn about some of its fundamental properties. To understand what the industry means by forecasting and the steps involved, let's visit a common misconception about the financial industry: only lending activities require forecasting. We need forecasting in order to grant personal loans, mortgages, overdrafts, or simply assess someone's eligibility for a credit card, as the industry uses forecasting to assess a borrower's affordability and their willingness to repay the debt. Even deposit products such as savings accounts, fixed-term savings, and bonds are priced based on some forecasts. How we forecast and the rationale for that methodology is different in borrowing or lending cases, however. All of these areas are related to time series, as we inevitably end up using time series data as part of the overall analysis that drives financial decisions. Let's understand the forecasts involved here a bit better. When we are assessing an individual's lending needs and limits, we are forecasting for a single person yet comparing the individual to a pool of good and bad customers who have been offered similar products. We are also assessing the individual's financial circumstances and behavior through industry-available scoring models or by assessing their past behavior, with the financial provider assessing the lending criteria.

In the case of deposit products, as long as the customer is eligible to transact (can open an account and has passed **know your customer (KYC)**, **anti-money laundering (AML)**, and other checks), financial institutions don't perform forecasting at an individual level. However, the behavior of a particular customer is primarily driven by the interest rate offered by the financial institution. The interest rate, in turn, is driven by the forecasts the financial institution has done to assess its overall treasury position. The treasury is the department that manages the central bank's money and has the responsibility of ensuring that all departments are funded, which is generated through lending and attracting deposits at a lower rate than a bank lends. The treasury forecasts its requirements for lending and deposits, while various teams within the treasury adhere to those limits. Therefore, a pricing manager for a deposit product will price the product in such a way that the product will attract enough deposits to meet the forecasted targets shared by the treasury; the pricing manager also has to ensure that those targets aren't overshot by a significant margin, as the treasury only expects to manage a forecasted target.

In both lending and deposit decisions, financial institutions do tend to use forecasting. A lot of these forecasts are interlinked, as we saw in the example of the treasury's expectations and the subsequent pricing decision for a deposit product. To decide on its future lending and borrowing positions, the treasury must have used time series data to determine what the potential business appetite for lending and borrowing in the market is, and would have assessed that with the current cash flow situation within the relevant teams and institutions.

Characteristics of time series data

Any time series analysis has to take into account the following factors:

- Seasonality
- Trend
- Outliers and rare events
- Disruptions and step changes

Seasonality

Seasonality is a phenomenon that occurs each calendar year. The same behavior can be observed each year. A good forecasting model will be able to incorporate the effect of seasonality in its forecasts. Christmas is a great example of seasonality, where retailers have come to expect higher sales over the festive period.

Seasonality can extend into months but is usually only observed over days or weeks. When looking at time series where the periodicity is hours, you may find a seasonality effect for certain hours of the day. Some of the reasons for seasonality include holidays, climate, and changes in social habits. For example, travel companies usually run far fewer services on Christmas Day, citing a lack of demand. During most holidays people love to travel, but this lack of demand on Christmas Day could be attributed to social habits, where people tend to stay at home or have already traveled. Social habit becomes a driving factor in the seasonality of journeys undertaken on Christmas Day therefore.

It's easier for the forecaster when a particular seasonal event occurs on a fixed calendar date each year; the issue comes when some popular holidays depend on lunar movement, such as Easter, Diwali, and Eid. These holidays may occur in different weeks or months over the years, which will shift the seasonality effect. Also, if some holidays fall closer to other holiday periods, it may lead to individuals taking extended holidays and travel sales may increase more than expected in such years. The coffee shop near the office may also experience lower sales for a longer period. Changes in the weather can also impact seasonality; for example, a longer, warmer summer may be welcome in the UK, but this would impact retail sales in the autumn as most shoppers wouldn't need to buy a new wardrobe. In hotter countries, sales of air-conditioners would increase substantially compared to the summer months' usual seasonality. Forecasters could offset this unpredictability in seasonality by building in a weather forecast variable. We will explore similar challenges in the chapters ahead.

Seasonality shouldn't be confused with a cyclic effect. A cyclic effect is observed over a longer period of generally two years or more. The property sector is often associated with having a cyclic effect, where it has long periods of growth or slowdown before the cycle continues.

Trend

A trend is merely a long-term direction of observed behavior that is found by plotting data against a time component. A trend may indicate an increase or decrease in behavior. Trends may not even be linear, but a broad movement can be identified by analyzing plotted data.

Outliers and rare events

Outliers and rare events are terminologies that are often used interchangeably by businesses. These concepts can have a big impact on data, and some sort of outlier treatment is usually applied to data before it is used for modeling. It is almost impossible to predict an outlier or rare event but they do affect a trend. An example of an outlier could be a customer walking into a branch to deposit an amount that is 100 times the daily average of that branch. In this case, the forecaster wouldn't expect that trend to continue.

Disruptions

Disruptions and step changes are becoming more common in time series data. One reason for this is the abundance of available data and the growing ability to store and analyze it. Disruptions could include instances when a business hasn't been able to trade as normal. Flooding at the local pub may lead to reduced sales for a few days, for example. While analyzing daily sales across a pub chain, an analyst may have to make note of a disruptive event and its impact on the chain's revenue. Step changes are also more common now due to technological shifts, mergers and acquisitions, and business process re-engineering. When two companies announce a merger, they often try to sync their data. They might have been selling x and y quantities individually, but after the merger will expect to sell $x + y + c$ (where c is the positive or negative effect of the merger). Over time, when someone plots sales data in this case, they will probably spot a step change in sales that happened around the time of the merger, as shown in the following screenshot:

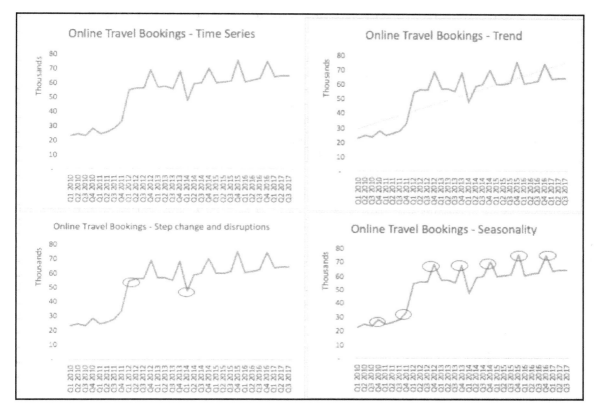

Figure 1.2: Online travel booking chart showing characteristics of time series

In the trend graph, we can see that online travel bookings are increasing. In the step change and disruptions chart, we can see that Q1 of 2012 saw a substantive increase in bookings, where Q1 of 2014 saw a substantive dip. The increase was due to the merger of two companies that took place in Q1 of 2012. The decrease in Q1 of 2014 was attributed to prolonged snow storms in Europe and the ash cloud disruption from volcanic activity over Iceland. While online bookings kept increasing after the step change, the disruption caused by the snow storm and ash cloud only had an effect on sales in Q1 of 2014. In this case, the modeler will have to treat the merger and the disruption differently while using them in the forecast, as disruption could be disregarded as an outlier and treated accordingly. Also note that the seasonality chart shows that Q4 of each year sees almost a 20% increase in travel bookings, and this pattern continues each calendar year.

Challenges in data

If your client says they have an abundance of good quality data, be sure to take it with a pinch of salt. Data collection and processing are cost – and time-intensive tasks. There is always a chance that some data within the organization may not be of as high a quality as another data set. The problems in time series are often compounded by the time element. Due to challenges in data, organizations need to recalculate metrics and make changes to historical data, source additional data and build a mechanism to store it, as well as reconcile data when there are different definitions of data or a new data source doesn't reconcile with the previous sources. Data processing and collection may not be difficult for an organization if the requirement was for data going forward; historical data recalibration across a large time period, on the other hand, will present some challenges, as shown in the following diagram:

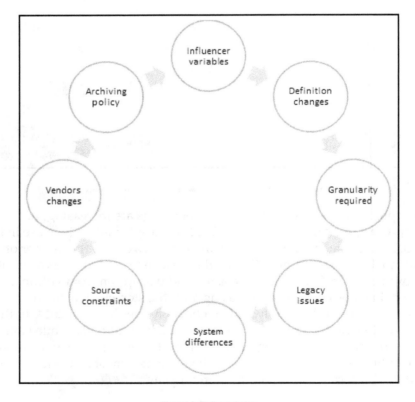

Figure 1.3: Challenges in data

Influencer variables

The relationship between the forecasted and dependent variable and other influencer or independent variables changes over a period of time. For example, most forecasting models weren't able to predict the global economic crash of 2008. Post-crash, modelers in a leading bank tried to rebuild their models with new variables that would be able to predict behavior better. Some of these new influencer variables weren't available in the central database. A vendor was selected to provide history and a continuing data feed to enable the availability of such variables in the future. In this case, since the influencer variables changed, the modeler had to look outside the scope of available variables in the central database and try to find better fitting variables.

Definition changes

A financial institution recently changed its definition of defaulting as it moved from a standard approach to an advanced, internal rating-based approach to potentially reduce its capital requirements and credit risk. The change to the Basel definition means that the institution's entire historical database needed to be modified. In this case, the new default definition in the institution is calculated using at least six other variables that need to be stored and checked for data quality across several years.

Granularity required

After changing influencer variables and running models for a couple of years, a modeler was informed by a data team that the central bank is planning to stop providing granular data for one of the modeling variables and that the metric would still be published but in an aggregated manner. This may impact the usability of such data for modeling purposes. A change in a variable in a regulatory environment has multiple overheads. In this scenario, the modeler would have to engage with the data team to understand which variable can be used as a substitute. The IT team would then have to ensure that variable (if not already available as a regular feed) is made available to the data team and the modeler. The material impact of the change in the variable on the modeling output would also have to be studied and documented. There might be an instance where a modeling governance team has to be notified of changes in the model. In an ideal governance environment, if code changes are to accommodate a new variable, testing would be undertaken before any change is implemented. A simple change in variable granularity can trigger the need for multiple subsequent tasks.

Legacy issues

Legacy issues may mean that some amount of information isn't available in the central database. This could be due to the fact that a system was upgraded recently and didn't have the capability to capture some data.

System differences

System differences arise because of a user's behavior or the way systems process data. Users of a telephone banking **customer relationship management** (**CRM**) system, for example, may not be capturing the incoming details of its callers, whereas branch officers using a different CRM frontend will be. The branch data may only be sparsely available (only when the customer divulges income), but has the potential to be more accurate.

Source constraints

Source constraints could arise simply because of the way some systems are designed. A system designed to store data at a customer level will not be able to efficiently store data that has been aggregated at an account level, for example. Vendor changes may impact data quality or the frequency of when data is available. Organizations also have differing archival policies, so if a modeler is looking to use time series data that goes as far back as a decade, some of this data may have already been archived and retrieval may be a time-consuming affair.

Vendor changes

Most organizations end up using a particular vendor for a long period of time. In some instances, it is the bank's transactional data system, in others the CRM tool or data mining software. In all of these cases, there is dependency on a vendor. Most vendors would like to develop a relationship with their client and grow alongside them, where contracts would be re-negotiated but with greater functionality and scalable software provided. There are times, however, when a client and a vendor decide to part ways. Be mindful that this can be a painful exercise and a lot of things can go wrong. Such a transition might lead to temporary or long-term breaks in data; some systems may be switched off and the new system replacing it might not be able to capture data in the same manner. A vendor who supplied customer leads or risk ratings may no longer be contracted and data quality may even suffer from a new vendor. Businesses and modelers need to be aware of these challenges.

Archiving policy

There is an archiving and retrieval policy in place in most organizations. However, retrieval can take time and may also lead to higher costs for sourcing data. These constraints could easily put off a modeler from exploring historical data that may have been archived. Archiving policy should therefore be based on the importance of the data, the regulatory requirement, and the ease of data retrieval.

Good versus bad forecasts

Forecasting plays a fundamental role in ensuring the success and future viability of an organization. The famous camera and film company Kodak failed to forecast the growth of digital photography, for example, and has now fallen behind its peers. Coca-Cola had to famously ramp up its own production after pulling the curtains on its revamped Coke New in response to a surge in popularity of Pepsi in the 1980s. Because of this, Coke miscalculated the potential popularity of its new formula and branding and instead went back to its core formula and started calling it Classic Coke. As we can see, most business decisions involve estimates or forecasts. These decisions can range from opening a new manufacturing facility to launching a new product range, opening up more stores, or even launching a new mobile application.

Since forecasting is so integral to the whole business process, it is important to get the forecast as accurate as possible. Seldom will you see a forecast that is the exact quantity of the observed event. However, it isn't rare to see forecasts miss their objective by a wide margin either. There are various statistical measures that we will cover in upcoming chapters that will help us to assess the probable success of a model's forecast. For now, let's first assess the following factors that define the quality of forecasts produced:

- **Subject area**: Forecasting accuracy depends on what is being forecasted and its application. In the earlier example of a spacecraft being readied for launch, the accuracy of the weather forecast cannot be wrong by a significant margin as the cost of getting it wrong will be high. However, if you are simply planning a picnic, the costs of getting the weather forecast wrong are completely different.

- **Consistency**: One of the most difficult tasks in the corporate world is to get peers in various teams to trust the model that generates forecasts. An inconsistent model isn't going to help in convincing others to support the model through budget allocation or ensuring that the output is consistently used. Any model needs testing, and validation data in ideal circumstances, before it is formally signed off. If a model is replacing a manual process, then it might be a good idea to conduct a pilot or parallel run where the model and the manual input both act as inputs. This might help overcome any teething problems when making the model operational, and may also highlight any concerns before the model gets a reputation.

- **Error margins**: In most cases, the brief for any forecasting model is to get it right–but get it right by what percentage? Is there an acceptable tolerance? And should a model be right all the time? A model isn't a crystal ball, and there will be instances when forecasts aren't right or miss the mark within a reasonable level. While sharing forecasts, a modeler should provide a confidence level that implies a margin for error. A business' expectation of the error margin may be different, so it is best to discuss this prior to building.

- **Rare events**: In hindsight, rare events are relatively simple to model. You will probably see a big crest or trough in a time series line plot and will therefore be able to make out a significant event. If it's a rare event, dummy variable creation should help smooth out its effect. If another rare event occurs in the future, a model might not be able to deal with it effectively. There is always a possibility of this happening and the impact of rare events is unpredictable. A modeler should be able to interpret an event's effects and communicate with stakeholders on the relationship between the event and their forecast, as well as if the model needs recalibrating.

- **Judgment versus modeled forecasts**: In any large organization, there will be individuals who might think they can predict a scenario better than a model. They might deal with the forecasted scenario more closely than the modeler, they might have some inherent bias towards an outcome, or they might feel that the model doesn't take into account factors that they think are important. Rather than taking a skeptical view of such individuals, a modeler should try and engage them to see if their model can learn from their experiences.

- **Volatile environment**: Will a model's performance be the same in both a volatile and stable period? Post-Lehman crisis, the interest rates of major central banks have nosedived. The two scenarios that a model would probably forecast in this scenario is that the central bank will hold rates or revise them downwards. Once the US Federal Bank starts revising rates upwards, other banks might follow. So, will the model be able to correctly forecast the rate rise and be able to effectively predict for an alternative scenario? A model that incorporates good explanatory variables should ideally be able to predict rate rises and accommodate for other scenarios; however, not all models continue to perform well and any deterioration may prompt the need for model recalibration or a rebuild.

- **Assessing period**: Some models are built for a one-off objective, whereas others are built into **business as usual** (**BAU**) processes and will generate forecasts for years to come. The benchmark for judging forecasts as good or bad should depend on the assessing period. Another aspect of the assessing period to take note of is its length. A weather model might be more accurate when forecasting a day ahead but not when forecasting a month ahead, for example. The monthly forecast model might need to use different variables and methodology, and so this model might not be fit for purpose in this case. A modeler should therefore try to build separate models for predicting the risk of default by a customer at any point in time versus any time in the next 12 months. A regulator might also require that certain businesses and models are validated every few months or years to ensure they are fit for purpose.

Use of time series in the financial industry

The financial industry has managed to find varied uses for time series. Some of the uses we are going to cover are as follows:

- Predicting stock prices and making portfolio decisions
- Adhering to Basel norms
- Demand planning
- Inflation forecasting
- Managing customer journeys and maintaining loyalty

Predicting stock prices and making portfolio decisions

Stock price prediction is based on the assumption that the efficient market hypothesis doesn't hold true. The efficient market hypothesis states that, at any point, the price of stock is already reflective of all information and rational expectations. Hence, no amount of insight generated from historical price trends or influencer variables will predict the stock price movement effectively. There is academic evidence to support the efficient market hypothesis, but also an acknowledgement that there are some individuals and institutions who have managed to beat the average returns of the stock market by using their judgment. However, it is worth noting that stock prices are highly reactive to news and events, and also seem to be driven by both rational and irrational expectations. Time series data does have a role to play in predicting stock prices but its application is changing. In predicting stock prices, the problem isn't the availability of data but rather about cancelling out the noise and finding the real reasons that a stock moves.

Time series is also helpful when making portfolio decisions. Unlike stock prices, which can change by the second, portfolio decisions are taken over a slightly longer time-frame, ranging from a day to years. Time series data can help us understand the elements of an investment portfolio, the expected returns in a number of years, and even the probable behavior of investors once they re-invest their money from a maturity fixed bond into available products in the market.

Adhering to Basel norms

Basel norms were introduced by the **Basel Committee on Bank Supervision (BCBS)**, which set out the minimum capital requirements that financial institutions need to hold to minimize credit risk. What started out as a voluntary framework that institutions were free to adopt is now a key requirement for some central banks. The Basel norms have been revised to safeguard against the growing risks that financial institutions face. Time series data is used to build various models related to the probability of default and various other metrics that help in assessing credit risk and deciding the level of capital that institutions need to hold to offset risk. The **Prudential Regulatory Authority (PRA)** in the UK and similar federal organizations regulate and monitor adherence to the Basel norms.

Demand planning

Any organization, industry sector, or government body needs to estimate demand for products or services. The estimation needs to be primarily done at the firm and industry level, as there might be many more models required within one firm to estimate demand. A finance team may use demand estimation models to assess its funding needs; an inventory management team may assess consumer demand and its current production levels to assess stock needs and plan production accordingly. At times, forecasting might happen at a macro level, for example involving the economy, market sizing, and so on. A company planning to diversify into a new sector will want to know what the current market demand is, how much is it expected to grow by, and what proportion of this market can be captured as a new entrant in what might be a crowded marketplace of established players. Demand planning helps with all of these scenarios.

Inflation forecasting

Inflation is a measure that affects all aspects of our life, including earnings and spending power. It is produced by central banks, or some other nominated government institution, and is used as a benchmark to assess the health of the economy and set expectations on the level of future earnings to ensure sufficient returns on investment. Various levels of inflation can highlight different problems in the economy. Japan can be considered as a classic example of experiencing deflation, where a government tries to increase spending through various measures to get the inflation rate higher. Run-away inflation in Zimbabwe and Venezuela has caused havoc for its residents, on the other hand, while the Eurozone is struggling to get inflation to a meaningful growth rate. Whatever the rate of inflation, forecasting it using time series data is of the utmost importance.

Managing customer journeys and maintaining loyalty

Managing customer journeys and maintaining loyalty aren't the most obvious uses of time series data, but by assessing the history of customers' past product choices, transactional data, and their engagement with an organization, you can try to manage this customer journey. After all, in most instances, it is much cheaper to keep a customer loyal and onboard than to acquire a new customer.

Summary

In this chapter, we defined time series and learned why it is important for forecasting. We looked at the characteristics of time series data, and we also explored the challenges associated with it when we try to make forecasts. Lastly, we looked at the use of time series in various industries. In the next chapter, we will learn how to forecast stock prices using time series data modeling.

References

Please refer to the following articles:

- Lo, A.W. and Mackinlay, A.C. *A Non-Random Walk Down Wall Street* 5th Ed. Princeton University Press, 2002
- Shumway, R. H. (1988). *Applied statistical time series analysis*. Englewood Cliffs, NJ: Prentice Hall. ISBN0130415006.
- Gershenfeld, N. (1999). *The Nature of Mathematical Modeling*. New York: Cambridge University Press. pp. 205-208. ISBN0521570956.

2
Forecasting Stock Prices and Portfolio Decisions using Time Series

I wish I had put more money into this stock. I should have trusted my technical analysis. I need to trust my broker. My gut feeling told me I should have cut my losses. Aren't these all statements that we have heard individuals involved in stock markets say at some point?

With a stock price, you can instantly see the impact of getting forecast right or wrong. It pays to be right. But if it were so simple, anyone could forecast the closing price of a blue-chip share and make millions. Maybe if it were so simple, there wouldn't be anything to distinguish investors, and the returns for everyone investing would be smaller, as the winning prize would be split across millions of investors. The ability to make the right call on investment decisions is what differentiates successful and unsuccessful investors and brokers.

In this chapter, we will look at statistical methodologies for forecasting stock prices. Is the financial world only interested in forecasting the price of one stock, or a basket of stocks? Are statistical models supposed to behave independently of the other intricacies of the decision process about where to invest? To answer these questions, we will explore:

- Portfolio forecasting
- Decisions involved in managing portfolios
- The forecasting process
- Visualizations of time series data
- Modeling techniques to solve a business problem
- Evaluating techniques to select the best solution

Portfolio forecasting

The use of forecasting, and, in particular, using time series forecasting, goes beyond the scope of a few stocks. Hence, in this chapter, we will also cover the forecasting of portfolios. A portfolio can be defined as simply a range of investments held by a person or organization. An individual may have multiple stocks. Thus, the need to look at the scenarios where investment in a single stock needs to be assessed against holdings in other stocks. Certainly, there must also be other investment instruments that a person can hold. What about gold, bonds, real estate, and the now in vogue cryptocurrencies, such as Bitcoin?

Most organizations deal with multiple items in a portfolio. These items are usually spread across asset and liability classes. The portfolio usually isn't compiled in a day. It evolves over a period of time, and there are entrants and leavers. There is also competition among the various constituents of a portfolio. Are this year's retained earnings for a company going to be invested in fixed deposits, or are a part of the earnings going to be invested in government bonds? There's bound to be questions about the best avenue for investing the money. At the time of investment, the most logical choice would be to go for the option that offers the highest rate of return.

A portfolio demands decisions

A company that decides to invest all of its money in fixed deposits, rather than in government bonds, will have more decisions to make. At some point in time, the cash flow of the company will increase or decrease. If it increases, there might be further investment decisions, and a need to decide between various investment choices. Again, the easiest choice would be to go for the option that offers the highest rate of return. But what about putting all of your eggs in one basket? Shouldn't the company think about the need to diversify? Is the option of fixed deposits as attractive as last time? Interest rates might have moved, or the fixed term on offer could be different. And what about using the funds to expand, rather than investing? Suppose that this tranche of funds available for investment is expected to be invested for a longer time period than the previous tranche was invested. If a longer-term product isn't available, or isn't the best choice available for investment, then the matured funds will probably need to be invested again, until they reach the time horizon when the company wishes to utilize them again for non-investment purposes:

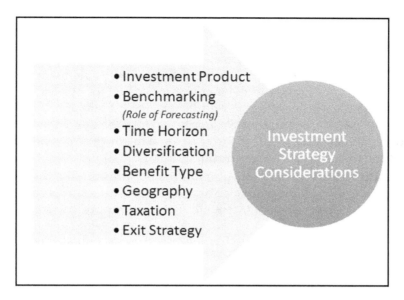

Figure 2.1: Investment strategy considerations and role of forecasting

Now, let's discuss investment strategy considerations in detail:

- **Investment product**: The modeler needs to understand investment strategy considerations in order to play an effective role. The investment strategy considerations aren't ordered by a particular sequence, as each element is important. The relative weight of the elements will vary, on a case-by case basis. The product is an element that needs to be considered in each case. Apart from the statistical aspect, the modeler will need to understand the product features and nuances of the market that operates it. In the majority of cases, modelers are experts in a particular asset class, owing to the focus of their team in the organization.

- **Benchmarking**: The role of a forecasting model is to help benchmark the various investment products being considered. When dealing with multiple options to invest, an informed choice is what the investor is looking for. At times, the product being considered guarantees certain payments over a period of time. A fixed deposit states the percentage of interest that will be earned by investing a certain capital amount over a particular period of time. In this instance, the time period is known, the capital requirement known, and we even know how much interest can be earned. Even with all of the information, forecasting has a role to play in benchmarking this investment product against various available scenarios.

- **Time horizon**: We already briefly touched on a company's dilemma of investing a second tranche for a longer time horizon than the first tranche of retained earnings, invested in fixed deposits. Within the five years that the company wants to invest the money for, the country where the company operates is going to see federal elections, and the markets are poised for at least a 200 basis points increase (a 2% rate increase over the central bank's rate). Further, inflation is expected to hover around the 3% mark, up from the low 1% where it currently stands. The company will have to take these factors into consideration when investing over the five-year time horizon.

- **Diversification**: The company also has the opportunities to diversify and spread the risk across multiple asset classes. The real estate sector is something that the company has been eyeing for a while. They could purchase something with an eye to sell in five years, or further develop the real estate into a commercial enterprise. Diversification into various asset classes helps when gains from one asset class balance out lower growth in another asset class.

- **Benefit type**: Some asset classes also provide a particular benefit. A bond or a fixed deposit could guarantee a coupon rate or a regular interest payment over the course of an investment. This is a regular inflow that could help the company's overall cash flow. Buying US Treasury bonds may seem less exciting than investing in the stock market, but the former gives the benefit of a practically risk-free investment. The nature of benefits offered by investments may swing investment decisions. Cryptocurrencies are non-regulated to a large extent, and that's been one of the reasons for the rise of Bitcoin. However, major stock markets, and the stocks that trade on them, are regulated. If the company in question is large and has a variety of shareholders, there might be differing opinions on whether investments should be headed for a regulated or unregulated market. These benefits seem to be intangible, but they could weigh heavily on investment decisions.

- **Geography**: Some portfolios focus on certain markets. This doesn't mean that they aren't exposed to markets that they aren't explicitly present in. An upheaval in the credit market in China would have an impact on all major economies, irrespective of whether a country is invested in China. Diversification isn't just about investing in various products. One way to diversify is to invest in various geographies. There are rules and regulations about various geographies that need to be contemplated before investing. These relate to how much can be invested, what assets can be bought, taxation, and so on.

- **Taxation**: Many government projects are funded by giving a tax break to investments made by the general public. The tax-free threshold of an individual's personal income is also guaranteed at times when the taxpayer invests the funds in a certain type of government or privately held fixed deposit, bond, mutual fund, and so on. Furthermore, a proportion of interest earned on some schemes is declared tax-free. The interest rates in these schemes may not be the market leading rates. However, some of these schemes retain their popularity. Apart from the tax breaks offered, the scheme might be popular because it has been around for a long time, there is a government guarantee to protect the funds in case of a fiscal crisis, the product is available to invest every year, or because recently offered interest rates or the threshold that can be invested in these schemes have increased. Usually, any profit made via an asset sale is subject to tax. In some asset classes, there is a tax on acquiring the asset. Real estate is typically taxed by a stamp duty at the time of acquisition. A value-added tax on the transaction costs of buying and selling stocks is another way the government taxes investments. Some countries tax an inheritance that is passed over to loved ones. The modeler, in all probabilities, won't be dealing with the accountancy aspect of the tax, but needs to be aware of how a tax on a product influences the investment choice.

- **Exit strategy**: This is an element that is relevant to all investment decisions. A fixed term deposit can be exited at the end of a term. Still, it is worth reading the fine print on the cost of exiting before the end of the fixed term. The investor may have found a better deal somewhere, or may just need the invested capital for other purposes. Pensions usually tend to have the longest lock-in period. A risk-averse person may contribute more to such a product, to average out the earnings over the years, whereas a risk taker may only invest a minimum amount, trying to test his luck with investments in other areas. Hence, the exit strategy will always influence the investment decision, and the level of weight assigned to this element will vary on a case-to-case basis.

Forecasting process

The forecasting process, illustrated in the following diagram, represents a typical process flow that can be applied to both time series and other models. There isn't a stage in the process that is more important than others. However, a good understanding of the business problem should be the building block of any modeling process:

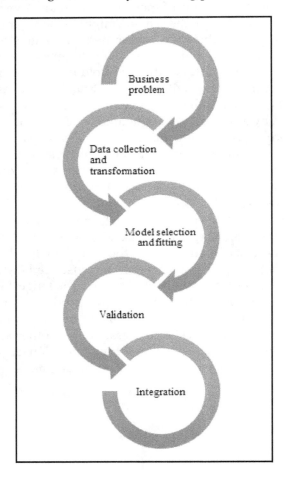

Figure 2.2: Forecasting process

Let us walk through the process of forecasting:

1. Define the business problem and state what the model expects to achieve.
2. Collect data from various sources and systems and transform it to clean data.
3. Plot the data, run statistical tests, fit the model, and interpret the results.
4. Validate the model by using a holdout sample.
5. Obtain a model sign after it meets the technical and the business requirements. Integrate it into the business process.

Most modelers spend a disproportionate amount of time on data, modeling, and validation tasks. At times, the business problem gets modified by the addition or deletion of scope. This causes problems for the modeler, as modeling times seldom get adjusted to deal with a retrospective change in scope. Another aspect related to the business problem that isn't explicitly mentioned in the forecasting process is the interaction with the **subject matter experts** (**SMEs**). The back and forth dialogue with the SMEs adds quality and perspective to the modeling process. This can also be a challenging task, given the timelines involved. However, a conversation during the modeling process can ensure that there are no surprises for anyone involved in the project. This aids in the integration of the model into the business process.

The larger the organization, the greater the risk that the modeler will not be involved in the integration of the modeling output. Modeling becomes a specialized unit in large organizations, and the modeler is involved only indirectly in the implementation. However, feedback processes do exist, and the modeler should request an update and ensure that the model is performing as expected. In some of the models, where there is an operational need to keep running the model, a monitoring aspect is also involved. This is a more formal process, where interaction with the business is higher than with a model that was built as a one-off.

Visualization of time series data

With an increase in software, there is also the option to use fancy charts to visualize data, while creating a better understanding of the underlying story. However, some charts don't work as well with time series data. The line chart is the one that works best for almost all business cases. Let's explore the case of the growth over lending in the last three years:

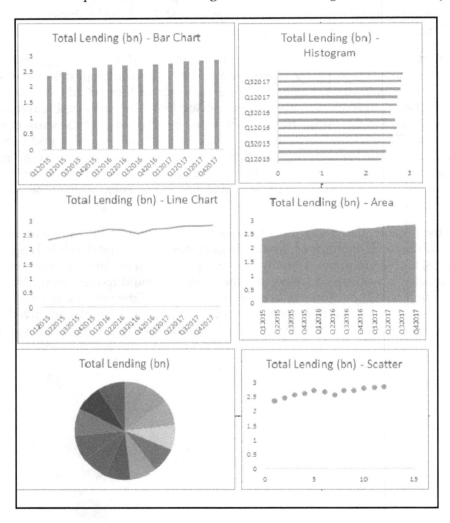

Figure 2.3: Visualization of time series

All of the six charts are trying to tell the same story. The bank has seen lending grow from £2.35 billion to £2.84 billion between 2015 and 2017. However, some of the charts are much better placed to tell the story. The best placed is the line chart, which depicts the time on the x-axis and the value of lending on the y-axis. As we read the chart, it becomes apparent that the line shows a growth in lending. The bar chart gives us the scale of the lending by highlighting the level of lending in the various sizes of the bars across the time. However, the bars seem like a pointless addition to the line. The area chart suffers from the same issue, where the shaded area region is an extra bit of information below the line that it depicts. In both the bar and the area chart, the shaded area doesn't add much value. The histogram confuses matters slightly, as it is a bit difficult to realize the upward trajectory of lending over the years, since the volume of lending is on the x-axis, rather than the y-axis. The scatter plot is quite similar to the line chart in the way it depicts the growth of lending. With more history to plot, we would be better off going with the line chart and having an explicit line connecting the points, rather than just seeing a scatter plot. The pie chart is the most unsuited to describe the growth in lending, as it would be a painful exercise to add up the information represented by each chart. The pie chart would have to be labeled more accurately, and even then it wouldn't be as good a representative of the data in this instance.

These six charts help to illustrate how the visualization of the data is important. The same data shown using different mediums can alter the story it conveys. As a data consumer, publisher, or analyst, it's important to be conscious of the way charts are used to visualize the data. The line chart is the best suited to convey simple growth or a decrease of numbers over a time period. Other charts do have uses when evaluating time series data. Scatter plots can help us evaluate the relationship between two variables that explain a growth in lending. We will be using scatter plots later on in the chapter to depict such relationships.

Business case study

Let's discuss the need for modeling a hedge fund. Mr. Jefferson has just switched over to a niche hedge fund. He has years of experience in handling larger portfolios, but he has decided to shift to a smaller hedge fund as a partner. The place isn't as organized as the larger hedge funds with access to proprietary algorithms that run based on machine learning principles and manage a lot of the buy and sell transactions based on the hedge fund's goals. In this smaller and newer hedge fund, the aim is to slowly build a portfolio that delivers market-leading returns, thereby attracting newer clients. Mr. Jefferson has been asked, by the director, to recommend stocks that he would like to invest in, and his initial first-month portfolio has been assigned £10 million.

One of the stocks that Jefferson noticed that the hedge fund doesn't invest its client money in is a particular mobile phone manufacturer. It seemed peculiar to him that the fund has resisted the temptation to invest in a stock that most clients would like to hold.

To convince his director to invest in this stock, Jefferson needed to write a research report describing various aspects of the stock. Apart from doing the technical analysis, qualitative research, and other tasks for the report, he wanted to build a forecasting model. The research report would probably convince the director to invest. But the forecasting model would showcase that the hedge fund could predict the stock movement with a certain degree of accuracy. This would enable the hedge fund to actively manage the investments. Jefferson's goal wasn't just to invest his portfolio allocation; he wanted to create a proprietary algorithm for managing funds at the hedge fund. The forecasting model was just a start, to get the conversation going with the director.

Jefferson summarized the business problem:

- Build a forecasting model to predict the stock of a mobile phone manufacturer
- Assess its predicting power

Data collection and transformation

The stock price information was readily available from multiple sources. The modeler stored the stock price over the last couple of years. This information was collected on a daily basis. While getting the historical price movement wasn't a challenge, assessing which predictor variables could be important for the model was definitely intriguing. The modeler decided to use a bunch of financial ratios, econometric variables, and competitor-related information to build the model.

Financial ratios were important, as Mr. Jefferson wanted to test the significance of ratios used in the industry to predict the share price. A portfolio manager should always assess these sorts of ratios. The manager may decide to place a varying level of weight while investing, but these ratios are hard to ignore. The econometric variables, according to the modeler, were important, as there are a lot of economic factors that may be driving the share price. The competitor-related information is important, as the manufacturer of interest is one of many in a crowded mobile market. The fates of the manufacturers are interlinked. Product launches happen frequently, and customers switch loyalties at times, depending on the features and pricing of the products.

Let's take a look at the variables selected for modeling:

- Financial ratios and information:
  - **Earnings per share** (**EPS**): This is the earnings per outstanding shares of common equity of a company. It is one of the most important indicators of a company's performance. This ratio informs on the value that is available to stockholders. The higher the EPS, the more attractive it is for investors.
  - **Price (PE) ratio**: This is related to the EPS, as it is used as the denominator when calculating the PE ratio. A high PE ratio may be considered to be an average level for stocks of a different industry. However, given the stocks of two similar companies, the company with the lower PE ratio might be more attractive to the investor, as the upside potential of the stock price may be higher.
  - **M1 money supply**: This is the money supply of a country that is monitored by the central banks. The modeler, in this instance, created an index of the M1 money supply of the top 10 economies in the world.
- Econometric variables:
  - **Gross Domestic Product (GDP) of selected economies**: The modeler has created an index of the GDP of the top 10 economies in the world.
  - **Inflation of selected countries**: The modeler has created an index of the inflation of the top 10 economies in the world.
- Competitor and market related:
  - **Global market share**: This is the percentage of the global market share that the mobile manufacturer in question has.
  - **Competitor basket index**: This is an index of the growth of stock prices of major mobile manufacturing competitors.

- **Media analytics index**: All of the news stories from major publications, opinions, and social media chatter are aggregated by certain media companies and given a score. The score represents how favorably the company is being perceived. The modeler wanted to include this as a probable significant predictor, as the product launches are debated intensively in the mainstream and social media.

The transformation that was done by the modeler was primarily to create various indexes. The indexes show the changes in value or percentage across various time periods. The base value of the indexes has been kept as 100 (or 100%). Any decrease in the value pushes the index below 100, and any increase keeps it above the base level. Different indexes used by the modeler are updated at various time intervals. The media analytics index is updated monthly, the GDP index quarterly, and the global market share on a six-monthly basis.

The predictor variables were sourced by the modeler from various sources, and underwent some sort of transformation or data cleaning. The stock price data didn't undergo any transformation. The modeler decided to do a data check prior to modeling. He ran the PROC UNIVARIATE code and produced the following output:

PROC UNIVARIATE code:

```
PROC UNIVARIATE DATA=raw;
ID date;
VAR stock;
RUN;
```

The PROC UNIVARIATE partial output was as follows:

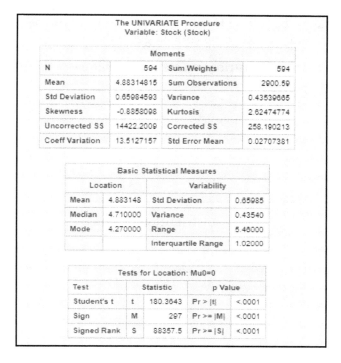

Figure 2.4.1: Data quality check using PROC UNIVARIATE

To understand the computation of the basic statistical measures, the modeler turned his attention to the output box of the extreme observations. These observations had the biggest hand in the variance that was captured by the statistical measures. He noticed that the value 0.37 of stock stood out as being quite low, given that the mean, median, and mode of the variable were all above 4:

Extreme Observations					
Lowest			Highest		
Value	Date	Obs	Value	Date	Obs
0.37	07/13/2016	203	5.81	12/21/2017	585
3.43	11/11/2015	30	5.81	12/24/2017	588
3.43	11/06/2015	27	5.82	12/22/2017	586
3.43	11/03/2015	24	5.82	12/26/2017	589
3.43	11/02/2015	23	5.83	12/23/2017	587

Figure 2.4.2: Data quality check using PROC UNIVARIATE

He wanted to understand the impact that this observation had on the normal distribution plot of the variable. He ran the following code to generate the normal distribution plot.

The `PROC UNIVARIATE` normal distribution code is as follows:

```
PROC UNIVARIATE DATA=raw;
HISTOGRAM Stock / normal(percents=20 40 60 80 midpercents)
                   name='MyPlot';
INSET n normal(ksdpval) / pos = ne format = 6.3;
RUN;
```

The output is as follows:

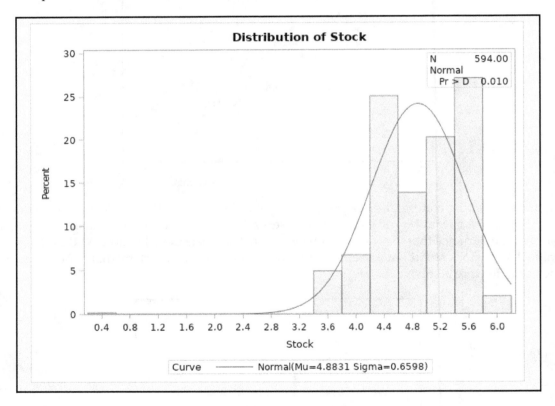

Figure 2.5: Normal distribution plot

The normal distribution is just one of many distributions used to describe the spread of the data. The normal distribution is among the most widely used distributions, and is also called a bell curve. It plots the probability distribution of stock, in this case. Most of the values of stock are expected to be around the mean, and the variables are expected to be equally distributed around the center. A normal distribution is defined by its mean and standard deviation. A standard normal curve has a mean $\mu = 0$, and standard deviation $\sigma = 1$. If the dataset is normal distributed, then 68% of all observations are within $\sigma = 1$, and 95% of them fall within $\sigma = 2$.

In the case of the stock, the modeler noticed a couple of things. Towards the mean, most distributions have a value of around 4.5 or 5.5 U.S. dollars. He also noticed that there seems to be a particular data point with a very high standard deviation that is falling outside the bell curve, and is located towards the left side of the distribution. Upon further investigation, the modeler realized that there is a stock value of 0.37 on July 13, 2016. This was an error in the creation of the SAS dataset, and, in fact, the value of stock observed on July 13, 2016, was 4.37. After correcting this, another PROC UNIVARIATE was performed. The result is as follows.

The PROC UNIVARIATE normal distribution code is as follows:

```
PROC UNIVARIATE DATA=model;
HISTOGRAM Stock / normal(percents=20 40 60 80 midpercents)
                name='MyPlot';
INSET n normal(ksdpval) / pos = ne format = 6.3;
RUN;
```

| Extreme Observations | | | |
| Lowest | | Highest | |
Value	Obs	Value	Obs
3.43	30	5.81	588
3.43	27	5.82	586
3.43	24	5.82	589
3.43	23	5.83	587
3.44	34	5.96	583

Figure 2.6.1: PROC UNIVARIATE after data cleansing

As we can now see from *Figure 2.6.1*, the change in the value from 0.37 to 4.37 has meant that the extreme observations have a lower range than when compared to *Figure 2.4.2*:

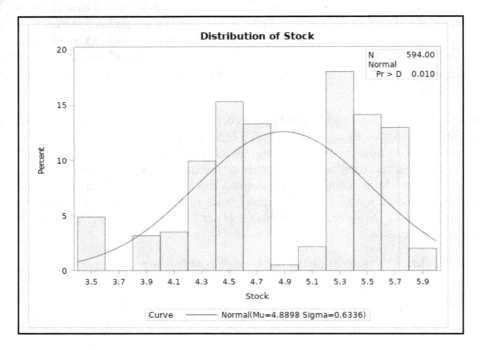

Figure 2.6.2: PROC UNIVARIATE after data cleansing

After changing the value of one observation from 0.37 to 4.37, the modeler observed a marked difference in the normal distribution plot. This plot looks more symmetrical than the earlier plot. The earlier plot had a bit of a negative skew, or what could be called a left tail. The distribution was spread towards the right side of the chart, with the outlier of 0.37 creating a longer left tail. The range of the value of the stock has also reduced, and the minimum and maximum observed values look more in sync with the observed stock prices of the mobile manufacturer.

Model selection and fitting

The modeler decided to test which of the variables could be important in predicting the variable stock. PROC CORR was run to test the relative strength of the predictor (independent/regressor) variables and the outcome (dependent) variable.

The PROC correlation code is as follows:

```
PROC CORR DATA=model outp=corr nosimple;
ID Date;
WITH Stock;
VAR Basket_index -- M1_money_supply_index;
RUN;
```

The correlation was run across all of the eight independent variables. The correlation values were expected to be between -1 and 1. The negative sign denotes that the dependent and independent variables are inversely correlated. The higher the value of the correlation coefficient close to -1 or 1, the greater the strength of the variables concerned:

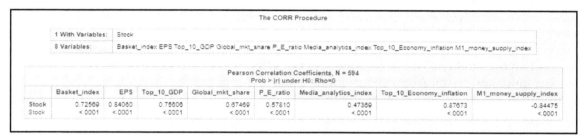

Figure 2.7: Correlation output

The least correlated variable seems to be the media analytics index. However, at this point, the modeler was cautious to not confuse the strength of the correlation with the significance. Later on, the modeler was planning to test for significance. The modeler wanted to do that to ascertain whether something that is strongly correlated is also significant in explaining the variation in the dependent variable. One other check that he was planning to do later on was for multicollinearity. Multicollinearity is said to occur when two or more similar, independent variables are highly correlated with a dependent variable. For example, if we are trying to predict the on-time arrival of a train, instances where a particular train has the highest speed and also the fewest stops might both show a high correlation with the on-time arrival of a train. However, both the highest speed and fewest stops could be highly correlated themselves, as the railways might have given the least stops to the fastest trains. Such relationships between dependent variables may deteriorate the quality of the model, if both of these variables are selected in the final model.

The modeler now decided to build the regression model. The correlation measured the strength of the relationship between the two variables. However, in testing the correlation, the dependent and independent variables aren't explicitly assigned their roles. Regression goes a step further than correlation and tests the strength of the relationship between the independent and dependent variable. The model can also help us determine variables that are significant, and provide us with an equation that showcases the relationship between all variables. Before we look at the regression model of stock, let's delve into the concepts of regression.

Let's think about multiple examples, spanning economy, marketing, and education, to make things simpler. The GDP of the economy can be dependent on various factors, including the rate of employment, the growth rate of manufacturing and services, any adverse weather events, oil prices, and so on. In marketing, the sales of a new beauty cream can be dependent on the size of the target market, the brand perception of the company, the advertising budget, and so on. In the education sector, the performance of a student can be depend on the quality of teachers, time spent in activities outside of class, family background, and so on. All three instances—GDP, sales of new beauty cream, and performance of a student—are seemingly dependent on multiple factors, such as the price of oil, the advertising budget, the quality of teachers, and so on.

But not all of the independent variables will have an equal influence on the dependent variables. The extremely poor quality of teachers in a school might not be fully compensated by a student's parents being highly literate. In this case, the performance of a student (the dependent variable) might be influenced in a different magnitude by the quality of teachers and family background. Hence, the measure of this relationship becomes important, and that's what regression tries to do. Consider the mathematical equation that users of regression analysis have come across in the past:

$$Y = a_1 X_1 + b_2 X_2 + c_3 X_3 + Z$$

The sales of a new beauty cream can be predicted if we use the target size of the market, the brand perception, and the advertising budget, and assign each of these independent variables a weight that they need to be multiplied with. The weight is the influence that each independent variable has in determining the dependent variable, *Sales*. The simplified equation of multiple regression – the marketing application – is give here:

Sales = Target Size*X_1 + Perception*X_2+ Ad Budget*X_3+ Unknown

In the preceding formula, the following applies:

- *Sales* is the dependent variable, influenced by multiple variables
- X_1-X_3 are the measures of influence that each variable has on the dependent variable (*Sales*)
- If 100% of *Sales* can be determined by adding all of the three variables in the equation, then *Unknown/intercept* will have the value 0

The unknown (Z) is also called the constant, or the *intercept*. If all independent variables had a value of 0, then Z will be the value of the mean of the dependent. We spoke about the independent variables as though they have a positive relationship with the dependent variable. Quite often, this isn't true. The relationship can be inverse/negative:

Sales = Target Size*X$_1$ + $_{Perception*}$X$_{2+}$ Ad Budget*X$_3$- CompetitorCampaign*X$_4$ + Unknown

Competitor campaigns on similar products are thought to have a negative impact and reduce the sales of the company in the previous example. By now, we have an overview of what regression does. But how does the regression equation get formulated? Because this is a two-dimensional environment, let us look at a simple regression equation, rather than multivariate regression:

Sales = Ad Budget*X$_1$ + Constant

Looking at the scatter plot of *Sales* and *Ad Budget*, it seems that there is a linear relationship between budget and sales. As the budget (*x*-axis) keeps on increasing for most of the data points, it seems that there is an increase in the sales:

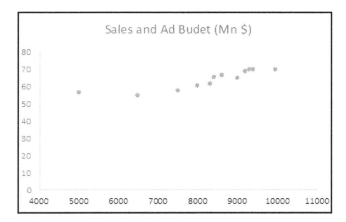

Figure 2.8: Scatter plot of ad budget and sales

Let's now try to draw a straight line that represents the regression equation in *Figure 2.9*:

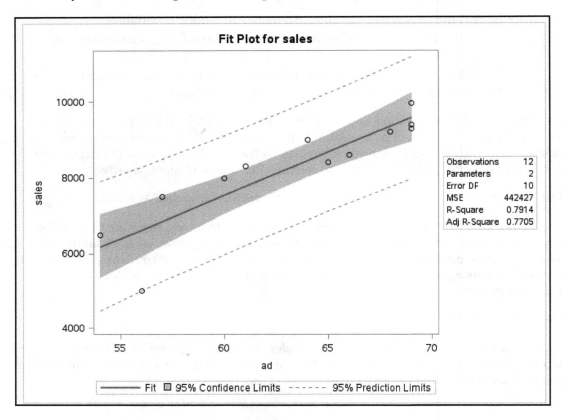

Figure 2.9: Regression line plot - regression fundamentals

Rather than just drawing a line through the scatter plots, the aim is to draw a line in a way that:

- Most points fall on or around the regression line that we draw across the scatter plot
- The distances of the individual observations from the regression line are as small as possible

We have also added a confidence limit around the regression equation, showing the scatter of the data points around the line. Most of the data points falling on or around the regression equation are within the 95% confidence limit. However, some points near the middle of the line and the top part are far from the regression line. In modeling, we do measure the distances of these data points from the regression line, to understand the predictive power of the regression equation. The data points when sales are 5,000 million against an ad budget of 56 million don't fall on the regression line. This could happen, because at this inflexion point of budget and sales, the impact of the budget on sales may be higher or lower in magnitude than the linear relationship effect that we saw at other inflexion points.

There could be some other factors contributing to the sales that have not been captured in the regression equation. Maybe some of the customers were paid a bonus at this point, and sales increased. The variable bonus could be added at this inflection point. This could be added as a dummy variable with the value 1, at the inflection points of budget and sales, where we think it has a role to play. The regression line could be redrawn after the addition, to see if the dummy variable is significant.

Having explored the basics of regression, let's turn back to the main business problem of forecasting the stock value of our mobile phone manufacturer. Our modeler has just run a regression model on the data. Let's evaluate its results.

The PROC regression code is as follows:

```
PROC REG DATA=build plots=diagnostics(unpack);
ID date;
MODEL stock = basket_index -- m1_money_supply_index;
RUN;
```

Part A – Fit statistics

Did you notice that the observations used have decreased in the regression model? Earlier in the univariate procedure, we had 594 rows of data, and they have now reduced to 564. We have called the new data the build data. The last 30 observations in the data have been left out of the model-building process, and have been put in a dataset called validation.

We will use the validation dataset later in the chapter:

The REG Procedure
Model: MODEL1
Dependent Variable: Stock Stock

Number of Observations Read	564
Number of Observations Used	564

Analysis of Variance					
Source	DF	Sum of Squares	Mean Square	F Value	Pr > F
Model	8	188.80094	23.60012	541.20	<.0001
Error	555	24.20194	0.04361		
Corrected Total	563	213.00287			

Root MSE	0.20882	R-Square	0.8864
Dependent Mean	4.84254	Adj R-Sq	0.8847
Coeff Var	4.31227		

Figure 2.10: Fit statistics for regression model

In the **analysis of variance (ANOVA)** table, the eight degrees of freedom refer to the eight independent variables that are available to estimate the parameters of predicting the dependent variable. The total degrees of freedom represent the sources of variance, which are usually denoted by *N-1*. Since we did not exclude the *intercept* from the modeling statement, we have *N-1 (eight independent variables - 1) + intercept*, which gives us eight degrees of freedom.

The error mentioned in the ANOVA table is something that most modelers don't actively consider when assessing the results of regression. However, if the error is equal to 0, then no F or P statistic will be produced in ANOVA, and the modeler will probably have to collect more data before the regression model can be run. The error term refers to the residual degrees of freedom, which in our case will be *563-8=555*.

The sum of squares in ANOVA is associated with the variance for the model, error, and the corrected total. The mean square refers to the sum of squares divided by the degrees of freedom. The *F* value is compiled by dividing the mean square model by the mean square error. The *F* value, used in conjunction with the *P* value informs us whether the independent variables are reliable variables for predictions of the dependent variable `stock`.

The next important statistics that the modeler referred to in the ANOVA output were the values of the R square and the adjusted R square. The R square is the value that depicts the percentage of the variance in the variable stock that can be explained by the independent variable. In this case, 88.59% of the variance can be explained by the use of the independent variables selected for modeling. As the independent variables keep getting added on to the model, the prediction power of the model increases, in general. Some of this increase happens by chance. To negate the chance factor, we observe the adjusted R square. Having a close R square and adjusted R square is always a good sign in the model. One of the reasons that the adjusted R square could vary significantly from the R square is the low number of observations and high number of predictor variables. Apart from this, if the two values differ significantly, then the modeler should ensure that the model is thoroughly scrutinized. A higher adjusted R square value is a positive sign in interpreting the model, but it isn't the only measure that the modeler should rely on:

Parameter Estimates						
Variable	Label	DF	Parameter Estimate	Standard Error	t Value	Pr > |t|
Intercept	Intercept	1	-2.98841	4.46899	-0.67	0.5040
Basket_index	Basket_index	1	-0.00578	0.00234	-2.47	0.0137
EPS	EPS	1	1.63835	0.16086	10.19	<.0001
Top_10_GDP	Top_10_GDP	1	0.29955	0.11731	2.55	0.0109
Global_mkt_share	Global_mkt_share	1	103.61091	23.89472	4.34	<.0001
P_E_ratio	P_E_ratio	1	-0.12295	0.01067	-11.52	<.0001
Media_analytics_index	Media_analytics_index	1	0.01439	0.00223	6.46	<.0001
Top_10_Economy_inflation	Top_10_Economy_inflation	1	-1.28481	0.28984	-4.44	<.0001
M1_money_supply_index	M1_money_supply_index	1	-0.12957	0.00813	-15.93	<.0001

Figure 2.11: Parameter estimates for regression model

The parameter estimate table is critical for the model – building exercise, as this is the section that helps to identify the significant variables for prediction, and informs us of the value of the parameter estimate that is to be used in the regression equation. However, some modelers overlook the observations that can be made from looking at the diagnostic plots. Before accepting the results from the model, it is necessary to review the diagnostic plots. But for now, let's focus on the value of the information in the parameter estimates table.

According to the table , there are six variables that are statistically significant in predicting the variable stock. All of these variables have a *Pr> |t| <0.001*. We can set our significance level (alpha level) at 95%, or 0.05, to accept or reject the null hypothesis. All of the six significant variables have a *P* value less than 0.05. The null hypothesis tested here is that the explanatory variables don't have a significant explanatory power (as the regression coefficient is assumed to be zero) for the response variable of stock price. In the case of these six variables, as the *P* value is <0.05 (our significance level), we can reject the null hypothesis and conclude that these variables can be used for explaining the relationship with the stock price movement.

For every change in one unit of the significant variable of EPS, there is a 1.63450 unit change in the value of the stock price. This level of change per unit is provided to us by the parameter estimate. The parameter estimate also provides the direction of the relationship. Three of the six significant variables are inversely related to the stock price. These are the *P/E* ratio, the weighted inflation of the top 10 economies, and the weighted index of the M1 money supply for the top 10 economies. The modeler expected that the *P/E* ratio could be inversely related to the stock price, as a lower *P/E* ratio is what investors are typically looking for, with the expectation that investing in such a stock will lead to higher returns. Hence, the negative relationship between the *P/E* ratio and stock price makes intuitive sense.

Inflation does impact consumer spending and corporate profits. As inflation rises, consumers may hold back their spending. The raw material costs may increase, and the corporations may be forced to either reduce profitability or pass the high costs onto the consumer, thereby further pushing up the cost of goods. A higher inflation rate may also be a sign of wage growth, giving consumers a bit of extra cash every month. Each company's stock price may react to changes in inflation differently, due to the many factors at play in the economy. However, for the mobile manufacturer in question, it seems that a rise in inflation would negatively impact the stock price.

The modeler expected that the M1 money supply would have a positive impact on the stock price. The assumption was that the higher the money supply in the top 10 economies of the world, the greater the chance that consumers would splurge on new mobile phones. However, here, a bit of recent history might come into play. Almost a decade ago, there was a major worldwide financial crisis, and, as a result, central banks started a program of quantitative easing. Although quantitative easing doesn't strictly increase the M1 money supply directly, there is a chance that it could end up helping it.

A reduction in the M1 index may be interpreted in the current context, with the tightening or stopping of quantitative easing by a section of the large economies. This may, in turn, be a positive indicator for the economy. The modeler was nevertheless surprised with the negative parameter estimate for the variable, and had to consider the reasons why the model assigned it an inverse relationship.

If you recollect the correlation output, you might have noticed that only variable the M1 money supply index should an inverse relationship when we measured the strength of each variable and stock price. However, in the regression model output, we have three significant variables with an inverse relationship with the stock price. Remember, we also said earlier that the correlation doesn't test the significance, and we do not assume any independent or dependent variable relationship in the correlation. Furthermore, the correlation was just a measure of two variables. It didn't take into account the effects of other variables in measuring the strength of the relationship between two variables; whereas in the regression model, all independent variables are collectively trying to explain the variance seen in the stock price movement. This interplay between various independent variables is different from the correlation phenomenon. Hence, the output of the correlation and regression should be viewed in the correct perspective.

So far, in this section, we have analyzed the output of ANOVA and studied the relevance of the parameter estimates. We have also highlighted how any one statistic shouldn't be interpreted in isolation, and diagnostic plots should also be evaluated. Let's move on to assessing the diagnostic plots.

Part B - Diagnostic plots

The residual fit spread for the variable stock shows two charts boxed together. These are the fit-mean and the residual. The fit-mean refers to the spread of the fitted values, and the residual graph refers to the spread of the residuals. The residuals are calculated based on the differences between the observed (actual) and the fitted (predicted). In the case of our model, the spread of the fitted is more than the spread of the residual, which means that the spread of the residual is less than the fitted, and the model can be used.

The flatter or more horizontal the shape of the residual, the better the chances of the spread of fitted being more favorably distributed:

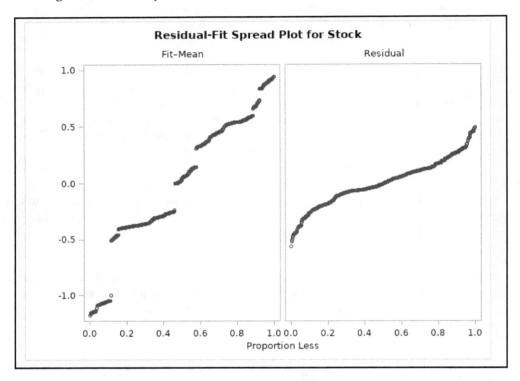

Figure 2.12.1: Residual fit spread plot for stock

The Q-Q plot of residuals does point to some observations at the lower and top end of the quantile that have higher residuals, and don't fit as well as the rest of the population. When the stock price is low, then the model is under-predicting the stock value in some cases, and when the stock price is at the higher end, the model is over-predicting the value in some cases.

This is an observation that the modeler noted down, in case this bias can be overcome by building an alternative model:

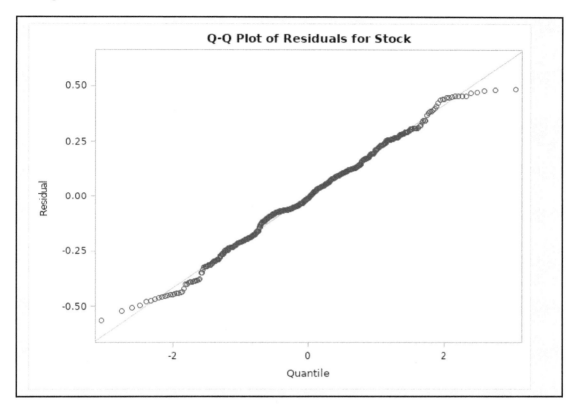

Figure 2.12.2: Q-Q plot for regression model

The distribution of residuals is fairly normally distributed, with no particular skewness observed:

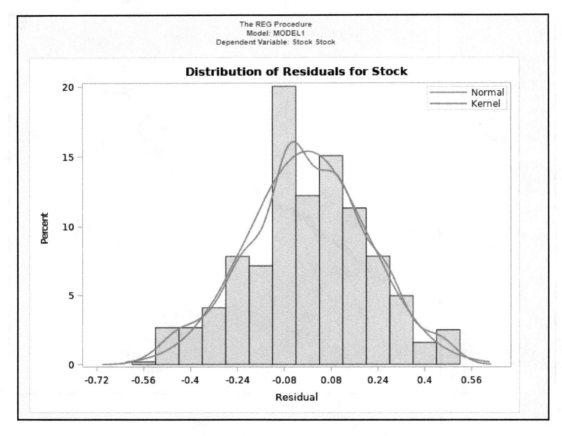

Figure 2.13: Distribution of residuals for regression model

Another main assumption of regression is that the residuals shouldn't form any pattern. Looking at the residual predicted stock chart, it seems that the residuals do not form any particular patterns. Hence, this assumption about regression also holds true for the model:

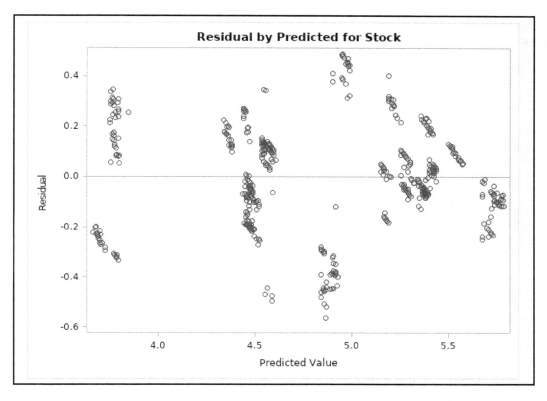

Figure 2.14.1: Residuals by predicted for regression model

The residuals from the predicted chart show that the residuals of predicted observations are higher when the stock price is around $4.80-$4.90. This chart reaffirms the observation made earlier, that the model is over-predicting the stock price when dealing with higher observed stock prices. Most of the residuals beyond the $5.50 stock price are negative. It is important for the modeler to decide whether the spread of the residuals is acceptable. This is a subjective call at times, and the level of acceptance around the spread differs from one business problem to another.

One of the main assumptions of a regression is that the residuals are normally distributed. By looking at the Q-Q plot, we can say that this assumption holds in this case:

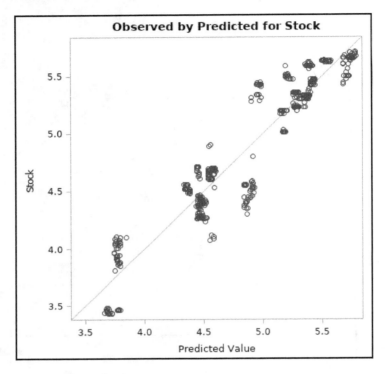

Figure 2.14.2: Observed by predicted for regression model

The RStudent and the Cooks D plots can be used to assess the model output. A significant number of observations over the value of 2 on the RStudent plot should be of concern to the modeler. The RStudent and Cooks D plots highlight that there are at least a couple of data points that have high leverage and are influencing the overall model fit disproportionately. Remember that these aren't data quality related observations.

We already had a data point, 0.37, that was changed to 4.37, as the earlier observation was a data quality issue. Let us try to identify these two data points by altering our model statement:

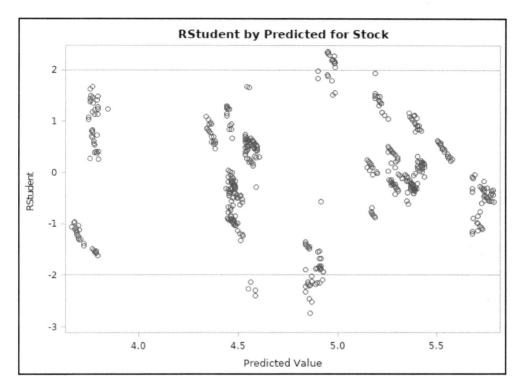

Figure 2.15.1: RStudent for regression model

In the RStudent outlier chart, we can see that there are a couple of points with a leverage of more than 0.03 that seem to extreme observations.

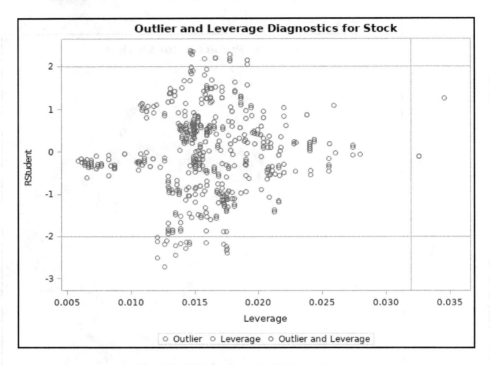

Figure 2.15.2: RStudent, outlier, and Cook's D for regression model

In *Figure 2.15.3*, the Cook's D chart doesn't point to any particular data points that need investigation. Usually, a value greater than 2 merits investigation.

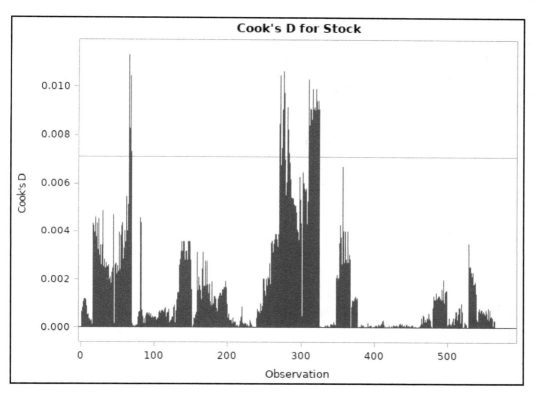

Figure 2.15.3: Cook's D for regression model

The PROC REG code for identifying high leverage observations is as follows:

```
PROC REG DATA=build plots(only label)=(RStudentByLeverage CooksD);
ID date;
MODEL stock = basket_index -- m1_money_supply_index;
RUN;
```

As we can see from the partial output of the code run to highlight the leveraged data points, the stock prices observed on December 31, the 7th of March and April, and the 5th of July, 2017, are have a high influence. Having checked the values of the stock prices and other variables, the modeler did not find any reason why these shouldn't be included in the analysis dataset. Hence, these values were retained. No transformation or data treatment was deemed necessary:

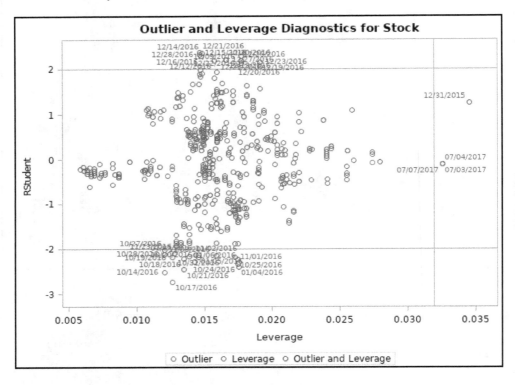

Figure 2.16: Outlier labels for regression model

In this section, we validated that the model abides by two of the underlying principles of regression. We also understood the significance of various charts, and created a slightly modified version of an existing chart, to better understand our model.

Part C - Residual plots

The residual plots of each independent variable are plotted against the dependent variable. We can attempt to evaluate the significance of the spread of the residuals. None of the residuals plotted are forming any particular pattern, in this instance:

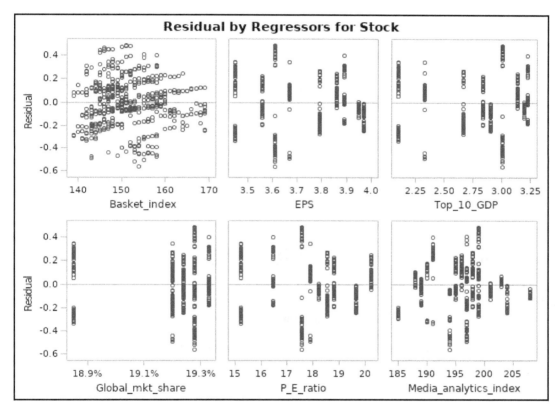

Figure 2.17.1: Residuals by regressors

Similar to *Figure 2.17.1*, in *Figure 2.17.2*, we see no particular pattern of residuals for both of the regressors plotted:

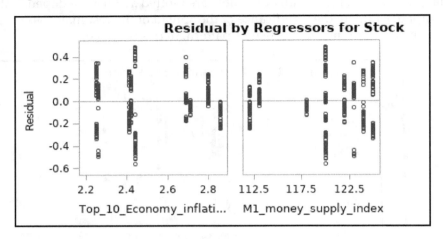

Figure 2.17.2: Residuals by regressors

Dealing with multicollinearity

The modeler still wasn't sure that the model was robust enough. He remembered that he hadn't tested the model for any effects of multicollinearity. We spoke briefly about this phenomenon when we studied the correlation of stock prices with each of the eight independent variables proposed for the regression model. The multicollinearity test was run using the tolerance and the **variance inflation factor (VIF)**.

The `PROC REG` code for multicollinearity is as follows:

```
PROC REG DATA=build plots(only label)=(RStudentByLeverage CooksD);
ID date;
MODEL stock = basket_index -- m1_money_supply_index/tol vif;
RUN;
```

Parameter Estimates								
Variable	Label	DF	Parameter Estimate	Standard Error	t Value	Pr > |t|	Tolerance	Variance Inflation
Intercept	Intercept	1	-2.98841	4.46899	-0.67	0.5040	.	0
Basket_index	Basket_index	1	-0.00578	0.00234	-2.47	0.0137	0.30540	3.27438
EPS	EPS	1	1.63835	0.16086	10.19	<.0001	0.10049	9.95127
Top_10_GDP	Top_10_GDP	1	0.29955	0.11731	2.55	0.0109	0.03968	25.20264
Global_mkt_share	Global_mkt_share	1	103.61091	23.89472	4.34	<.0001	0.06925	14.44052
P_E_ratio	P_E_ratio	1	-0.12295	0.01067	-11.52	<.0001	0.32415	3.08500
Media_analytics_index	Media_analytics_index	1	0.01439	0.00223	6.46	<.0001	0.57829	1.72923
Top_10_Economy_inflation	Top_10_Economy_inflation	1	-1.28481	0.28964	-4.44	<.0001	0.02053	48.70007
M1_money_supply_index	M1_money_supply_index	1	-0.12957	0.00813	-15.93	<.0001	0.06544	15.28155

Figure 2.18: Partial output for multicollinearity

The tolerance is computed as *1-R²*. When the R^2 is high, the tolerance value is very low. Such low values of tolerance are indicative of multicollinearity. The VIF is derived by taking the inverse of tolerance; that is, 1/tolerance. A high VIF isn't good for the model. A VIF above 10 is definitely a matter of concern. Some academics also consider values between 2-10 to be indicative of multicollinearity. In our model's case, we have very high values of VIF. There could be multiple variables driving higher VIF, or even a single variable interacting with other predictor variables that might be leading to higher VIF. The modeler decided to remove the variable showing the inflation of the top 10 economies. Inflation is a factor that might be related to the GDP growth among other variables.

The `PROC REG` code for multicollinearity, after the removal of a variable, is as follows:

```
PROC REG DATA=build plots(only label)=(RStudentByLeverage CooksD);
ID date;
MODEL stock = basket_index eps p_e_ratio global_mkt_share
media_analytics_index m1_money_supply_index top_10_gdp/tol vif;
RUN;
```

			Parameter Estimates					
Variable	Label	DF	Parameter Estimate	Standard Error	t Value	Pr > |t|	Tolerance	Variance Inflation
Intercept	Intercept	1	-19.14146	2.63381	-7.27	<.0001	.	0
Basket_index	Basket_index	1	-0.00683	0.00236	-2.89	0.0040	0.30855	3.24098
EPS	EPS	1	1.02645	0.08412	12.20	<.0001	0.37976	2.63326
P_E_ratio	P_E_ratio	1	-0.11987	0.01083	-11.07	<.0001	0.32552	3.07200
Global_mkt_share	Global_mkt_share	1	176.10894	17.72143	9.94	<.0001	0.13013	7.68471
Media_analytics_index	Media_analytics_index	1	0.01187	0.00219	5.42	<.0001	0.61854	1.61672
M1_money_supply_index	M1_money_supply_index	1	-0.10408	0.00585	-17.79	<.0001	0.13065	7.65409
Top_10_GDP	Top_10_GDP	1	-0.12292	0.06963	-1.77	0.0780	0.11641	8.59007

Figure 2.19: Partial regression output for multicollinearity after the removal of a variable

As you can see, the VIF has gone down substantially, after the removal of a single variable related to the inflation of the top 10 economies. This was also a significant variable, and earlier, the model had six significant variables; now we are left with only five. This shouldn't impact the model negatively, as now, by reducing the multicollinearity, the model is much more stable.

Role of autocorrelation

One of the assumptions for ordinary least squares regression is that the error terms are independent. However, with time series data, much of the time, the error terms are correlated. This is also known as autocorrelation. The regression tests performed up until now don't test for autocorrelation. If autocorrelation is present in the model, then the parameter estimates may not be accurate, and the standard error estimates will be biased.

While the `AUTOREG` procedure should ideally be used for regressing time series data, we can still try to evaluate the model for autocorrelation by using `PROC REG`, which was used earlier. The statistic that is going to help us explore the autocorrelation is the **Durbin-Watson (DW)** statistic.

The `PROC REG` code for autocorrelation is as follows:

```
PROC REG DATA=build;
ID date;
MODEL basket_index eps p_e_ratio global_mkt_share media_analytics_index
m1_money_supply_index top_10_gdp = /dw;
RUN;
```

If the value of the DW statistic is close to 2, then the errors are uncorrelated. The highest level of the statistic observed was 0.256 for the variable basket index. However, in our model, there seems to be autocorrelation in all of the variables. We will ignore the following autocorrelation figures for now, and try to explore them in-depth when we discuss **Auto-Regressive Integrated Moving Average (ARIMA)**:

Dependent	Label 1	Value 1
Stock	1st order autocorrelation	0.993
Basket index	1st order autocorrelation	0.881
EPS	1st order autocorrelation	0.989
PE ratio	1st order autocorrelation	0.988
Global market share	1st order autocorrelation	0.988
Media analytics index	1st order autocorrelation	0.977
M1 money supply index	1st order autocorrelation	0.993
Top 10 GDP	1st order autocorrelation	0.995

Figure 2.20: DW statistic

Scoring based on PROC REG

Once we have built the regression model, we need to generate scores for a holdout sample. The holdout sample contains one month of observed data. At times, when building the model, we over fit the data. It is always a good idea to have a holdout sample on which the model can be fitted. There isn't anything better than using the observed values to see how well the predictions were made. The holdout sample shouldn't be too short or too future looking when compared to what has been built into the model.

We cannot expect the model that we have built for daily stock prices using almost three years of data to help us predict three years ahead. Also, using our model to predict just one day ahead and using that as a holdout sample would be too lenient on the model, and would not check for its practical use with a decent data size.

We will write the model parameters to the `REGOUT` dataset. We have stored our holdout data in a table called `predict`. The regression equation will be used to generate forecasts on this dataset.

The code to generate a `PROC REG` based forecast is as follows:

```
PROC REG DATA=build OUTEST=REGOUT;
ID DATE;
MODEL Stock = basket_index eps p_e_ratio global_mkt_share
media_analytics_index
m1_money_supply_index top_10_gdp;
RUN;

PROC SCORE DATA=validation
SCORE=REGOUT OUT=RSCOREP TYPE=PARMS;
var basket_index eps p_e_ratio global_mkt_share media_analytics_index
m1_money_supply_index top_10_gdp;
RUN;
```

Before we discuss the results of the preceding code, let us explore ARIMA in some detail.

ARIMA

ARIMA models are also referred to as Box-Jenkins models, owing to the approach made popular by the statisticians George Box and Gwilym Jenkins. It is worth noting that along with ARIMA, there are other terms, such as AR, MA, and ARMA, which help to form the ARIMA approach. *George Box* and *Gwilym Jenkins* are remembered for their contributions, as they bought together the AR and the MA approach. The ARIMA approach was developed in three parts. Let's first explore why ARIMA is relevant to time series forecasting. We can then focus on understanding the nuances of ARIMA.

One of the reasons we want to use ARIMA is to compare our multivariate model to a different methodology. We do occasionally see multivariate regression used for forecasting in the financial world, but most people prefer to use ARIMA. When we want to forecast something, we need to know what is influencing or driving the behavior of the variable we want to forecast. On a lot of occasions, we don't know what is driving the behavior. Yes, we can attempt to gather hundreds of independent variables and try to make our variable of interest as the dependent variable, and we can try to generate a regression model to identify drivers, get the parameter estimates, and create an equation for forecasting the dependent variable. But collecting, storing, and analyzing these independent variables takes time. Also, we are limited by the number and nature of variables we select.

At times, some users of the models may feel that the right influencing factors were never assessed, as they weren't part of the independent variables tested for their significance in forecasting. Stock prices are a perfect example of people having differing views on what influences them. Someone will point out that the financial ratios are important, others will talk about the recommendations from brokers, some will mention the global factors, and others will talk about their gut feelings. There is a cost associated with testing all of these potential influencers.

Moreover, the multivariate regression methodology doesn't incorporate any learnings from the residual errors generated during the forecasting process. The ARIMA models use information from past data points and the residuals generated. We can still use independent variables to generate forecasts in ARIMA, but these so-called independent variables in the ARIMA context may just be transformations of the variable (or, in this case, the dependent) of interest. The equation of such a model could be, simply, $Pt = Pt\text{-}1 + error$. The $Pt\text{-}1$ term is an independent variable in some sense, but it is merely a transformation of the dependent variable. Due to this particular way of using independent variables, this type of analysis is also called a univariate analysis. In our business problem, we are only concerned about the variable stock.

Let's run our first ARIMA model code:

PROC ARIMA code:

```
PROC ARIMA Data=build;
IDENTIFY VAR=STOCK;
RUN;
```

Figure 2.21.1 shows the autocorrelation test at various lags. By default, the first lag that is shown in the output is lag 6:

The ARIMA Procedure

Name of Variable = Stock	
Mean of Working Series	4.842535
Standard Deviation	0.614544
Number of Observations	564

Autocorrelation Check for White Noise

To Lag	Chi-Square	DF	Pr > ChiSq	Autocorrelations					
6	3229.48	6	<.0001	0.993	0.984	0.976	0.968	0.960	0.952
12	6160.10	12	<.0001	0.944	0.935	0.926	0.917	0.907	0.898
18	8770.20	18	<.0001	0.888	0.879	0.870	0.861	0.850	0.839
24	9999.99	24	<.0001	0.828	0.816	0.805	0.794	0.783	0.771

Figure 2.21.1: PROC ARIMA output - autocorrelation

Notice that the code statement only had a single variable of interest. This is different from the REG procedure, to begin with. Later on, we will try to explore the effect of other variables on our main variable of interest, stock.

We didn't act on the autocorrelation that we found in the multivariate regression model. It's now time to explore the autocorrelation using the ACF, or the autocovariance plot. The *x*-axis plots the lag, and the *y*-axis, the autocovariance level. The lag is simply the time between the observations. As we can see, in this case, the reduction in autocovariance is a smooth process.

The reduction is happening at a constant, but a, gradual pace. Although this makes the graph look symmetric, it is an indication of an issue that creeps into time series data. The issue, in this case, is called non-stationarity. We want our autocorrelations to exhibit stationarity:

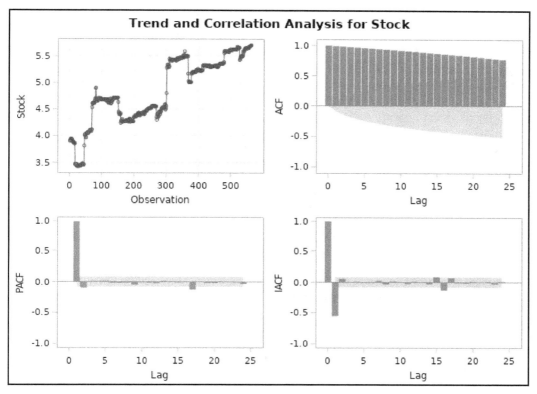

Figure 2.21.2: PROC ARIMA output - trend and correlation

When we spoke about multivariate regression, we explored the role of the constant value in a regression equation. Time series has two components: the deterministic aspect and the stochastic aspect. The stochastic aspect, in theory, is loosely related to the role of the constant in the regression. The non-error part, which explains the relationship of the dependent with the independent variables (a lagged form of dependent, or some other transformation, in the case of time series), is the deterministic aspect. It is something that, in plain language, we can determine by assigning a weight or parameter value to the independent variable, whereas the error of the equation is the stochastic part that explains the time series.

The stochastic part relates to the random error in forecasting. This random error captures the autocorrelation between two lags of the time series. For instance, the stock price is $5 today, and there is more of a likelihood that it will be $5 or +- 0.1 in a world with slow-moving factors. Hence, today's stock price is more likely to be related to yesterday's, and maybe even the day of the stock price recorded a week ago. This is a non-stationary process. A stationary process can be defined as one where the mean, variance, and autocorrelation don't change over time.

So, why is stationarity important? With stationarity, we have no trend, as the mean doesn't vary over time. The variance is constant, rather than fluctuating all over. The autocovariance depends only on a lag of, let's say, the most recent period. In our case, we can say that with a stationarity series, the autocovariance is only dependent on yesterday's closing stock price. Having a stationarity series makes forecasting more robust.

In our stock price example, a non-stationary series is being observed, due to the following reasons:

- The trend of the stock price is generally increasing since the start of the data period. This is clearly demonstrated by the output of `PROC ARIMA` in the plot where the *x*-axis charts the observation number, and the *y*-axis, the price of the stock.
- Variance is changing, and we have observed this in the residual charts that were produced as part of `PROC REG`.

There are probably seasonal effects, relating to the product launches or the Christmas time period. Just prior to the holiday season, the mobile manufacturer in question is launching new handsets. This could surely have a seasonal effect on the data. Again, the seasonal jumps we are referring to are probably the two spikes in the `PROC ARIMA` plot that we can observe. Overall, the trend is of a rising stock price, and there are two major jumps in the time series across the almost three years of data we have.

To make the series stationary, we could either difference it (the most popular method), try some log transformations (the second most popular approach in the industry), or use moving averages, based on some sort of judgment. Differencing tends to be the most popular option, as, from a practical consideration, it is an easier method to deploy. If, let's say, the first order differencing doesn't work, you can specify higher orders. But what is differencing?

Differencing is simply, $Y_i = Z_i - Z_{i-1}$.

Let's try to difference our data and observe the change in the ACF distribution.

The PROC ARIMA code for first order differencing is as follows:

```
PROC ARIMA Data=build;
IDENTIFY VAR=STOCK(1);
RUN;
```

The ARIMA Procedure

Name of Variable = Stock	
Period(s) of Differencing	1
Mean of Working Series	0.003215
Standard Deviation	0.049586
Number of Observations	563
Observation(s) eliminated by differencing	1

Autocorrelation Check for White Noise									
To Lag	Chi-Square	DF	Pr > ChiSq	Autocorrelations					
6	32.09	6	<.0001	0.226	0.006	-0.041	-0.052	0.017	0.033
12	39.21	12	<.0001	0.029	0.082	0.019	0.015	0.033	-0.056
18	40.88	18	0.0016	-0.036	-0.009	-0.023	0.013	0.020	0.021
24	55.92	24	0.0002	0.020	-0.037	-0.010	-0.005	0.052	0.144

Figure 2.22.1: First order differencing - autocorrelation

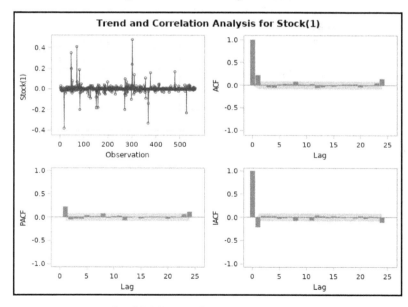

Figure 2.22.2: First order differencing - trend and correlation

So, what happened to the gradually declining autocovariance observed in the last run of PROC ARIMA? Well, the differencing has had its effect, and now, after the second lag, we can see that the series dramatically declines. We now have a stationary series, just by doing the first order differencing. Note that the only change in the two PROC ARIMA statements that we have seen until now is the addition of the syntax (1) in the code for differencing.

Also, notice the observation versus the stock (1) plot. Remember, without the differencing, we had a trend. It has now disappeared after the differencing. We no longer have seasonality in the chart. We do have some points where the variation is larger than most of the points. A large majority of the points have a variance close to zero. Hence, by looking at the plot, we can see that differencing seems to be delivering the required results.

Before exploring the partial autocorrelation function graph, let's spare some moments for the white noise table summary produced. Note the difference between the white noise summaries with and without differencing. Prior to differencing, for all of the four lags exhibited, we had a small p-value.

After differencing, lags 6 and 12 still have a small p-value. For lag 18, the p-value is not significant, but again, for lag 24, the lag value is significant. Remember that we are more concerned about the second lag after differencing, as this is when the autocovariance suddenly declines. Since the p-value at lag 2 after differencing is significant, we can state that there is no white noise; that is, at least some of the autocorrelations up to lag 2 are not zero. If the autocorrelation at all lags is zero, and we determine that there is white noise, then there is no point to model ahead. Remember that we aren't using a multivariate approach to use a lot of variables as independent variables. We are trying to use the autocorrelations in the stock variable series to forecast values. If there are no autocorrelations, then this is the point when the modeling needs to stop. Yes, we want a stationary process, but no, we don't want white noise where there is no autocorrelation.

The ARIMA function has p, d, and q elements. The p element relates to the autoregressive order. The d element is the differencing order, and the q element is related to the moving average. Having analyzed the ACF plot and ruled out white noise, we can now explore the PACF plot, to find out the autoregressive order.

The partial autocorrelation, or the PACF plot, needs to be analyzed, ignoring the negative values. We are again looking to establish at which lag the partial autocorrelations have reduced substantially and are no longer relevant. Again, at the first lag, the autocorrelations have reduced a lot. We could also consider saying that after lag 2, they stop reducing by a lot, but they are still substantial at lag 2. For our model purposes, let's go with lag 1 as the point after which the partial autocorrelations reduce substantially.

Hence, for our model purposes, the autoregressive, or AR, order is 1. What we can interpret is that we need only one number of previous data points in the series to predict the present data point. Hence, our model will have first order autoregression.

The **inverse autocorrelation function (IACF)** plot could be used to interpret some models. It is particularly useful if we have over-differenced the series. In this case, expect that the IACF could look like the ACF did when we had a non-stationary series. If our model is a purely autoregressive model, with no moving average element, then we would expect the series to decay dramatically after a value greater than p. In our case, p is 1, but the IACF doesn't decay at that point. In fact, it does this at lag 2. This might be related to the previous discussion, where we were uncertain whether the p-value should be 1 or 2, after estimating the PACF plot. The actual moving average order can again be derived by reviewing the ACF plot. The series only stops declining at the second lag. However, since the decay at lag 2 is only marginal, we will retain moving the average component (q) for our ARIMA process as 1. Now, we have $p=1$, $d=1$, and $q=1$. We have now completed the first stage of the ARIMA process. This first stage is known as the identification stage, where we need to achieve stationarity, check for white noise, and determine the components of p, d, and q. We haven't done cross-correlations, where the variable stock can be assessed along with other predictor variables used in the multivariate regression. The model that we have decided to estimate at this stage is the ARIMA (1,1,1) model.

Let us explore the second stage, which is known as the estimation stage. This stage incorporates the ARIMA model that we have identified. There will be a set of diagnostics that will help us assess the model. The significance of parameter estimates will also help to identify redundant information in the model. The white noise test of the residual will inform us on whether there is information that the current model has failed to capture.

The `PROC ARIMA` (1,1,1) code is as follows:

```
PROC ARIMA Data=build;
IDENTIFY VAR=STOCK(1);
ESTIMATE p=1 q=1;
RUN;
```

The ARIMA Procedure

Name of Variable = Stock	
Period(s) of Differencing	1
Mean of Working Series	0.003215
Standard Deviation	0.049586
Number of Observations	563
Observation(s) eliminated by differencing	1

Autocorrelation Check for White Noise									
To Lag	Chi-Square	DF	Pr > ChiSq	Autocorrelations					
6	32.09	6	<.0001	0.226	0.006	-0.041	-0.052	0.017	0.033
12	39.21	12	<.0001	0.029	0.082	0.019	0.015	0.033	-0.056
18	40.88	18	0.0016	-0.036	-0.009	-0.023	0.013	0.020	0.021
24	55.92	24	0.0002	0.020	-0.037	-0.010	-0.005	0.052	0.144

The preceding image shows the autocorrelation results at various lags.

Conditional Least Squares Estimation					
Parameter	Estimate	Standard Error	t Value	Approx Pr > |t|	Lag
MU	0.0032194	0.0025527	1.26	0.2078	0
MA1,1	-0.16718	0.18008	-0.93	0.3536	1
AR1,1	0.06783	0.18220	0.37	0.7098	1

Constant Estimate	0.003001
Variance Estimate	0.002342
Std Error Estimate	0.048394
AIC	-1809.24
SBC	-1796.24
Number of Residuals	563

* AIC and SBC do not include log determinant.

Correlations of Parameter Estimates			
Parameter	MU	MA1,1	AR1,1
MU	1.000	0.000	0.000
MA1,1	0.000	1.000	0.973
AR1,1	0.000	0.973	1.000

Autocorrelation Check of Residuals									
To Lag	Chi-Square	DF	Pr > ChiSq	Autocorrelations					
6	2.70	4	0.6099	0.000	-0.002	-0.030	-0.051	0.023	0.026
12	9.86	10	0.4526	0.004	0.081	-0.001	0.005	0.046	-0.062
18	10.92	16	0.8142	-0.023	0.003	-0.027	0.016	0.014	0.012
24	24.72	22	0.3108	0.027	-0.044	0.001	-0.012	0.023	0.142
30	33.33	28	0.2238	-0.008	-0.027	-0.022	0.044	-0.105	-0.017
36	38.43	34	0.2758	-0.015	-0.065	0.047	-0.003	0.029	-0.031
42	41.74	40	0.3953	-0.055	0.026	-0.014	-0.035	0.016	-0.003
48	43.02	46	0.5979	-0.004	0.007	-0.004	-0.014	-0.023	-0.036

Figure 2.23: Partial output of PROC ARIMA (1,1,1) estimation

Notice that at lag 6, the white noise hypothesis is accepted, and the model doesn't require any more transformation. However, none of the t values are statistically significant. This means that our ARIMA (1,1,1) model probably isn't the best-suited model for the series. Let us produce an ARIMA (1,1,0) model and evaluate its output.

The `PROC ARIMA` (1,1,0) code is as follows:

```
PROC ARIMA Data=build;
IDENTIFY VAR=STOCK(1);
ESTIMATE p=1;
RUN;
```

Conditional Least Squares Estimation					
Parameter	Estimate	Standard Error	t Value	Approx Pr > |t|	Lag
MU	0.0032230	0.0026320	1.22	0.2213	0
AR1,1	0.22557	0.04113	5.48	<.0001	1

Constant Estimate	0.002496
Variance Estimate	0.002342
Std Error Estimate	0.048394
AIC	-1810.23
SBC	-1801.57
Number of Residuals	563

* AIC and SBC do not include log determinant.

Correlations of Parameter Estimates		
Parameter	MU	AR1,1
MU	1.000	0.000
AR1,1	0.000	1.000

Figure 2.24: Partial output of PROC ARIMA (1,1,0) estimation

Just like the ARIMA (1,1,1) model, the white noise hypothesis is significant, and hence, there is no need to build a complex model to try and further deal with the issue of white noise. The ARIMA (1,1,0) model is better than the earlier model, as the t-value is statistically significant. **Akaike's information criterion** (**AIC**) and **Schwarz's Bayesian criterion** (**SBC**) are two information criteria produced by the model.

These come in handy when comparing multiple ARIMA models. The current model has lower AIC and SBC, and hence, it is a better model, as compared to the ARIMA (1,1,1) model:

To Lag	Chi-Square	DF	Pr > ChiSq	Autocorrelations					
6	3.75	5	0.5860	0.011	-0.037	-0.034	-0.052	0.023	0.026
12	10.81	11	0.4595	0.005	0.080	-0.002	0.005	0.046	-0.062
18	11.90	17	0.8059	-0.024	0.004	-0.026	0.015	0.014	0.013
24	26.03	23	0.2996	0.026	-0.043	-0.001	-0.015	0.024	0.143
30	34.59	29	0.2185	-0.007	-0.034	-0.018	0.044	-0.103	-0.017
36	39.56	35	0.2737	-0.014	-0.064	0.046	0.002	0.029	-0.033
42	42.95	41	0.3875	-0.056	0.028	-0.013	-0.036	0.017	-0.001
48	44.25	47	0.5871	-0.004	0.007	-0.003	-0.013	-0.023	-0.036

Table title: Autocorrelation Check of Residuals

The quantile plot shows that the residuals of predicting the stock price are not normally distributed:

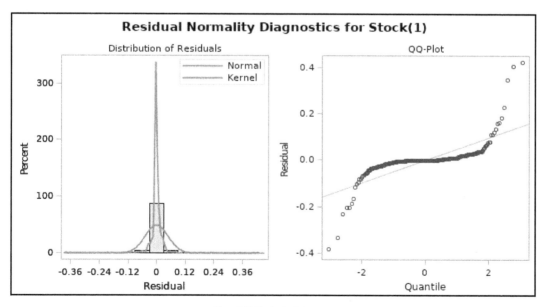

Figure 2.25: Further ARIMA output

We estimated two ARIMA models before selecting the appropriate model. The model selection was done on the basis of summary statistics, diagnostics, tests, and visual analysis of the charts. There is an option in SAS that helps us to identify the exact model, or to at least zero in on the most likely p, q, and d values for the model.

The code for automated model selection is as follows:

```
PROC ARIMA DATA=build;
IDENTIFY VAR=STOCK SCAN;
RUN;
```

SCAN Chi-Square[1] Probability Values						
Lags	MA 0	MA 1	MA 2	MA 3	MA 4	MA 5
AR 0	<.0001	<.0001	<.0001	<.0001	<.0001	<.0001
AR 1	<.0001	0.7628	0.4551	0.3126	0.5938	0.3720
AR 2	0.3163	0.4193	0.4363	0.3563	0.3759	0.7795
AR 3	0.5050	0.8714	0.3428	0.7151	0.4607	0.5666
AR 4	0.4533	0.3888	0.4282	0.4923	0.5699	0.2473
AR 5	0.3054	0.3326	0.4191	0.4243	0.3116	0.3619

ARMA(p+d,q) Tentative Order Selection Tests	
SCAN	
p+d	q
1	1
2	0
(5% Significance Level)	

Figure 2.26: Partial output using the SCAN function

As you can see, both of the models that we ran in ARIMA have already been suggested by the SCAN functionality. From an understanding of the process, it is better to avoid using the SCAN function, and so that it creates a deeper understanding of PROC ARIMA works.

We will now move on to the forecasting part of the ARIMA model.

The code for forecasting is as follows:

```
PROC ARIMA DATA=build;
IDENTIFY VAR=STOCK SCAN;
ESTIMATE p=1 q=0;
FORECAST LEAD=30 OUT=PREDICT;
RUN;
```

The forecasting of 30 data periods has been stored in a table called `PREDICT`. The output also generates a chart of the stored dataset, and contains the forecasted value, the standard error, and 95% confidence limits:

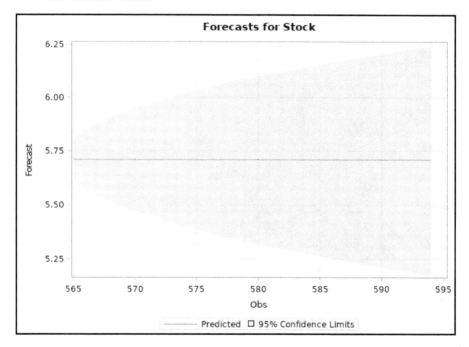

Figure 2.27: ARIMA forecasting output

Validation of models

We can now use the forecasts from the regression model and `ARIMA` and compare this against the observed values from our handout sample. As you can see, the `ARIMA` model forecasts are closer to the observed values. The regression forecasts tend to perform better during the latter part of the handout's observed values. Just a glance at the chart will surely lead to the decision of going with the regression methodology. But is the decision that simple?

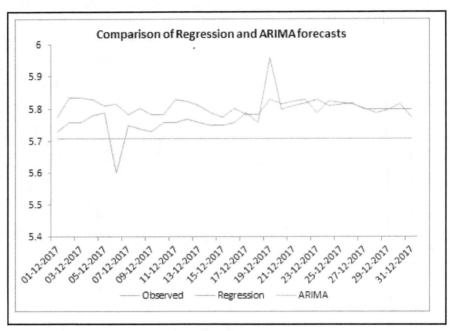

Figure 2.28: Model comparison

Remember, our modeler has $10 million to invest. What if he invested 10% of it in this mobile manufacturer's stock, based on the closing price of the last modeling data point we have? The last modeling data point that we have is November 30, 2017, and the stock price on this day was $5.71. On the first date of the investment, which also happens to be the first data point of our hold-out sample, the estimated value of the investment would be different, depending on the model. Let's compare the value of the estimated investment against the actual value of the investment.

Model implementation

We have observed that the regression model seems to be doing a better forecasting job. When integrating the model with our business, we need to further evaluate the impact of selecting a particular model:

	Portfolio Value of $1 Mn Investment			% Gain by Estimated Methodology	
	Observed	Regression	ARIMA	Regression	ARIMA
01/12/2017	5,730,000	5,775,297	5,710,000	-0.79%	1.13%
02/12/2017	5,760,000	5,836,741	5,710,000	-1.33%	2.17%
03/12/2017	5,760,000	5,836,741	5,710,000	-1.33%	2.17%
04/12/2017	5,780,000	5,829,914	5,710,000	-0.86%	2.06%
05/12/2017	5,790,000	5,809,433	5,710,000	-0.34%	1.71%
06/12/2017	5,600,000	5,816,260	5,710,000	-3.86%	1.83%
07/12/2017	5,750,000	5,782,124	5,710,000	-0.56%	1.25%
08/12/2017	5,740,000	5,802,606	5,710,000	-1.09%	1.60%
09/12/2017	5,730,000	5,782,124	5,710,000	-0.91%	1.25%
10/12/2017	5,760,000	5,782,124	5,710,000	-0.38%	1.25%
11/12/2017	5,760,000	5,829,914	5,710,000	-1.21%	2.06%
12/12/2017	5,770,000	5,823,087	5,710,000	-0.92%	1.94%
13/12/2017	5,760,000	5,809,433	5,710,000	-0.86%	1.71%
14/12/2017	5,750,000	5,788,952	5,710,000	-0.68%	1.36%
15/12/2017	5,750,000	5,775,297	5,710,000	-0.44%	1.13%
16/12/2017	5,760,000	5,802,606	5,710,000	-0.74%	1.60%
17/12/2017	5,790,000	5,782,124	5,710,000	0.14%	1.25%
18/12/2017	5,760,000	5,782,124	5,709,999	-0.38%	1.25%
19/12/2017	5,960,000	5,829,914	5,709,999	2.18%	2.06%
20/12/2017	5,800,000	5,816,260	5,709,999	-0.28%	1.83%
21/12/2017	5,810,000	5,823,087	5,709,999	-0.23%	1.94%
22/12/2017	5,820,000	5,829,914	5,709,999	-0.17%	2.06%
23/12/2017	5,830,000	5,788,952	5,709,999	0.70%	1.36%
24/12/2017	5,810,000	5,823,087	5,709,999	-0.23%	1.94%
26/12/2017	5,820,000	5,816,260	5,709,999	0.06%	1.83%
27/12/2017	5,800,000	5,802,606	5,709,999	-0.04%	1.60%
28/12/2017	5,800,000	5,788,952	5,709,999	0.19%	1.36%
29/12/2017	5,800,000	5,795,779	5,709,999	0.07%	1.48%
30/12/2017	5,800,000	5,816,260	5,709,999	-0.28%	1.83%
31/12/2017	5,800,000	5,775,297	5,709,999	0.43%	1.13%

Figure 2.29: Portfolio investment comparison

We now have the actual gain or loss position of the portfolio of $1 million that we would have held for the stock in December, 2017. The average gain, based on the regression and ARIMA estimate, would be -0.47% and +1.64%, respectively. This shows that for the investor, the positive news will be when the ARIMA model would have been the basis for investment. However, what would the investor's reaction have been if the gain percentage on regression and ARIMA was -10% or +10%? Well, certainly, some investors would have been disappointed, had we used the regression model estimates for investments. The investors would have been ecstatic, with a double-digit growth in a month, if we had used the ARIMA model for the forecast. As a modeler, both -10% and +10% hypothetical returns would have been a cause for worry. This significant shift in percentage from the estimated gains would have shown that the model is missing out on a great deal of explanatory power. It would have been a case of re-evaluating or re-building the model. Doing this in the first month of making the model live wouldn't have inspired a lot of trust in the model among the stakeholders.

We have concluded that we lose by using the regression model. But couldn't we gain by using the explanatory power of the independent variables of the regression model? As of now, our regression model suggests that the stock price is a function of the relationship between EPS, the PE ratio, the global market share, the media analytics index, and the M1 money supply index. We can use these variables to explain the variance in the stock price. However, using the ARIMA model, we can merely state that the previous price movements are determining the current price. This explanatory power gained by stating the role of various factors will be lost if we don't use the regression model. The regression model isn't too far off in terms of its forecasts, when compared to the actual. However, we did highlight earlier that there is autocorrelation present in the model. Yes, we could have also used estimates from a different sort of regression model by using the AUTOREG procedure. The ARIMA model used does take into consideration the autocorrelation element. It also makes the modeler's life easier, by not creating a dependency on the independent variables.

In a real-world business scenario, the modeler must now think of implementing this model. Implementing the regression model develops a dependency on the independent variables, and, at times, some other variables. For instance, in our case, if the modeler used the regression model, there would be a dependency on five independent variables, whereas the ARIMA model just utilized the stock price data. From an implementation perspective, the ARIMA model is easier to implement.

Hence, we recommend that the modeler use the `ARIMA` model, if the overall aim is to reduce variable dependability, while only increasing the forecasting inaccuracy marginally.

Recap of key terms

Some of the terms that we used in this chapter are:

- **ARIMA**: The `ARIMA` model was analyzed by looking at various aspects of the model. We gained an understanding of the auto-regressive and moving average component of `ARIMA`. We also looked at the *p*, *d*, and *q* elements of the model. We developed an understanding of how the process helps to deal with autocorrelation, in comparison to regression. We forecasted values from the model using the historical data from the variable of interest only.

- **Dependent**: The variable that we are trying to forecast or gain a better understanding of is the dependent. We can use a series of independent variables to try and forecast a dependent variable.

- **Differencing**: This is the transformation of the data that we have used to derive a new variable, based on the change of the series from one data point to another.

- **Independent**: The variables that help predict the business problem. The variation of these variables does not depend on other variables.

- **Multicollinearity**: Multicollinearity is said to occur when two or more similar, independent variables are highly correlated with the dependent variable.

- **Regression**: This is the statistical measure/model that evaluates the relationship between a dependent and a series of independent variables. We reviewed three different types of outputs from regression models. These are the fit statistics, diagnostic plots, and residual plots.

- **Seasonality**: A phenomenon that we see occurring over an at least one-year period, where the change is predictable.

- **Stationarity**: A stationarity process in one in which the mean, variance, and autocorrelation are constant across time. A non-stationarity process has many disadvantages, as we reviewed.

- **Trend**: This shows a pattern within the data. This could be simply a linear pattern on increasing the stock price, when plotted against the time series.

Summary

In this chapter, we explored aspects of portfolio forecasting, steps in the forecasting process, tips for the visualization of time series data, and model building for a business case. Both regression and ARIMA models were used, and we compared the results of the model by using a validation sample. In the next chapter, we will discuss risk modeling.

3
Credit Risk Management

Financial institutions lend to various organizations. At times, financial institutions also end up borrowing. The lending creates a risk of default. In the event of a default, the borrower might not fully pay back the principal and the interest on the borrowed sum. This scenario is termed **credit risk**. There are various actions that can be taken to mitigate this risk. These actions collectively form the credit risk management discipline. The probability of the borrower defaulting needs to be taken into account when forming a credit risk management policy for a bank. Credit risk management is necessary in order to meet regulatory requirements and also to manage the lender's capital adequacy and monitor the quality of the loan book. Lenders also have an obligation to ensure that there are no systematic failures in their credit risk management policies, as any such failure could put the lender at risk of bankruptcy and create ripples across the financial world, thereby impacting the small businesses that are the mainstay of any economy.

We will cover the following topics in this chapter:

- Risk types
- Basel norms
- Key credit risk metrics
- Important aspects of credit risk management
- Building a PD model using the Genmod procedure that fits a generalized linear model

Risk types

Although this chapter is primarily concerned with credit risk, there are other types of risk that the financial industry faces. Some of these risk types are:

- **Operational risk**: Risk emanating due to failure in processes, systems, and errors caused by human intervention. For example, transactions being credited to incorrect accounts due to the absence of adequate checks, or a system upgrade to the core banking system failing, thereby preventing customers from accessing their accounts.

- **Market risk**: Risk arises due to dramatic and adverse movements in market prices. Both the on-and off-balance sheet positions are vulnerable to factors that affect the overall performance of financial markets in which the firm is involved. It is also at times referred to as systematic risk. For example, a market that the organization is exposed to is suddenly faced with currency controls, an expected high interest rate movement catches the financial markets off-guard, or persistent high inflation significantly erodes the value of money.

- **Liquidity risk**: Risk arising when a financial institution may be unable to meet its short-term debt obligations. Such a risk happens when some of the assets cannot be sold at a fair market price. For example, as part of the sub-prime mortgage crisis, home owners found that there were no buyers for their houses at the valuation on which they took out mortgages. In a stock exchange meltdown scenario, the range of bid-ask spread increases to such a high level that many securities find no buyers. This leads to a liquidity crisis.

- **Reputation risk**: Risk arising due to the conduct of the financial institution. This could include the erosion of the brand's reputation, leading to the risk spreading to the bottom line and capital adequacy position. For example, a run on the bank due to any adverse rumor may lead to high withdrawals, thereby leading to a capital adequacy crisis.

One of the reasons credit risk management has taken center stage in the financial world is due to the Basel norms. Let's look at the history of these norms and how they have shaped the credit risk environment.

Basel norms

Credit risk management is a highly regulated discipline. Analysts, modelers, project managers, and individuals in various roles within the discipline are expected to have a knowhow of the Basel accords.

The Basel accord was formulated by the **Basel Committee on Banking Supervision** (**BCBS**). The accord is a set of recommendations for regulatory mechanisms in the banking world. While the accord isn't binding, major and emerging economies of the world have made their recommendations binding through their own legislative processes. In 1998, the Basel Committee first published a set of recommendations for the minimum capital requirements of banks. Initially, the G-10 countries enforced these recommendations as laws. These recommendations are known as Basel I. The recommendations are focused on credit risk and the risk-weighting of assets. One of the main takeaways was that the banks with international presences were asked to hold capital equal to 8% of their **risk-weighted assets** (**RWA**).

The accord assumed significance, as it was meant to ensure that the credit risk was effectively managed. On the flip side, it also meant that for every penny lent by some banks, they needed to keep 8% of it aside for the capital adequacy ratio to be maintained. While effective credit risk management is a priority for any bank, they are also interested in holding on to minimum capital reserves, so that there can be more money available to earn from increased lending. Basel II laid the foundation of the advanced approach, which provided more flexibility to banks for assessing capital adequacy to deal with credit risk.

The Basel II accord was formally proposed in 2004, but it was only implemented in 2008 in most economies, after the spread of the financial crisis. Basel II, which superseded the earlier accord of 1998, shifted the focus on capital adequacy to the kind and degree of risk that banks were exposed to. It placed certain disclosure requirements that would allow external stakeholders to better understand the capital adequacy of banks. It proposed the use of an advanced modeling approach, whereby the banks could build their own empirical models. The advantage to the banks was that they could assess whether they needed to hold less capital than what the regulator would recommend, based on a standard approach. The advantage to the central banks was that the advanced approach meant that banks were more hands-on with credit risk management. The Basel II accord proposed that central banks, or a regulatory authority, would have to sign off on a request by the bank to use the advanced modeling approach. This guaranteed that a control was in place to ensure there was no misuse to justify the advanced modeling approach as simply a means to lower capital adequacy requirements.

The Basel II norms were based on a three-pillar approach. The three pillars of the accord were:

- **Minimum capital requirements**: Capital needs to be maintained for dealing with credit risk, market risk, and operational risk
- **Supervisory review**: This provided a framework for regulators to deal with multiple risk types, including liquidity, systematic, and legal risk
- **Market discipline**: This ensured greater transparency for external stakeholders, as it mandated that banks would have to publish information on exposures, risk management processes, and capital adequacy ratio

The Basel III accord was first formally proposed in 2009, even though the deliberations had been going on for a number of years. It increased the capital requirements in response to the global banking crisis. It also recognized that banks go through a cyclic phase of expansion and contraction over a period of time. It mandated higher provision by banks during expansion years, and the opportunity for reduced capital provision during credit contraction. It also introduced financial ratios to monitor the liquidity that the banks maintained while trying to grow their lending book.

As a result of the Basel accords, there are a few industry terms that are at the heart of the advanced modeling approach.

Credit risk key metrics

Let's review the key terms for credit risk.

Exposure at default

This is the amount that a bank is exposed to when a counterparty defaults. It could be equal to the outstanding amount on a fixed loan. In the case of limits, this needs to be assessed based on the drawn and undrawn components. Having a high **exposure at default** (**EAD**) doesn't necessarily mean that the bank would lose an equivalent amount. The amount lost could be less, equal, or even higher than the EAD. The loss given default calculation would help the bank assess the loss in case of a certain EAD. The regulators are concerned about the bank's overall EAD figure and also the EAD figures, to some specific sectors, which may point to a credit risk situation developing.

Probability of default

This is the likelihood of default over a given time period. It is usually calculated as the **probability of default** (**PD**) over a year, or a point in time PD. Organizations using advanced approach modeling have to use a standard default definition. This is usually represented by scoring customers between 0 and 1. There are various types of PD models, but the most common ones are application and behavioral models. Application models, as the name suggests, are used when a customer is still a prospect wishing to join an organization. Behavioral PD models are used to assess and score existing customers. The data available for modeling tends to differ widely, as when building application models, the only available sources of information are what the prospect provides as part of the process and external bureau ratings. However, by the time you develop a behavioral scorecard, the customer has already on-boarded, and hopefully has made enough transactions for you to assess and understand the customer behavior.

Loss given default

This can be simply defined as the amount lost when a counterparty defaults on borrowing. The **loss given default** (**LGD**) could be equal to or less than the amount of exposure at the time of default. The LGD percentage will depend on the settlement terms, the collateral available, and the litigation actions that may happen once the customer goes into default.

Let's imagine a scenario where a social media startup has defaulted on a loan of $500,000. The founders had pledged collateral worth $150,000 when availing of the borrowing facility. Let's assume that the value of the pledged collateral is now $200,000. The LGD in this case would be:

$$LGD = Loss / EAD = \$300,000/500,000 = 60\%$$

The recovery rate in this case is *1-LGD*. We have assumed a very simple scenario. Usually, there will be overhead legal, administrative, and other costs involved in trying to recover the amount due or liquidate the collateral pledged.

The *LGD* could, in rare circumstances, go down below 0% or above 100%. The below 0% situation might arise if the value of the pledged security goes up after default, and the coupons (and so on) linked to the collateral are the property of the lender, as per the borrowing agreement. However, it is very rare for a regulator to allow for a 0% *LGD* rate assumption. There may be a floor that needs to be assigned to the *LGD* rate.

Expected loss

Expected loss (EL) can be stated as:

$$EL = EAD * PD * LGD$$

Since we will be using a mortgage dataset later on in the chapter to build a PD model, let's calculate EL for a hypothetical mortgage scenario.

Let's assume that a young couple has recently bought their first home for $200,000. They paid only a 5% deposit, and borrowed $190,000. The bank, at this time, had an EAD of $190,000. The couple's family pledged collateral of $5,000 at the time of agreeing with the borrowing facility. The house value due to recessionary effects, has gone down to an estimated $170,000. There is an additional cost of $10,000 for taking possession and selling the property that the bank provisions for a borrowing of this nature.

Hence, after selling the house, there will be a shortfall of $30,000. The borrowing is for $190,000 only. So, the net shortfall at this stage would be $20,000 of the amount borrowed. There is also collateral and a cost of recovery. The total shortfall would be $25,000. Hence, the *LGD* will be:

$$LGD = 25,000/190,000 = 13.16\%$$

The counterparty has still not defaulted. However, based on estimations, the PD is 25%. Hence, the *EL* will be:

$$EL = EAD * PD * LGD$$

$$EL = \$190,000 * 25\% * 13.16\%$$

$$EL = \$6,251$$

Having understood the key terms used for modeling, it may also be worthwhile to reflect on why credit risk management is, at times, a specialized area of modeling. Let's review the aspects of credit risk management that influence this area to become such a specialized modeling role.

Aspects of credit risk management

The following aspects of credit risk management make it a complex and challenging area of specialization.

Basel and regulatory authority guidelines

Earlier, we learned about the Basel norms. We have three versions of the Basel norms, but many more deliberations, consulting papers, and clarifications from the Basel Committee. There is already a Basel IV being spoken about, although there is no such formal name assigned to the extensions of certain aspects of Basel III that are currently being discussed by the Basel Committee.

In the case of the Eurozone and United Kingdom, the **European Central Bank (ECB)** and the **Prudential Regulatory Authority (PRA)** provide sign-offs for the advanced modeling approach. The regulators, at times, have their own interpretations of the Basel norms, in instances where there aren't sufficient clarity or guidelines issued. A modeler needs to be aware of not only the Basel framework, but the latest advice issued by the central regulator.

Governance

When we talk about modeling, at times, the governance aspect only comes in after building the model. In the case of credit risk, this aspect is at the core of the risk management strategy. If a behavioral scorecard is being built, it won't be prudent to keep on redeveloping it every few months. To stand the test of time, the underlying data system used must be robust. Also, there should be a stakeholder engagement process to kick off model development, discuss the outcomes, get a sign-off on the model, and help to implement the model. These activities entail that the governance process is set up initially, rather than at the time of submitting the model to the regulator for approval.

Validation

If the behavioral model has been built to last a few years, how is the regulator going to trust that the model is fit for purpose over time? Considerable time and other resources are spent on building these models. A large bank may have hundreds of such models built across various time periods. Some of these models might not even be representative of the current business scenario. As new data comes in, the model fit may not be accurate. To mitigate this, a validation exercise is usually carried out after a certain time period, to calibrate the model on the latest data and assess if the original model parameters are observed at the time of validation.

Data

Last but not least, in order to do all of the aforementioned activities, we need data. When dealing with credit risk management, the modeler may have to deal with various data systems. An understanding of these systems is required to build accurate models, explain the modeling process to the internal review team and the regulator, and also, to ensure that the model output can be implemented in one or multiple data systems. There may be one system to book the lending, another to manage the collaterals, and a third system to monitor the recoveries and write-offs. External bureau data may also be required, especially in the case of application scorecards. This adds to the complexity of ensuring that data quality is met and that the modeler has sufficient knowledge of the systems to leverage them for modeling.

PD model build

While a chapter cannot do justice to the whole credit risk modeling process, we will try to incorporate multiple approaches to model building. Let's start with exploring our data for the mortgage book of a retail bank.

The concept of link, customer, and account is something that most individuals dealing with credit risk modeling will become acquainted with. These concepts can be named differently in organizations, but the relationship remains similar. Individual customers may come together to form a relationship. The variable representing such relationships has been called a **link** in *Figure 3.1*. Each customer is also expected to have various lending needs. In the case of mortgages, these lending needs may be mortgage terms across various years, varying interest rates, differing **loan to values** (**LTVs**), and so on. Each of these combinations of needs may exist as a product within the bank.

Every borrowing instance from the customer is usually assigned an account or facility ID. This is usually a unique primary key. For simplicity's sake, the following figure only contains one year of data for each account.

In the following example, customers `5182106` and `6161840` have come together to open two accounts, `616135` and `616134`. These customers are linked together with the `Link` ID `5182106`. Customer `5182106` seems to be the primary customer in the link. However, in the last account that customer `6161840` has, it has broken its link with the other customer, and has instead become the sole and primary customer attached to the account. There can be many other variables forming a relationship with various ID variables. For instance, collateral pledged to the bank may have its own collateral ID. This will be needed when calculating LGD at a customer level.

A customer may not stay in default for a long period of time. Once the customer meets the obligations of a borrowing account, the account may be considered cured. However, as the following example shows, customer `1608830` has what can be called a double default. Some accounts are closed at default, whereas others return to a cured status. In some data systems, the account may still be kept active, as most recoveries or write-off actions will happen only after the defaults:

Link	Customer	Account	Date	Year	Default_date	Cure_date	Re_default_date
5182106	5182106	518225	02.07.2012	2012			
5182106	5182106	51821	03.06.2013	2013			
5182106	5182106	518273	08.06.2014	2014	08.06.2014	13.05.2015	
5182106	5182106	518296	09.06.2015	2015			
5182106	5182106	518263	31.03.2016	2016			
5182106	5182106	518211	30.06.2017	2017			
1608830	1608830	160894	06.02.2012	2012			
1608830	1608830	160818	07.12.2013	2013	07.12.2013	05.01.2014	05.12.2015
1608830	1608830	16089	04.12.2014	2014			
1608830	1608830	160843	05.12.2015	2015	05.12.2015		
1608830	1608830	160846	30.12.2016	2016			
1608830	1608830	160825	5.03.2017	2017			
5182106	6161840	616135	05.01.2014	2014			
5182106	6161840	616134	05.01.2015	2015			
6161840	6161840	616179	02.12.2016	2016			
8603912	8603912	860379	01.07.2009	2009			
8603912	8603912	860347	08.08.2010	2010			

Figure 3.1: Relationships between various IDs

The mortgage data in this instance is held in a time series format. The data contains observations from 2009 to 2017. This is a yearly snapshot of the customer's position. It shows the limit assigned to the customer, the drawn amount in the form of utilization, and the LTV ratio. The LTV ratio is calculated as borrowing/collateral. The collateral value may change over time, due to index linking of mortgage valuations over time. The customer may also provide more collateral for additional borrowing, and in some instances, such as account maturities, the collateral might be released, thereby reducing the collateral's value. Collateral, such as stocks and shares, may vary in value much more than fixed assets, such as properties. The collateral type is the nature of the collateral pledged. The portfolio value has been sourced from the credit application of the customer. The postcode index is a ranking of the postcode that has the mortgaged property. This isn't an index of the collateral property where the collateral type is property. The customer type is a flag to hold some profiling information about the customer. Arrears are instances when the customer is late on the account payment. Arrears don't mean that the customer is in default, or will go on to be in default. However, accounts with chronic arrear problems may have a higher probability of ending up in default. An account may be in arrears, but the customer may not be in arrears across various other accounts in the same time period. The following figure represents the independent variables:

Customer	Date	Utilisation	Limit	Borrowing	LTV	Collateral	Collateral type	Portfolio value	Borrowing portfolio ratio	Postcode index	Customer type	Arrears
5182106	02.07.2012	0.66	1287187	849,543	2.08	407,953	Guarantee	8,655,769	0.10	91	Overseas	1
5182106	03.06.2013	0.24	1545673	365,000	1.97	185,481	Guarantee	8,655,769	0.02	91	Overseas	1
5182106	08.06.2014	1.02	1324381	1,354,004	2.00	675,434	Guarantee	8,655,769	0.10	91	Overseas	0
5182106	09.06.2015	0.68	1545673	1,051,058	1.19	881,034	Guarantee	8,655,769	0.12	91	Overseas	0
5182106	31.03.2016	0.38	1545673	587,356	1.90	309,135	Guarantee	8,655,769	0.07	91	Overseas	0
5182106	30.06.2017	0.71	1545673	1,097,428	1.87	587,356	Guarantee	8,655,769	0.13	91	Overseas	0
1608830	06.02.2012	0.74	247086	182,844	2.85	64,242	Cash	1,823,118	0.10	78	Investor	0
1608830	07.12.2013	0.50	792660	396,330	1.25	317,064	Cash	1,823,118	0.22	78	Investor	0
1608830	04.12.2014	0.81	792660	642,055	2.19	293,284	Cash	1,823,118	0.35	78	Investor	0
1608830	05.12.2015	0.49	792660	388,403	4.08	95,119	Cash	1,823,118	0.21	78	Investor	0
1608830	30.12.2016	0.45	792660	356,697	2.25	158,532	Cash	1,823,118	0.20	78	Investor	0
1608830	5.03.2017	0.56	792660	443,890	2.15	206,092	Cash	1,823,118	0.24	78	Investor	0
6161840	05.01.2014	0.70	1503274	1,052,292	1.92	546,745	Stocks	4,839,078	0.22	71	Investor	1
6161840	05.01.2015	0.70	1237320	866,124	2.00	433,000	Stocks	4,839,078	0.18	71	Investor	1
6161840	02.12.2016	0.70	1385358	969,751	1.94	498,729	Stocks	4,839,078	0.20	71	Investor	0
8603912	01.07.2009	0.72	1813424	1,305,665	2.57	507,759	Cash	6,158,116	0.21	50	Overseas	0
8603912	08.08.2010	0.56	650803	364,450	1.75	208,257	Cash	6,158,116	0.06	50	Overseas	0

Figure 3.2: Independent variables available

Genmod procedure

Let's start the model building process by using the Genmod procedure. We will cover some aspects of data cleaning and transformation in more detail as we evaluate the initial results from modeling. The data has been rolled over to an account level where each customer only has one row per account, which showcases the customer's current position. Some new variables have been created to capture the past customer behavior. One of the new variables that we will use to assess the model fit is the length of the customer relationship.

The Genmod procedure fits generalized linear models, not just the traditional linear models. Readers may be aware that Proc logistic, a widely used procedure for primarily modeling binary outcomes, is a generalized linear model. This procedure is superior to Proc logistic, as it allows the response probability distribution to be any member of an exponential family of distributions. As a start, we will try to generate, from the Genmod procedure model, results that are similar to what we would generate using Proc logistic:

```
Proc Genmod data=model_latest_record descending;
Class collateral_type customer_type;
Model dflt = utilisation ltv collateral_type borrowing_portfolio_ratio
postcode_index customer_type arrears/ dist=binomial;
Output out=preds p=pred l=lower u=upper;
Run;
```

In *Figure 3.3*, the log of the model run shows that we have achieved model convergence, but the p-values we get for chi-square and most of the metrics are odd. There is something wrong with the model:

Analysis Of Maximum Likelihood Parameter Estimates							
Parameter	DF	Estimate	Standard Error	Wald 95% Confidence Limits		Wald Chi-Square	Pr > ChiSq
Intercept	1	-478.836	1.5438E9	-3.026E9	3.0258E9	0.00	1.0000
Utilisation	1	234.3617	1.212E9	-2.375E9	2.3754E9	0.00	1.0000
LTV	1	7.0403	70429581	-1.38E8	1.3804E8	0.00	1.0000
Collateral_type	1	1	-37.5175	1.337E9	-2.621E9	2.6206E9	0.00	1.0000
Collateral_type	2	1	-22.4757	9.1746E8	-1.798E9	1.7982E9	0.00	1.0000
Collateral_type	3	1	-28.2265	8.6701E8	-1.699E9	1.6993E9	0.00	1.0000
Collateral_type	4	0	0.0000	0.0000	0.0000	0.0000	.	.
Borrowing_portfolio_	1	72.1665	3.131E9	-6.137E9	6.1367E9	0.00	1.0000
Postcode_index	1	2.3862	22576426	-4.425E7	44248984	0.00	1.0000
Customer_type	1	1	-14.9370	9.0421E8	-1.772E9	1.7722E9	0.00	1.0000
Customer_type	2	1	10.4409	6.9651E8	-1.365E9	1.3651E9	0.00	1.0000
Customer_type	3	1	50.0915	7.6202E8	-1.494E9	1.4935E9	0.00	1.0000
Customer_type	4	1	-18.9441	8.313E8	-1.629E9	1.6293E9	0.00	1.0000
Customer_type	5	0	0.0000	0.0000	0.0000	0.0000	.	.
Arrears	1	87.6577	5.2247E8	-1.024E9	1.024E9	0.00	1.0000
Scale	0	1.0000	0.0000	1.0000	1.0000		

Figure 3.3: Output showing issues with the model

The roots of the problem can be traced immediately by looking at the response profile in *Figure 3.4*. In the non-aggregated data at the customer level, we observed 20 instances of defaults. In the aggregated data at the customer level, we are left with only five defaults. We have lost a lot of information about the defaults by only incorporating the latest records:

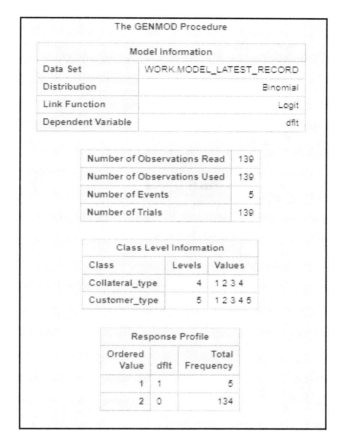

Figure 3.4: Model information showing lower defaults than expected

One of the key aspects for data preparation for modeling is to capture the information in the best way possible, when transforming or aggregating information. The defaults could have happened any time between 2009 and 2017. However, by only picking up the latest records, we ended up ignoring crucial default information when the defaults did not happen in the most recent record of the customer.

In the preceding model, we have specified the distribution as binomial. The assumption is that the profile of defaulted and non-defaulted customers is quite different. Let's test this assumption out, after ensuring that the right numbers of defaults are represented in the modeling dataset. In the data preparation step for the model rerun, the data was first bifurcated into defaulted and non-defaulted customers. In the case of defaulted customers, no transformation was carried out, and the records were incorporated into the modeling dataset. If a customer had double defaulted, then both of the records were included. For the non-defaulted customers, the latest available record was treated as being representative of the customer.

Additionally, a length of relationship variable was calculated at a customer level. If the customer had any arrears in its transaction history, the customer was assigned a value of 1 in the newly created `arrears_flag` variable. This was done to identify arrears at any point in time. Some of the customers at the point of default weren't recorded as being in arrears, which was deemed to be a data quality issue. The collateral type variable was adjudged to be of dubious quality, as most of the collateral for the borrowing should be the property that is being mortgaged, and not the populated values, such as cash, guarantees, and stocks and shares. The customer type variable was also removed; its accuracy was doubtful, since it was based on the free text data entered by the mortgage advisor, rather than the customer application verification process.

A validation dataset was also created. The randomly selected 10 records (defaulted and non-defaulted customers totaled five each) were not part of the training dataset. This was specified in the data using the weight statement. Since we have selected the validation records based on random sampling, each time the data cleaning code is run, we will get a different model output.

In *Figure 3.5*, the model information states that there are 14 observations with defaults. We have only selected five defaulted and five non-defaulted customers for validation. We have a total of 20 observations with defaults. There is a customer with a re-default that is part of the validation dataset. Hence, even though we have only five customers as part of the defaulted validation dataset, one customer in particular is contributing to two defaults.

Hence, we have six defaults in the validation dataset, and we are left with 14 only defaults (not 15) in the training dataset:

```
Proc Genmod data=model_validation descending;
Weight validation_sample;
Model dflt = utilisation ltv borrowing_portfolio_ratio postcode_index
arrears_flag
relationship_length/ dist=binomial;
Output out=preds(where=(validation_sample=0)) p=pred l=lower u=upper;
Run;
```

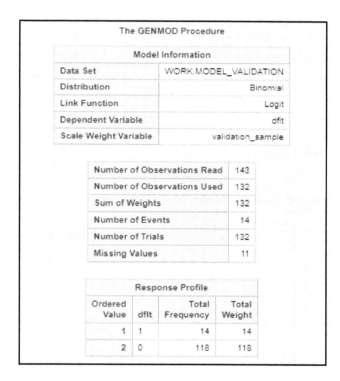

Figure 3.5: Model information for rerun model

In *Figure 3.6*, there is only one variable, `arrears_flag`, which is significant at p-value <0.05. At the <0.10 significance, the percentage of mortgage utilized is also significant. Remember that the significance changes with a different validation dataset created when a random sample of validation dataset is created by the `Proc surveyselect` data cleaning code (for further information, please download the data cleaning code):

Analysis Of Maximum Likelihood Parameter Estimates							
Parameter	DF	Estimate	Standard Error	Wald 95% Confidence Limits		Wald Chi-Square	Pr > ChiSq
Intercept	1	-24.2386	8.0649	-40.0455	-8.4317	9.03	0.0027
Utilisation	1	9.2090	4.8407	-0.2787	18.6966	3.62	0.0571
LTV	1	0.8409	0.5561	-0.2489	1.9308	2.29	0.1305
Borrowing_portfolio_	1	6.2435	4.7283	-3.0237	15.5107	1.74	0.1867
Postcode_index	1	0.0789	0.0505	-0.0201	0.1779	2.44	0.1183
arrears_flag	1	5.9412	2.5582	0.9272	10.9551	5.39	0.0202
relationship_length	1	0.2609	0.2891	-0.3057	0.8274	0.81	0.3668
Scale	0	1.0000	0.0000	1.0000	1.0000		

Figure 3.6: Model parameter estimates after removing collateral and customer type

In *Figure 3.7*, we have listed the defaulted customers selected for validation:

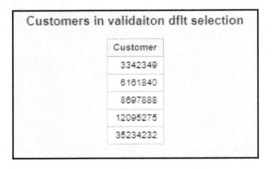

Customers in validaiton dflt selection
Customer
3342349
6161840
8697888
12095275
35234232

Figure 3.7: Defaulted customers in validation dataset

In *Figure 3.8*, we have listed the non-defaulted customers selected for validation:

Customers in validaiton non dflt selection
Customer
4232324
7567563
10870633
11228652
24123211

Figure 3.8: Non-defaulted customers in validation dataset

In *Figure 3.9*, we can see that the means for the variables in the defaulted (dflt=1) and non-defaulted (dflt=0) groups are different for all variables. The standard deviation of values is also quite different. Hence, a binomial distribution fit was chosen in the model. In terms of percentage differences, the mean of LTV and arrears is very different in the two groups. The defaulted customers have leveraged positions, and mostly tend to be in arrears at some point in their transaction history:

The MEANS Procedure

dflt=0

Variable	Label	N	Mean	Std Dev	Minimum	Maximum
Utilisation	Utilisaiton	123	0.5621138	0.2131160	0.0300000	0.8900000
LTV	LTV	123	2.0650402	1.3637526	0.0731707	6.5000000
Borrowing_portfolio_ratio	Borrowing_portfolio_ratio	123	0.1288171	0.1058244	0.0010996	0.5503003
Postcode_index	Postcode_index	123	73.6910569	14.0497536	50.0000000	99.0000000
arrears_flag		123	0.1626016	0.3705110	0	1.0000000
relationship_length		123	5.7235772	3.0922982	1.0000000	9.0000000

dflt=1

Variable	Label	N	Mean	Std Dev	Minimum	Maximum
Utilisation	Utilisation	20	0.9265874	0.2727838	0.5300000	1.8933874
LTV	LTV	20	9.2794160	17.1847257	0.2445092	67.1443259
Borrowing_portfolio_ratio	Borrowing_portfolio_ratio	20	0.4070063	0.2427159	0.1056738	0.8840264
Postcode_index	Postcode_index	20	82.3000000	11.7791073	55.0000000	98.0000000
arrears_flag		20	0.8000000	0.4103913	0	1.0000000
relationship_length		20	7.4500000	1.9861362	2.0000000	9.0000000

Figure 3.9: Variance between defaulted and non-defaulted groups

Figure 3.10 showcases the predicted value of the validation customer dataset. The predicted value, in this case, can be termed as the probability of default. The defaulted customers have a probability of default of 1. All but one instance of default sees our predicted probability being at least 0.90 for the defaulted customers. The non-defaulted customers have been assigned a very low probability of default predicted score. It seems that the model is able to predict accurately, to a large degree:

Prediction of validation dataset		
Customer	observed_default_status	Predicted Value
3342349	1	0.04695
4232324	0	0.00436
6161840	1	0.99257
7567563	0	0.00164
8697888	1	1.00000
10870633	0	0.00029
11228652	0	0.00781
12095275	1	0.93004
24123211	0	0.22609
35234232	1	0.89879
35234232	1	0.62372

Figure 3.10: Validation dataset prediction

Let's fit an ROC curve for the predicted values of the validation dataset. The Genmod procedure doesn't support an ROC curve. Let's utilize the logistic procedure without fitting any model. The predicted values have been used in the procedure to generate the ROC curve:

```
Proc logistic data=preds descending;
Model dflt = / nofit;
Roc "Genmod model" pred=pred;
Run;
```

Figure 3.11 contains the ROC curve. But what is the ROC curve, and what is its use?

ROC Model: Genmod model

ROC Model Information		
ROC Contrast Coefficients	pred	Predicted Value

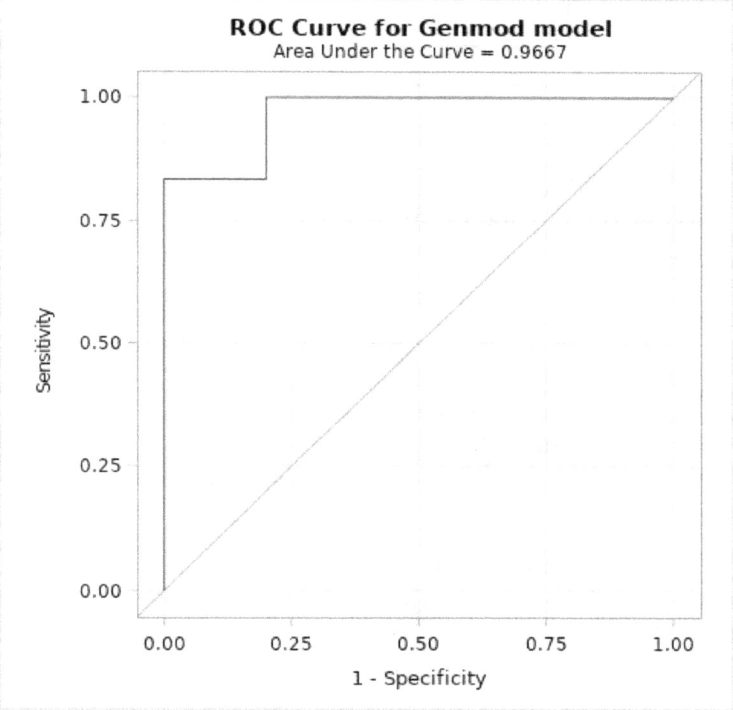

ROC Association Statistics							
	Mann-Whitney						
ROC Model	Area	Standard Error	95% Wald Confidence Limits		Somers' D	Gamma	Tau-a
Genmod model	0.9667	0.0471	0.8743	1.0000	0.9333	0.9333	0.5091

Figure 3.11: ROC curve

The ROC curve is an acronym for receiver operating characteristic curve. The ROC curve is used as a discriminatory test, to see how well the model has performed. Remember that our aim for modeling is to build a behavioral PD model. As part of that, we need to predict the PD. We have a validation dataset, and we just observed that we have had success in predicting accurately. But what are the scenarios that we might encounter when predicting? Let's look at the scenarios of an application scorecard where we will use some level of PD as a cut-off point to reject applications:

	Account performance	
	Good	Bad
Insufficient score	Rejected application but good performance (*false negative*)	Rejected and bad performance (*true negative*)
Sufficient score	Accepted and good performance (*true positive*)	Accepted and bad performance (*false positive*)

Figure 3.12: Application decision and outcome

The true positive and true negative scenarios from *Figure 3.12* are acceptable outcomes from implementing an application scorecard. However, the false negative and false positive scenarios aren't acceptable, but they are scenarios that are generally experienced. The false negative scenario is less costly than the false positive scenario. In the false negative scenario, there is only opportunity cost, whereas in the false positive scenario, the whole lending may have to be written off.

In an ROC curve, the true positive error is plotted on the *y*-axis, and the false positive error, on the *x*-axis. The *y*-axis is also known as the sensitivity, and the *x*-axis as 1-specifity. A perfect scenario with all true-positives in a prediction will have an ROC curve like the one shown in *Figure 3.13*. Somers' D can range between -1 to 1. Our model has a value of 0.93. In simplistic terms, this means that the model has good predictive ability. A perfectly predictive model will have a Somers' D value of 1:

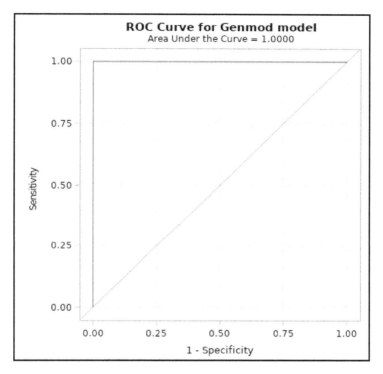

Figure 3.13: True positive perfect prediction

The **area under the curve** (**AUC**), in this case, is at the maximum (value 1). The AUC can be useful in comparing models. An AUC of 1 is rarely achieved in the practical world. In general, banks would assign the following **red, amber, and green** (**RAG**) statuses, based on the AUC:

AUC	RAG
0.9 - 1	Green
0.7-0.9	Amber
<0.7	Red

Figure 3.14: AUC and RAG status

Based on the ROC curve in *Figure 3.11*, the model would get an RAG status of green. However, this is just one of the metrics by which a model can be compared. Another useful metric is the GINI, or the Somers' D value.

With the limited data at hand, we have only built a model with one procedure. Most of the variables aren't significant. Let's build a PD model using `Proc logistic` and observe the output.

Proc logistic

Using `Proc logistic` on the same customers that are present in the training dataset of `Genmod`:

```
Proc logistic data=logistic;
Model dflt=utilisation ltv borrowing_portfolio_ratio postcode_index
arrears_flag
relationship_length;
Run;
```

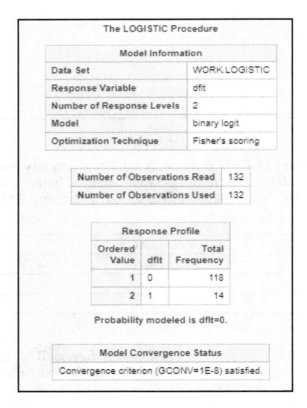

Figure 3.15: Proc logistic model information

When introducing `Genmod`, it was mentioned that we will build a model similar to what we will get by running `logistic`. Looking at *Figure 3.16*, you can see that the output is the same as *Figure 3.6*:

Analysis of Maximum Likelihood Estimates					
Parameter	DF	Estimate	Standard Error	Wald Chi-Square	Pr > ChiSq
Intercept	1	24.2386	8.0649	9.0327	0.0027
Utilisation	1	-9.2090	4.8407	3.6191	0.0571
LTV	1	-0.8409	0.5561	2.2870	0.1305
Borrowing_portfolio_	1	-6.2435	4.7283	1.7436	0.1867
Postcode_index	1	-0.0789	0.0505	2.4391	0.1183
arrears_flag	1	-5.9412	2.5582	5.3937	0.0202
relationship_length	1	-0.2609	0.2891	0.8145	0.3668

Odds Ratio Estimates			
Effect	Point Estimate	95% Wald Confidence Limits	
Utilisation	<0.001	<0.001	1.321
LTV	0.431	0.145	1.283
Borrowing_portfolio_	0.002	<0.001	20.568
Postcode_index	0.924	0.837	1.020
arrears_flag	0.003	<0.001	0.396
relationship_length	0.770	0.437	1.358

Association of Predicted Probabilities and Observed Responses			
Percent Concordant	98.8	Somers' D	0.977
Percent Discordant	1.2	Gamma	0.977
Percent Tied	0.0	Tau-a	0.187
Pairs	1652	c	0.988

Figure 3.16: Proc logistic output

Proc Genmod probit

Let's run a `probit` model. Only two values of the dependent are possible - defaulted and non-defaulted. We will use a `link` function to run a `probit` model:

```
Proc Genmod data=model_validation descending;
Weight validation_sample;
Model dflt = utilisation borrowing_portfolio_ratio postcode_index
arrears_flag
/ dist=binomial link=probit;
Output out=preds_link(where=(validation_sample=0)) p=pred l=lower u=upper;
Run;
```

Figure 3.17 contains the model information where the `probit link` function is mentioned:

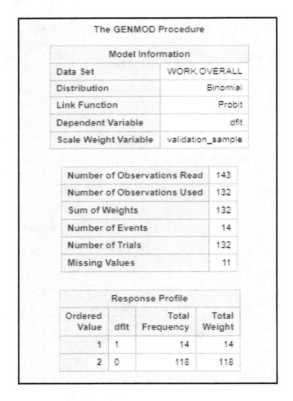

The GENMOD Procedure

Model Information	
Data Set	WORK.OVERALL
Distribution	Binomial
Link Function	Probit
Dependent Variable	dflt
Scale Weight Variable	validation_sample

Number of Observations Read	143
Number of Observations Used	132
Sum of Weights	132
Number of Events	14
Number of Trials	132
Missing Values	11

Response Profile			
Ordered Value	dflt	Total Frequency	Total Weight
1	1	14	14
2	0	118	118

Figure 3.17: Model information probit link

The specified model does not contain two of the variables that were present in the output shown in *Figure 3.6*. These are LTV and `relationship_length`. LTV and utilization both have borrowing as a common element. LTV is useful if one wants to understand the multiple of collateral that an individual has borrowed. However, in our case, the main focus is the exposure. Customers with high exposure ought to be a trigger in predicting PD as the business consensus. LTV can be useful, but most of the bank's mortgage book is highly leveraged, and a high LTV isn't necessarily going to capture the change in customer behavior over years. Utilization could have a better chance of changing around the default.

The length of a relationship has been compiled at a customer level. A customer who has defaulted in one account may do so in another account. However, at times, it is a specific product that triggers the customers into having a higher probability of default. While the overall model isn't being built at an account level, it feels like the relationship length at a customer level might not have anything to do with the probability of default. Hence, the length of relationship has also been dropped from the model building. *Figure 3.18* showcases the tests of significance for various variables. Utilization, borrowing portfolio ratio, and arrears flags are all statistically significant:

Algorithm converged.

Analysis Of Maximum Likelihood Parameter Estimates

Parameter	DF	Estimate	Standard Error	Wald 95% Confidence Limits		Wald Chi-Square	Pr > ChiSq
Intercept	1	-9.9197	2.6782	-15.1689	-4.6705	13.72	0.0002
Utilisation	1	6.2753	2.2933	1.7806	10.7700	7.49	0.0062
Borrowing_portfolio_	1	3.8592	1.9509	0.0355	7.6829	3.91	0.0479
Postcode_index	1	0.0265	0.0221	-0.0168	0.0698	1.44	0.2302
arrears_flag	1	2.3629	0.7564	0.8805	3.8454	9.76	0.0018
Scale	0	1.0000	0.0000	1.0000	1.0000		

Note: The scale parameter was held fixed.

Figure 3.18: Variable significance test and metrics

While we can see the parameter estimates in *Figure 3.18,* we can request an output of the parameter estimates at a higher precision level if we want to export the parameters outside of SAS to score data:

```
Proc Print data=parms noobs;
format estimate 12.10;
var parameter level: estimate;
Run;
```

Figure 3.19 contains the parameter estimates at a higher decimal precision:

Parameter	Estimate
Intercept	-9.919741832
Utilisation	6.2753186044
Borrowing_portfolio_	3.8591911182
Postcode_index	0.0265093379
arrears_flag	2.3629197893
Scale	1.0000000000

Figure 3.19: Parameter precision values

The requested ROC curve in *Figure 3.20* has the same AUC and other metrics as the ones in *Figure 3.11.* By removing two variables, we have the same AUC in the `probit` model, compared to what we had in the earlier model. From an implementation perspective, a model with fewer variables is desirable. However, the available data isn't exhaustive, and more data should be used before finalizing the PD model, in this instance:

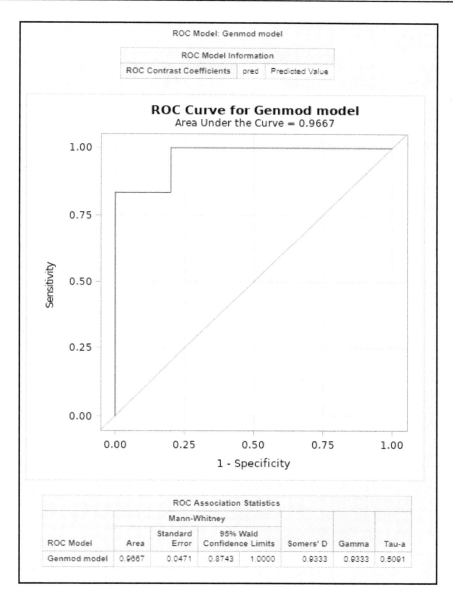

Figure 3.20: ROC curve

Summary

In this chapter, we reviewed the regulatory influences on credit risk, and understood key aspects and metrics. We also introduced the concept of a generalized linear model using `Proc Genmod`. We showcased how a logistic model can be built using `Genmod`. We also discussed how ROC curves can help us compare models.

In the next chapter, we will introduce methodologies for budget and demand forecasting.

4
Budget and Demand Forecasting

Budget and demand forecasting are important aspects of any finance team. Budget forecasting is the outcome, and demand forecasting is one of its components. Contrary to popular belief, the finance team cannot make demand forecasting decisions without consulting various other teams. The marketing team may need to be involved to figure out the impact of a brand-new commercial series on potential sales in the next 12 months. This needs to be an input in demand forecasting to calculate revenue. The risk management team needs to be consulted to calculate the impact of risk modeling on capital provision requirements. This needs to be an input in budget estimation. These examples are more apt for a mid-range or larger organization. New customers joining and churn in an organization are aspects that also impact small organizations. This would impact budget planning for a small organization.

Hindsight is a luxury that the budget-forecasting process doesn't have. Hence, demand forecasting becomes an important component of the budgeting process. There are various qualitative and quantitative ways in which demand forecasting can be done. These could range from the de-briefing of sales staff, updating a model on a spreadsheet with basic assumptions, conducting a primary research survey, advanced statistical modeling, and so on.

Some of the topics that we will cover in the chapter include:

- Understanding the Markov model and exploring its use
- Forecasting using a Markov model
- Comparing Markov model forecasts with ARIMA generated forecasts
- Showcasing the use of the Markov model Monte Carlo method for data imputation

The need for the Markov model

Given the range of models we are discussing in this book, is there a need to discuss Markov models? When we speak about forecasting, one of the main inputs is the historical information. This could be in the form of a time series. However, Markov models don't need historical information to be able to forecast. When we build a Markov model, we are interested in the state (value/behavior/phenomenon) of a subject at the present time. We are also interested in the states that the subject can get transitioned to and the transition probabilities involved. A textbook definition of the Markov model would be a stochastic model describing a sequence of possible events in which the probability of each event depends only on the state attained in the previous event. To understand the terms better, let's look at the states that a car being driven may experience:

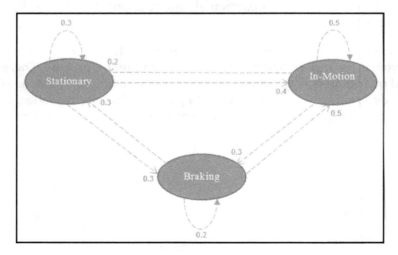

Transition state flow

P(Stationary | Stationary)=0.3

P(In motion | Stationary)=0.4

P(Braking | Stationary)=0.3

— — — — — — — — — — — — — —

Total Probability of transition from Stationary State = 1

The possible transition states are as follows:

Original state	Transitioned state
Stationary	Stationary
Stationary	In motion
Stationary	Braking
In motion	In motion
In motion	Stationary
In motion	Braking
Braking	Braking
Braking	Stationary
Braking	In motion

Figure 4.1: Inter-state transition probability of a car

While considering transition states, you have to bear in mind that a state can continue to remain the same. Hence, a car in a stationary state can remain in the same state (P(Stationary | Stationary)) or move to a different state, such as in motion (P(In motion | Stationary)). The rules of probability hold true in this case: the transition probabilities from a state always add up to 1. *Figure 4.1* contains the flow of the transitional probabilities in a diagram and a tabular format. If we want to estimate the probability of reaching a particular state, we can use the transitional probability. If the car is in motion, then the probability of it being in the same state? The answer to this is P(In motion | In motion)=0.5. To take this illustration a step further, the probability of the next state being in motion and the one after that being stationary is P(In motion | In motion)P(Stationary | In motion)=0.5*0.2=0.1.

Markov models don't need to use time series data as a direct input. Later on, we will see how, by using data points for only one time period, we can build a forecasting model. However, the model does use the transition matrix of probabilities. This transition matrix is derived from the time series data. There is an indirect dependency on time series data in certain business situations, and this will be highlighted in our business problem.

But can Markov models be used only for forecasting? There are various other uses of Markov models. One of the issues that modelers have to deal with is when there is missing information for a variable over various time periods. There exist various imputation methodologies that a modeler could use. One of the methods to impute missing values is to use the Markov model. In this case, the model doesn't need to be used for forecasting but can enable forecasting by helping with imputation. The missing data points can be part of a time series. The Markov model thereby has an important relationship with time series data. It can be used to impute missing values into time series, leverage the time series to generate a transition matrix, or be used for both these purposes.

This chapter will help to distinguish the benefits of the ARIMA and Markov model forecasting techniques. Additionally, we will learn how the Markov method can be used to impute missing values for a time series.

Business problem

While a few decades ago, retail banks primarily made profits by leveraging their treasury office, recent years have seen fee income become a major source of profitability. Accepting deposits from customers and lending to other customers is one of the core functions of the treasury. However, charging for current or savings accounts with add-on facilities such as breakdown cover, mobile and other insurances, and so on, has become a lucrative avenue for banks. One retail bank has a plain vanilla classic bank account, mid-tier premier, and a top-of-the-range, benefits included platinum account. The classic account is offered free and the premier and platinum have fees of $10 and $20 per month respectively. The marketing team has just relaunched the fee-based accounts with added benefits. The finance team wanted a projection of how much revenue could be generated via the premier and the platinum accounts.

Markovian model approach

Even though we have three types of account, the classic, premier, and the platinum, it doesn't mean that we are only going to have nine transition types possible as in *Figure 4.1*. There are customers who will upgrade, but also others who may downgrade. There could also be some customers who leave the bank and at the same time there will be a constant inflow of new customers. Let's evaluate the transition states flow for our business problem:

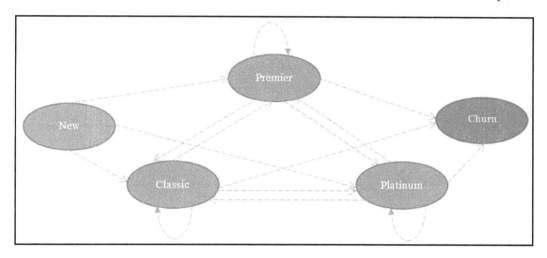

Figure 4.2: Transition flow of customers across account types

In *Figure 4.2*, we haven't jotted down the transition probability between each state. We can try to do this by looking at the historical customer movements, to arrive at the transitional probability. Be aware that most business managers would prefer to use their instincts while assigning transitional probabilities. They may achieve some merit in this approach, as the managers may be able to incorporate the various factors that may have influenced the customer movements between states. A promotion offering 40% off the platinum account (effective rate $12/month, down from $20/month) may have ensured that more customers in the promotion period opted for the platinum account than the premier offering ($10/month). Let's examine the historical data of customer account preferences. The data is compiled for the years 2008 – 2018. This doesn't account for any new customers joining after January 1, 2008 and also ignores information on churned customers in the period of interest.

Figure 4.3 consists of customers who have been with the bank since 2008:

Year	Active customer counts (Millions)			
	Classic (Cl)	Premium (Pr)	Platinum (Pl)	Total customers
2008 H1	30.68	5.73	1.51	37.92
2008 H2	30.65	5.74	1.53	37.92
2009 H1	30.83	5.43	1.66	37.92
2009 H2	30.9	5.3	1.72	37.92
2010 H1	31.1	4.7	2.12	37.92
2010 H2	31.05	4.73	2.14	37.92
2011 H1	31.01	4.81	2.1	37.92
2011 H2	30.7	5.01	2.21	37.92
2012 H1	30.3	5.3	2.32	37.92
2012 H2	29.3	6.4	2.22	37.92
2013 H1	29.3	6.5	2.12	37.92
2013 H2	28.8	7.3	1.82	37.92
2014 H1	28.8	8.1	1.02	37.92
2014 H2	28.7	8.3	0.92	37.92
2015 H1	28.6	8.34	0.98	37.92
2015 H2	28.4	8.37	1.15	37.92
2016 H1	27.6	9.01	1.31	37.92
2016 H2	26.5	9.5	1.92	37.92
2017 H1	26	9.8	2.12	37.92
2017 H2	25.3	10.3	2.32	37.92

Figure 4.3: Active customers since 2008

Since we are only considering active customers, and no new customers are joining or leaving the bank, we can calculate the number of customers moving from one state to another using the data in *Figure 4.3*:

Year	Customer movement count to next year (Millions)									
	Cl-Cl	Cl-Pr	Cl-Pl	Pr-Pr	Pr-Cl	Pr-Pl	Pl-Pl	Pl-Cl	Pl-Pr	Total customers
2008 H1	-	-	-	-	-	-	-	-	-	-
2008 H2	30.28	0.2	0.2	5.5	0	0.23	1.1	0.37	0.04	37.92
2009 H1	30.3	0.1	0.25	5.1	0.53	0.11	1.3	0	0.23	37.92

2009 H2	30.5	0.32	0.01	4.8	0.2	0.43	1.28	0.2	0.18	37.92
2010 H1	30.7	0.2	0	4.3	0	1	1.12	0.4	0.2	37.92
2010 H2	30.7	0.2	0.2	4.11	0.35	0.24	1.7	0	0.42	37.92
2011 H1	30.9	0	0.15	4.6	0	0.13	1.82	0.11	0.21	37.92
2011 H2	30.2	0.8	0.01	3.8	0.1	0.91	1.29	0.4	0.41	37.92
2012 H1	30.29	0.4	0.01	4.9	0.01	0.1	2.21	0	0	37.92
2012 H2	29.3	0.9	0.1	5.3	0	0	2.12	0	0.2	37.92
2013 H1	29.2	0.1	0	6.1	0.1	0.2	1.92	0	0.3	37.92
2013 H2	28.6	0.3	0.4	6.5	0	0	1.42	0.2	0.5	37.92
2014 H1	28.7	0.1	0	7.2	0.1	0	1.02	0	0.8	37.92
2014 H2	28.7	0	0.1	8.1	0	0	0.82	0	0.2	37.92
2015 H1	28.6	0	0.1	8.3	0	0	0.88	0	0.04	37.92
2015 H2	28.3	0	0.3	8	0.1	0.24	0.61	0	0.37	37.92
2016 H1	27.6	0.8	0	8.21	0	0.16	1.15	0	0	37.92
2016 H2	26	1	0.6	8.21	0.5	0.3	1.02	0	0.29	37.92
2017 H1	25	0.5	1	8	0.5	1	0.12	0.5	1.3	37.92
2017 H2	25.3	0.1	0.6	9	0	0.8	0.92	0	1.2	37.92

Figure 4.4: Customer transition state counts

In *Figure 4.4*, we can see the customer movements between various states. We don't have the movements for the first half of 2008 as this is the start of the series. In the second half of 2008, we see that 30.28 out of 30.68 million customers (30.68 is the figure from the first half of 2008) were still using a classic account. However, 0.4 million customers moved away to premium and platinum accounts. The total customers remain constant at 37.92 million as we have ignored new customers joining and any customers who have left the bank. From this table, we can calculate the transition probabilities for each state:

Year	Cl-Cl	Cl-Pr	Cl-Pl	Pr-Pr	Pr-Cl	Pr-Pl	Pl-Pl	Pl-Cl	Pl-Pr
2008 H2	98.7%	0.7%	0.7%	96.0%	0.0%	4.0%	72.8%	24.5%	2.6%
2009 H1	98.9%	0.3%	0.8%	88.9%	9.2%	1.9%	85.0%	0.0%	15.0%
2009 H2	98.9%	1.0%	0.0%	88.4%	3.7%	7.9%	77.1%	12.0%	10.8%
2010 H1	99.4%	0.6%	0.0%	81.1%	0.0%	18.9%	65.1%	23.3%	11.6%
2010 H2	98.7%	0.6%	0.6%	87.4%	7.4%	5.1%	80.2%	0.0%	19.8%
2011 H1	99.5%	0.0%	0.5%	97.3%	0.0%	2.7%	85.0%	5.1%	9.8%
2011 H2	97.4%	2.6%	0.0%	79.0%	2.1%	18.9%	61.4%	19.0%	19.5%
2012 H1	98.7%	1.3%	0.0%	97.8%	0.2%	2.0%	100.0%	0.0%	0.0%

2012 H2	96.7%	3.0%	0.3%	100.0%	0.0%	0.0%	91.4%	0.0%	8.6%
2013 H1	99.7%	0.3%	0.0%	95.3%	1.6%	3.1%	86.5%	0.0%	13.5%
2013 H2	97.6%	1.0%	1.4%	100.0%	0.0%	0.0%	67.0%	9.4%	23.6%
2014 H1	99.7%	0.3%	0.0%	98.6%	1.4%	0.0%	56.0%	0.0%	44.0%
2014 H2	99.7%	0.0%	0.3%	100.0%	0.0%	0.0%	80.4%	0.0%	19.6%
2015 H1	99.7%	0.0%	0.3%	100.0%	0.0%	0.0%	95.7%	0.0%	4.3%
2015 H2	99.0%	0.0%	1.0%	95.9%	1.2%	2.9%	62.2%	0.0%	37.8%
2016 H1	97.2%	2.8%	0.0%	98.1%	0.0%	1.9%	100.0%	0.0%	0.0%
2016 H2	94.2%	3.6%	2.2%	91.1%	5.5%	3.3%	77.9%	0.0%	22.1%
2017 H1	94.3%	1.9%	3.8%	84.2%	5.3%	10.5%	6.2%	26.0%	67.7%
2017 H2	97.3%	0.4%	2.3%	91.8%	0.0%	8.2%	43.4%	0.0%	56.6%

Figure 4.5: Transition state probability

In *Figure 4.5*, we have converted the transition counts into probabilities. If 30.28 million customers in 2008 H2 out of 30.68 million customers in 2008 H1 are retained as classic customers, we can say that the retention rate is 98.7%, or the probability of customers staying with the same account type in this instance is .987. Using these details, we can compute the average transition between states across the time series. These averages can be used as the transition probabilities that will be used in the transition matrix for the model:

	Cl	Pr	Pl
Cl	98.2%	1.1%	0.8%
Pr	2.0%	93.2%	4.8%
Pl	6.3%	20.4%	73.3%

Figure 4.6: Transition probabilities aggregated

The probability of classic customers retaining the same account type between semiannual time periods is 98.2%. The lowest retain probability is for platinum customers as they are expected to transition to another customer account type 26.7% of the time. Let's use the transition matrix in *Figure 4.6* to run our Markov model.

Use this code for `Data` setup:

```
DATA Current;
input date CL PR PL;
datalines;
2017.2 25.3 10.3 2.32
;
Run;

Data Netflow;
input date CL PR PL;
datalines;
2018.1 0.21 0.1 0.05
2018.2 0.22 0.16 0.06
2019.1 .24 0.18 0.08
2019.2 0.28 0.21 0.1
2020.1 0.31 0.23 0.14
;
Run;

Data TransitionMatrix;
input CL PR PL;
datalines;
0.98 0.01 0.01
0.02 0.93 0.05
0.06 0.21 0.73
;
Run;
```

In the current data set, we have chosen the last available data point, 2017 H2. This is the base position of customer counts across classic, premium, and platinum accounts. While calculating the transition matrix, we haven't taken into account new joiners or leavers. However, to enable forecasting we have taken 2017 H2 as our base position. The transition matrix seen in *Figure 4.6* has been input as a separate dataset.

Here is the Markov model code:

```
PROC IML;
use Current; read all into Current;
use Netflow; read all into Netflow;
use TransitionMatrix; read all into TransitionMatrix;


Current = Current [1,2:4];
Netflow = Netflow [,2:4];

Model_2018_1 = Current * TransitionMatrix + Netflow [1,];
```

```
Model_2018_2 = Model_2018_1 * TransitionMatrix + Netflow [1,];
Model_2019_1 = Model_2018_2 * TransitionMatrix + Netflow [1,];
Model_2019_2 = Model_2019_1 * TransitionMatrix + Netflow [1,];
Model_2020_1 = Model_2019_2 * TransitionMatrix + Netflow [1,];

Budgetinputs =
Model_2018_1//Model_2018_2//Model_2019_1//Model_2019_2//Model_2020_1;

Create Budgetinputs from Budgetinputs;
append from Budgetinputs;
Quit;

Data Output;
Set Budgetinputs (rename=(Col1=Cl Col2=Pr Col3=Pl));
Run;

Proc print data=output;
Run;
```

Obs	Cl	Pr	Pl
1	25.3492	10.4192	2.51160
2	25.4113	10.5708	2.65792
3	25.4840	10.7431	2.77293
4	25.5655	10.9282	2.86624
5	25.6547	11.1208	2.94442

Figure 4.7: Model output

The Markov model has been run and we are able to generate forecasts for all account types for the requested five periods. We can immediately see that there is an increase forecasted for all the account types. This is being driven by the net flow of customers. We have derived the forecasts by essentially using the following equation:

*Forecast = Current Period * Transition Matrix + Net Flow*

Once the 2018 H1 forecast is derived, we replace the *Current Period* with the 2018 H1 forecasted number while trying to forecast the 2018 H2 numbers. We are doing this as, based on the 2018 H1 customer counts, the transition probabilities will determine how many customers move across states. This will help generate the forecasted customer count for the required period.

Now, since we have our forecasts let's take a step back and revisit our business goals. The finance team wants to estimate the revenues from the revamped premium and platinum customer accounts for the next few forecasting periods. As we have seen, one of the important drivers of the forecasting process is the transition probability. This transition probability is driven by historical customer movements, as shown in *Figure 4.4*. What if the marketing team doesn't agree with the transitional probabilities calculated in *Figure 4.6*? As we discussed, 26.7% of platinum customers aren't retained in this account type. Since we are not considering customer churn out of the bank, this means that a large proportion of platinum customers downgrade their accounts. One of the reasons the marketing teams revamped the accounts is due to this reason. The marketing team feels that it will be able to raise the retention rates for platinum customers and want the finance team to run an alternate forecasting scenario. This is, in fact, one of the pros of the Markov model approach as by tweaking the transition probabilities we can run various business scenarios. Let's compare the base and the alternate scenario forecasts generated in *Figure 4.8*:

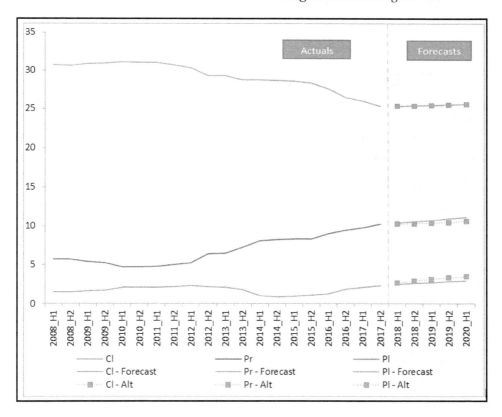

A change in the transition probabilities of how platinum customers moved to various states has brought about a significant change in the forecast for premium and platinum customer accounts. For classic customers, the change in the forecast between the base and the alternate scenario is negligible, as shown in the table in *Figure 4.8*. The finance team can decide which scenario is best suited for budget forecasting:

	Cl	Pr	Pl
Cl	98.2%	1.1%	0.8%
Pr	2.0%	93.2%	4.8%
Pl	5.0%	15.0%	80.0%

Figure 4.8: Model forecasts and updated transition probabilities

In Chapter 2, *Forecasting Stock Prices and Portfolio Decisions Using Time Series*, we introduced the concept of ARIMA. Let's try and use it to generate forecasts for our business problem, and compare it to the Markov model.

ARIMA model approach

To explore the basic concepts of ARIMA, please refer to Chapter 2, *Forecasting Stock Prices and Portfolio Decisions Using Time Series*. In this section, we will try and find the best suited ARIMA model to our three series: classic, premium, and platinum account types. We will be using historic time series data (*Figure 4.3*) to generate forecasts for five periods.

This is the data setup and ARIMA identification for the classic account:

```
Data Past;
input Cl Pr Pl;
datalines;
30.68 5.73 1.51
30.65 5.74 1.53
30.83 5.43 1.66
30.9 5.3 1.72
31.1 4.7 2.12
31.05 4.73 2.14
31.01 4.81 2.1
30.7 5.01 2.21
30.3 5.3 2.32
29.3 6.4 2.22
29.3 6.5 2.12
28.8 7.3 1.82
28.8 8.1 1.02
28.7 8.3 0.92
```

```
28.6 8.34 0.98
28.4 8.37 1.15
27.6 9.01 1.31
26.5 9.5 1.92
26 9.8 2.12
25.3 10.3 2.32
;
Run;

Ods Graphics On;
PROC ARIMA Data=Past;
identify var=Cl scan esacf;
RUN;
```

The first step in the ARIMA model is to identify the **autoregressive (AR)** – p, differencing – d, and **moving average (MA)** – q components of the model. We have used the `scan` and the `esacf` options, which will help us in identifying the values of p, d, and q.

The chi-square probability values for the `scan` option in *Figure 4.9* show that 0.701 (AR2, MA0) and 0.0671 (AR0, MA2) are the first instances when at a five percent level of significance we failed to reject the hypothesis of no correlation:

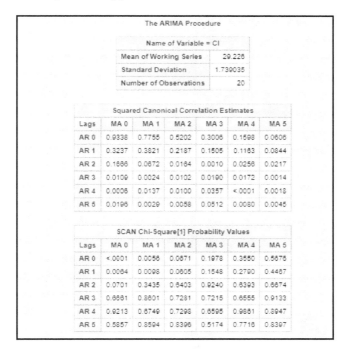

The ARIMA Procedure

Name of Variable = Cl	
Mean of Working Series	29.226
Standard Deviation	1.739035
Number of Observations	20

Squared Canonical Correlation Estimates

Lags	MA 0	MA 1	MA 2	MA 3	MA 4	MA 5
AR 0	0.9338	0.7755	0.5202	0.3006	0.1598	0.0606
AR 1	0.3237	0.3821	0.2187	0.1505	0.1163	0.0844
AR 2	0.1666	0.0672	0.0164	0.0010	0.0256	0.0217
AR 3	0.0109	0.0024	0.0102	0.0190	0.0172	0.0014
AR 4	0.0006	0.0137	0.0100	0.0357	<.0001	0.0018
AR 5	0.0196	0.0029	0.0058	0.0512	0.0080	0.0045

SCAN Chi-Square[1] Probability Values

Lags	MA 0	MA 1	MA 2	MA 3	MA 4	MA 5
AR 0	<.0001	0.0056	0.0671	0.1978	0.3550	0.5676
AR 1	0.0064	0.0098	0.0605	0.1548	0.2790	0.4467
AR 2	0.0701	0.3435	0.6403	0.9240	0.6393	0.6674
AR 3	0.6661	0.8601	0.7281	0.7215	0.6555	0.9133
AR 4	0.9213	0.6749	0.7298	0.6595	0.9861	0.8947
AR 5	0.5857	0.8594	0.8396	0.5174	0.7716	0.8397

Let us also look at the chi-square test for the `esacf` option. It shows that the first instance where at a 5 percent level of significance we failed to reject the hypothesis of no correlation is 0.2419 (AR1, MA0) and 0.0598 (AR0, MA1). We have other values of p and q also suggested by the `esacf` option. For the classic account customers, we have seven model choices: ARMA (2,0), ARMA (0,2), ARIMA (1,1,0), and ARIMA (0,2,0) based on scan output, and ARMA (1,0), ARIMA (0,1,0) or ARMA (0,1) based on `esacf` output:

Extended Sample Autocorrelation Function						
Lags	MA 0	MA 1	MA 2	MA 3	MA 4	MA 5
AR 0	0.8201	0.6446	0.4576	0.3224	0.2245	0.1341
AR 1	0.2685	0.3248	0.2347	0.2680	0.0560	-0.1934
AR 2	0.4830	0.2466	0.3743	0.1709	-0.1061	0.0356
AR 3	-0.0419	0.6598	0.0053	0.0833	0.1224	0.0189
AR 4	-0.2556	0.6356	0.3666	0.2567	0.0913	-0.0796
AR 5	0.7310	0.5196	-0.2981	-0.0722	-0.2879	

ESACF Probability Values						
Lags	MA 0	MA 1	MA 2	MA 3	MA 4	MA 5
AR 0	0.0002	0.0598	0.2509	0.4470	0.6067	0.7614
AR 1	0.2419	0.2448	0.4661	0.4438	0.8595	0.5212
AR 2	0.0404	0.3062	0.3171	0.5566	0.7351	0.9344
AR 3	0.8629	0.0076	0.9870	0.8464	0.7893	0.9614
AR 4	0.3067	0.0357	0.4146	0.5951	0.8454	0.8253
AR 5	0.0046	0.0448	0.3918	0.8243	0.3888	

ARMA(p+d,q) Tentative Order Selection Tests			
SCAN		ESACF	
p+d	q	p+d	q
2	0	1	0
0	2	0	1
		4	2
		5	2

(5% Significance Level)

Figure 4.9: ARIMA identification classic account customers

Figure 4.10 contains some of the plots of classic account customers without any model estimation. There is a gradual decline in the ACF plot, indicating a stationary time series. It may be a better idea to use at least one of the differencing models to compare the available options for modeling the classic account customers via the ARIMA methodology.

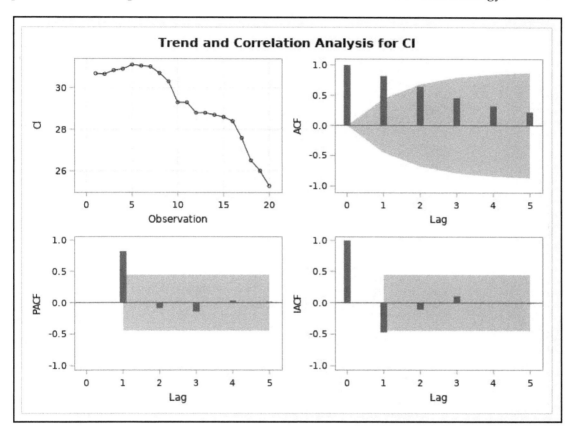

Figure 4.10: ARIMA identification plots classic account customers

Here is the code for estimating models for classic account customers:

```
PROC ARIMA Data=Past;
identify var=Cl(1);
estimate p=1;
forecast lead=5 interval=semiyear out=Cl1;
identify var=Cl;
estimate p=2;
forecast lead=5 interval=semiyear out=Cl2;
identify var=Cl;
```

```
estimate q=1;
forecast lead=5 interval=semiyear out=Cl3;
RUN;
```

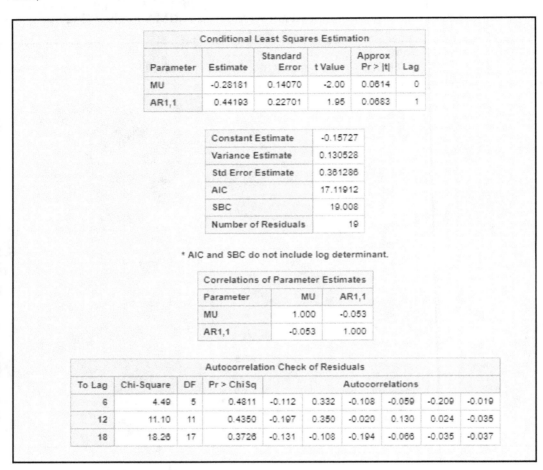

Figure 4.11: ARIMA estimation classic – differencing ARIMA (1,1,0)

In *Figure 4.11*, the first drawback of the ARIMA (1,1,0) model is that although the *t* value of autoregressive parameter AR1,1 shows that the term is significant, the p value indicates that at a 0.05 level, the term is insignificant. As soon as we move to the autocorrelation check of residuals, we encounter another problem. This section of the output relates to the white noise test. The null hypothesis is that no autocorrelations of the series are significantly different from 0 for the given lags.

Remember that ARIMA is based on autocorrelations being present. Given the p values >0.05 we cannot reject the null hypothesis. This means that autocorrelations are present for none of the lags. There is no need for an ARIMA model when we have used p=1, d=1, and q=0.

In *Figure 4.12*, let's evaluate our next model, ARMA (2,0). The term AR1, 1 is significant. The term AR (1,) is insignificant and doesn't add any value to the model, as shown in the following table:

	Conditional Least Squares Estimation				
Parameter	Estimate	Standard Error	t Value	Approx Pr > |t|	Lag
MU	30.11611	0.40917	73.60	<.0001	0
AR1,1	1.38761	0.25675	5.40	<.0001	1
AR1,2	-0.38762	0.31097	-1.25	0.2295	2

In this model too, we have an issue with the white noise null hypothesis. Since it cannot be rejected at the given p values, we should ideally discard this model and look for another alternative. See the following tables:

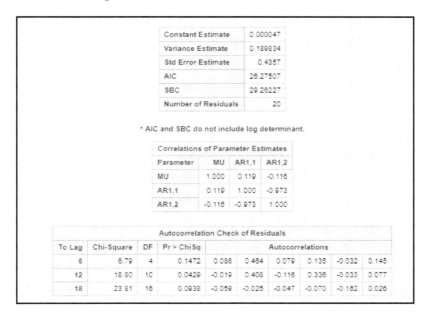

Constant Estimate	0.000047
Variance Estimate	0.189834
Std Error Estimate	0.4357
AIC	26.27507
SBC	29.26227
Number of Residuals	20

* AIC and SBC do not include log determinant.

Correlations of Parameter Estimates			
Parameter	MU	AR1,1	AR1,2
MU	1.000	0.119	-0.116
AR1,1	0.119	1.000	-0.973
AR1,2	-0.116	-0.973	1.000

Autocorrelation Check of Residuals									
To Lag	Chi-Square	DF	Pr > ChiSq	Autocorrelations					
6	6.79	4	0.1472	0.086	0.464	0.079	0.135	-0.032	0.145
12	18.80	10	0.0429	-0.019	0.408	-0.116	0.336	-0.033	0.077
18	23.81	16	0.0938	-0.059	-0.025	-0.047	-0.070	-0.162	0.026

Figure 4.12: ARIMA estimation classic – ARMA (2, 0)

In *Figure 4.13*, we have the output of the ARMA (0,1) model. A quick check shows that we can reject the null hypothesis at all the default lags that have been tested. This shows the need for an ARIMA model. The *t* value and the p statistic indicate that the term MA1,1 is significant. Usually, we should go with a lower AIC and BIC model. In both *Figure 4.11* and *Figure 4.12*, we have a lower AIC and BIC. However, due to the inability to reject the white noise null hypothesis, it would be prudent to go with the higher AIC and BIC in ARMA (0,1). A lower AIC and BIC would be preferable when comparing models, but due to the inability to reject the white noise null hypothesis, we are going ahead with the relatively higher AIC and BIC. Remember, we have six potential models for the classic account types that we can test. We aren't going to test for all of them and will now continue to look at some more diagnostics of the classic account series ARMA (0,1) model. See the following table:

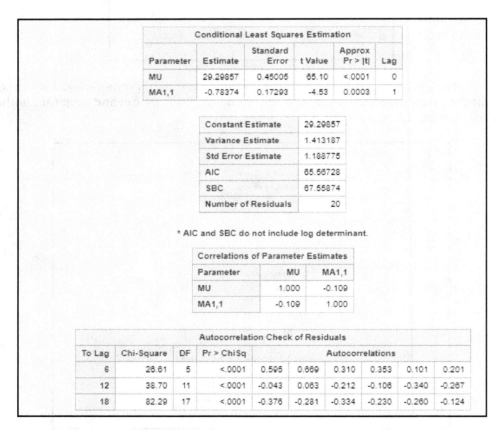

Conditional Least Squares Estimation

Parameter	Estimate	Standard Error	t Value	Approx Pr > |t|	Lag
MU	29.29857	0.45005	65.10	<.0001	0
MA1,1	-0.78374	0.17293	-4.53	0.0003	1

Constant Estimate	29.29857
Variance Estimate	1.413187
Std Error Estimate	1.188775
AIC	65.56728
SBC	67.55874
Number of Residuals	20

* AIC and SBC do not include log determinant.

Correlations of Parameter Estimates

Parameter	MU	MA1,1
MU	1.000	-0.109
MA1,1	-0.109	1.000

Autocorrelation Check of Residuals

To Lag	Chi-Square	DF	Pr > ChiSq	Autocorrelations					
6	26.61	5	<.0001	0.595	0.669	0.310	0.353	0.101	0.201
12	38.70	11	<.0001	-0.043	0.063	-0.212	-0.106	-0.340	-0.267
18	82.29	17	<.0001	-0.376	-0.281	-0.334	-0.230	-0.260	-0.124

Figure 4.13: ARIMA estimation classic – ARMA (0, 1)

When comparing the ACF plot in *Figure 4.10* and *Figure 4.14*, you can observe that ACF decreases significantly more in the latter figure where we have plotted the ARMA (0,1) model. However, there still seems to be some stationarity and the ACF plot doesn't show sudden declines till **Lag 3** in *Figure 4.14*:

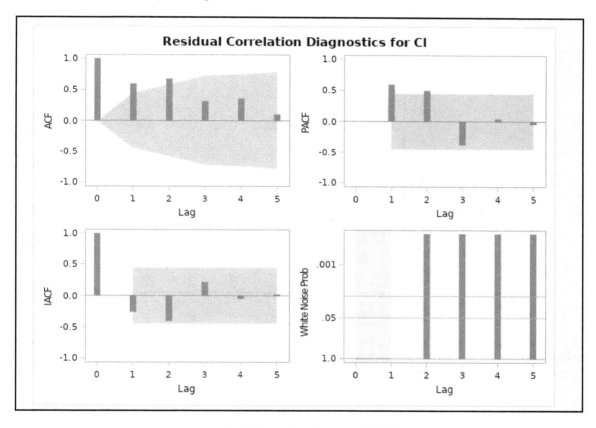

Figure 4.14: ARIMA residual correlation classic - ARMA (0, 1)

On examination of the residual normality diagnostics in *Figure 4.15*, it seems that the residuals are normally distributed. We can go ahead and have a look at the forecasts:

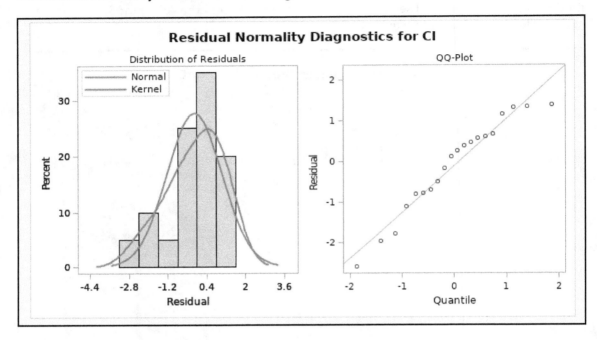

Figure 4.15: ARIMA residual normality classic - ARMA (0, 1)

In *Figure 4.16*, we have the forecasts for classic customer account types for five periods. We will compare the ARIMA forecasts with Markov model output once we have generated output for the premium and platinum customer accounts:

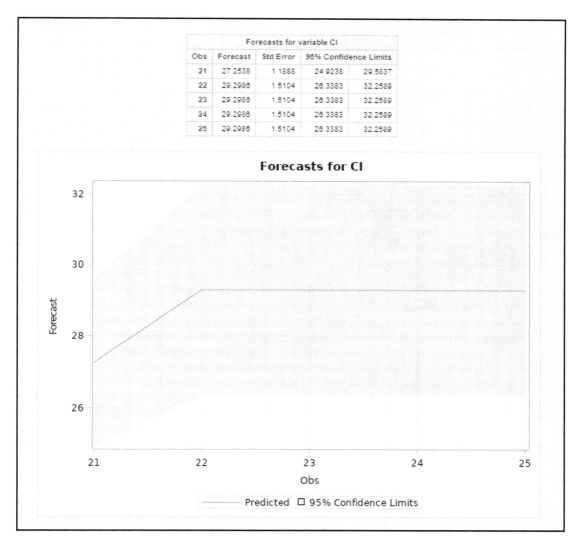

Forecasts for variable CI				
Obs	Forecast	Std Error	95% Confidence Limits	
21	27.2538	1.1888	24.9238	29.5837
22	29.2986	1.5104	26.3383	32.2589
23	29.2986	1.5104	26.3383	32.2589
24	29.2986	1.5104	26.3383	32.2589
25	29.2986	1.5104	26.3383	32.2589

Figure 4.16: ARIMA forecasts classic - ARMA (0, 1)

This is the ARIMA identification code for premium and account:

```
Ods Graphics On;
PROC ARIMA Data=Past;
identify var=Pr scan esacf;
identify var=Pl scan esacf;
RUN;
```

From the chi-square probability values from the scan option, $p+d = 2$ and $q = 0$ seems to be a fair model option given that the first value in the matrix greater than 0.05 in *Figure 4.17* is AR2 MA0:

SCAN Chi-Square[1] Probability Values						
Lags	MA 0	MA 1	MA 2	MA 3	MA 4	MA 5
AR 0	<.0001	0.0084	0.0769	0.2132	0.4102	0.7374
AR 1	0.0166	0.0940	0.1925	0.1709	0.2757	0.2773
AR 2	0.4044	0.8951	0.7750	0.8476	0.8097	0.6988
AR 3	0.6271	0.8543	0.8628	0.9255	0.9436	0.8886
AR 4	0.4692	0.8387	0.9231	0.9294	0.9050	0.9745
AR 5	0.6366	0.7941	0.9393	0.9920	0.9476	0.8799

For the `esacf` option, AR1 MA0 and AR0 MA2 fit the criterion of first value greater than 0.05. We already have AR1 MA0 and hence AR3 MA0 doesn't look like an attractive option, unless of course higher-order differencing is needed to achieve a stationary time series. Let's fit an ARIMA (1,1,0), ARMA (1,0), and ARMA (0,2) model and select the best possible option for forecasting premium account customer counts:

ESACF Probability Values						
Lags	MA 0	MA 1	MA 2	MA 3	MA 4	MA 5
AR 0	<.0001	0.0372	0.1682	0.3539	0.5637	0.8041
AR 1	0.2143	0.2912	0.5400	0.8802	0.3206	0.2534
AR 2	0.0289	0.6507	0.5412	0.9893	0.2788	0.9201
AR 3	0.8883	0.0650	0.9469	0.9183	0.1979	0.8688
AR 4	0.0038	0.1339	0.3990	0.6333	0.3454	0.9933
AR 5	0.0299	0.2344	0.7499	0.6051	0.2405	

Figure 4.17: ARIMA identification premium account customers

Here is the code for estimating models for premium account customers:

```
PROC ARIMA Data=Past;
identify var=Pr(1);
estimate p=1;
forecast lead=5 interval=semiyear out=Pr1;
identify var=Pr;
estimate p=1;
forecast lead=5 interval=semiyear out=Pr2;
identify var=Pr;
estimate q=2;
forecast lead=5 interval=semiyear out=Pr3;
RUN;
```

In *Figure 4.18*, the first drawback of the ARIMA (1,1,0) model is that although the *t* value of autoregressive parameter AR1, 1 shows that the term is significant, the p value indicates that at a 0.05 level, the term is insignificant. As soon as we move to the autocorrelation check of residuals, we encounter another problem. This section of the output relates to the white noise test. The null hypothesis is that no autocorrelations of the series are significantly different from 0 for the given lags. Remember that ARIMA is based on autocorrelations being present. Given the p values >0.05, we cannot reject the null hypothesis. This means that autocorrelations are present for none of the lags. There is no need for an ARIMA model when we have use p=1, d=1, and q=0.

This is exactly the same result we got when we used a similar model to test the robustness of the model on the classic account series:

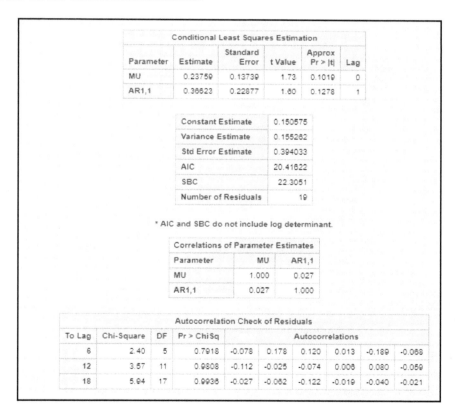

Conditional Least Squares Estimation

Parameter	Estimate	Standard Error	t Value	Approx Pr > |t|	Lag
MU	0.23759	0.13739	1.73	0.1019	0
AR1,1	0.36623	0.22877	1.60	0.1278	1

Constant Estimate	0.150575
Variance Estimate	0.155262
Std Error Estimate	0.394033
AIC	20.41622
SBC	22.3051
Number of Residuals	19

* AIC and SBC do not include log determinant.

Correlations of Parameter Estimates

Parameter	MU	AR1,1
MU	1.000	0.027
AR1,1	0.027	1.000

Autocorrelation Check of Residuals

To Lag	Chi-Square	DF	Pr > ChiSq	Autocorrelations					
6	2.40	5	0.7918	-0.078	0.178	0.120	0.013	-0.189	-0.068
12	3.57	11	0.9808	-0.112	-0.025	-0.074	0.006	0.080	-0.059
18	5.94	17	0.9936	-0.027	-0.062	-0.122	-0.019	-0.040	-0.021

Figure 4.18: ARIMA estimation premium – differencing ARIMA (1,1,0)

In *Figure 4.19*, let's evaluate our next model, ARMA (1,0). The term AR1,1 is significant. Compared to the model in *Figure 4.18*, we do not have an issue with the white noise null hypothesis. Since it can be rejected at the given p values, we can proceed to assess the model:

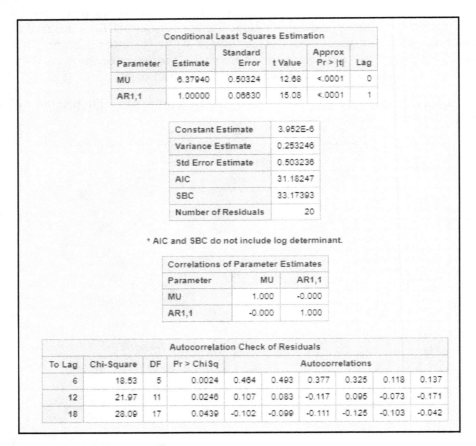

| | | | | Conditional Least Squares Estimation | | |

Parameter	Estimate	Standard Error	t Value	Approx Pr > |t|	Lag
MU	6.37940	0.50324	12.68	<.0001	0
AR1,1	1.00000	0.06630	15.08	<.0001	1

Constant Estimate	3.952E-6
Variance Estimate	0.253246
Std Error Estimate	0.503236
AIC	31.18247
SBC	33.17393
Number of Residuals	20

* AIC and SBC do not include log determinant.

Correlations of Parameter Estimates		
Parameter	MU	AR1,1
MU	1.000	-0.000
AR1,1	-0.000	1.000

				Autocorrelation Check of Residuals					
To Lag	Chi-Square	DF	Pr > ChiSq	Autocorrelations					
6	18.53	5	0.0024	0.464	0.493	0.377	0.325	0.118	0.137
12	21.97	11	0.0246	0.107	0.083	-0.117	0.095	-0.073	-0.171
18	28.09	17	0.0439	-0.102	-0.099	-0.111	-0.125	-0.103	-0.042

Figure 4.19: ARIMA estimation premium – ARMA (1.0)

In *Figure 4.19*, let's evaluate our next model ARMA (1,0). The term AR1,1 is significant. Compared to the model in *Figure 4.18*, we do not have an issue with the white noise null hypothesis. Since it can be rejected at the given p values, we can proceed to assess the model.

The model in *Figure 4.20* is also fitting well and has the white noise diagnostic test, and also has a significant *t* value. However, the model in *Figure 4.19*, which is the ARMA (1,0) model, has lower AIC and BIC values. Hence, this model will be suitable for forecasting the premium account series:

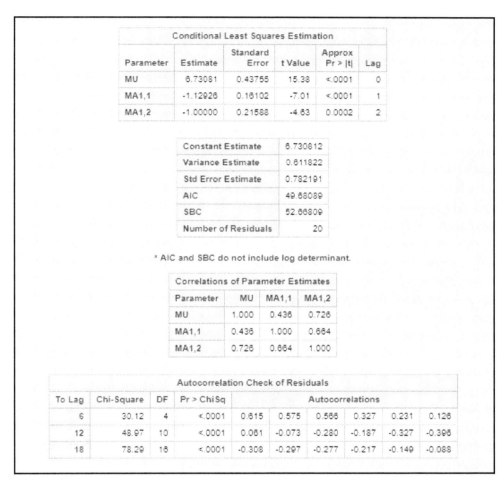

Figure 4.20: ARIMA estimation premium – ARMA (0,2)

Figure 4.21 contains the forecasts for premium account customers based on the ARMA (1,0) model:

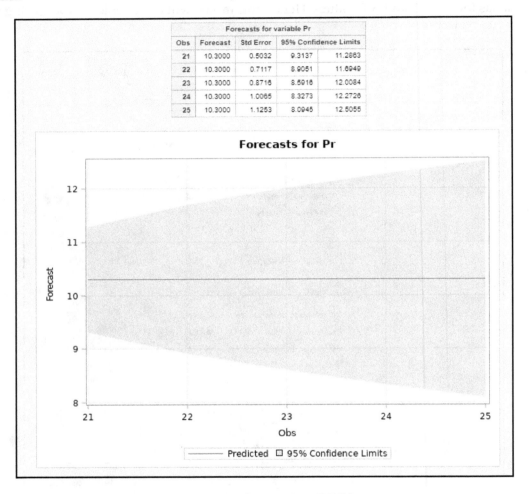

Figure 4.21: ARIMA forecasts premium – ARMA (1,0)

For the platinum account customers, let's try a slightly different approach to test the various models that fit the distribution. We will pick up the top recommendation from the scan and `esacf` table:

This is the ARIMA identification for the platinum account:

```
PROC ARIMA Data=Past;
identify var=Pl scan esacf;
RUN;
```

SCAN Chi-Square[1] Probability Values						
Lags	MA 0	MA 1	MA 2	MA 3	MA 4	MA 5
AR 0	<.0001	0.2682	0.7636	0.2429	0.0813	0.0788
AR 1	0.0002	0.0119	0.0360	0.0623	0.0702	0.3162
AR 2	0.1694	0.8862	0.1177	0.1213	0.2428	0.5541
AR 3	0.7905	0.4002	0.1521	0.8311	0.8363	0.7569
AR 4	0.0163	0.0342	0.2683	0.8727	0.7746	0.7680
AR 5	0.6653	0.1089	0.0672	0.6870	0.7857	0.8565

Since we have decided to pick the top recommendation, let's use the first recommendation from the tentative order selection tests in *Figure 4.22*:

ESACF Probability Values						
Lags	MA 0	MA 1	MA 2	MA 3	MA 4	MA 5
AR 0	0.0005	0.1939	0.9247	0.4204	0.1710	0.1770
AR 1	0.0044	0.1971	0.7647	0.6394	0.1337	0.4190
AR 2	0.0360	0.8998	0.8226	0.5292	0.2109	0.3466
AR 3	0.1044	0.7027	0.6846	0.4673	0.1867	0.8656
AR 4	0.1113	0.3143	0.5780	0.4732	0.2697	0.2787
AR 5	0.0135	0.4266	0.9948	0.2747	0.2538	

ARMA(p+d,q) Tentative Order Selection Tests			
SCAN		ESACF	
p+d	q	p+d	q
0	3	0	1
2	2	1	1
5	0	3	0
		2	1
		4	0
(5% Significance Level)			

Figure 4.22: ARIMA identification platinum account customers

Here is the code for estimating models for platinum account customers:

```
PROC ARIMA Data=Past;
identify var=Pl;
estimate q=3;
forecast lead=5 interval=semiyear out=Pl1;
identify var=Pl;
estimate q=1;
forecast lead=5 interval=semiyear out=Pl2;
RUN;
```

Now have a look at the following tables:

Conditional Least Squares Estimation					
Parameter	Estimate	Standard Error	t Value	Approx Pr > |t|	Lag
MU	1.72510	0.12569	13.73	<.0001	0
MA1,1	-1.10469	0.28524	-3.87	0.0013	1
MA1,2	-1.01996	0.33165	-3.08	0.0072	2
MA1,3	-0.91527	0.46860	-1.95	0.0685	3

Constant Estimate	1.725105
Variance Estimate	0.061174
Std Error Estimate	0.247334
AIC	4.414002
SBC	8.396931
Number of Residuals	20

* AIC and SBC do not include log determinant.

Correlations of Parameter Estimates				
Parameter	MU	MA1,1	MA1,2	MA1,3
MU	1.000	0.230	0.234	0.134
MA1,1	0.230	1.000	0.762	0.675
MA1,2	0.234	0.762	1.000	0.753
MA1,3	0.134	0.675	0.753	1.000

Autocorrelation Check of Residuals									
To Lag	Chi-Square	DF	Pr > ChiSq	Autocorrelations					
6	6.03	3	0.1103	0.116	0.080	0.047	-0.031	-0.377	-0.203
12	12.79	9	0.1722	-0.177	-0.346	0.068	0.029	0.094	0.109
18	17.88	15	0.2689	0.153	0.014	0.093	0.115	-0.093	-0.023

Figure 4.23: ARIMA estimation platinum – ARMA (0,3)

For the ARMA (0,3) model, the *t* value is insignificant in *Figure 4.23* for the MA1,3 model, whereas the *t* value is significant for the MA1,1 and MA1,2 models. The white noise test can't be rejected for any. However, for the ARMA (0,1) model in *Figure 4.24*, we see that the *t* value is significant and the white noise test can also be rejected:

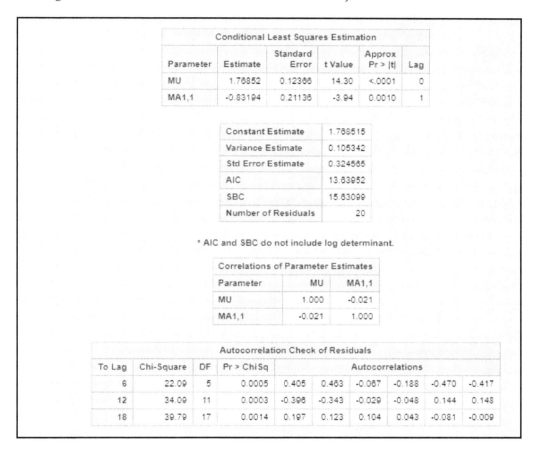

Figure 4.24: ARIMA estimation platinum – ARMA (0,1)

Let's combine the forecasts of the Markov model and ARIMA, and compare them:

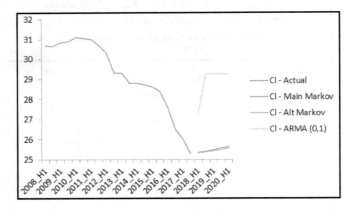

Figure 4.25: Forecasts for classic account

In the premium account forecast in *Figure 4.26*, the three model forecasts are close to the actuals:

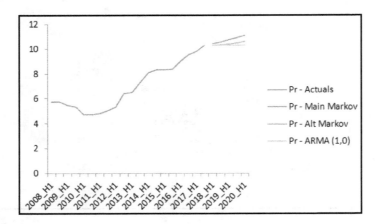

Figure 4.26: Forecasts for premium account

For the classic and the platinum accounts, the forecasts from the selected ARMA models in *Figure 4.25* and *Figure 4.27* seem to deviate significantly from the trend of the historical data:

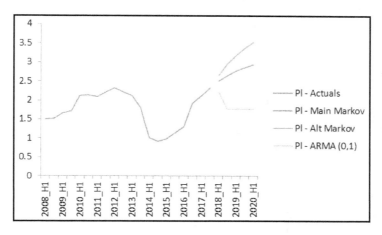

Figure 4.27: Forecasts for platinum account

The finance team now has the option of choosing the forecast they want from any of the three models: the main forecasts from the observed transition matrix, forecasts from the alternate transition matrix based on marketing team inputs, and the forecasts from ARMA models.

Markov method for imputation

In real-world scenarios, data is never perfect. There will be anomalies that a trained eye will be able to spot. Issues with data may occur due to the way the data is being sourced and as a result of the process used to store it. Data-retrieval issues related to technology, level of understanding of the data, the audited and controlled process for extraction, archiving issues, and understanding the data requirements of the business can further impact data quality. These are just a few examples of what can go wrong while trying to ensure that a firm has the best data quality. Thankfully, help is at hand when left with missing or poor quality data. Using various statistical methods, imputation can be performed to ensure there are no missing values. Imputation of missing values is an important step prior to modeling as a lot of the statistical procedures will ignore cases with missing values. This could mean that the entire information held by the other populated variables for this case will be neglected when analyzing the dataset.

The subject of which imputation methodology to use in a given scenario is so wide ranging that it cannot be covered in this chapter. However, we can explore a powerful procedure in SAS that uses the **Markov Chain Monte Carlo** (**MCMC**) method. This method should be used when the missing data is not due to any particular patterns. It is best suited to when the missing data is due to a random effect. While MCMC is just a method, we can use it as part of the MI procedure. The MI procedure can also use other methods to impute. So, what is the MI procedure?

MI is an acronym for multiple imputations. When we use the mean, standard deviation, or some other methodology to impute missing values, we are doing simple imputation. In simple imputation, we assume that the value we are imputing will be representative of the series, whereas in MI we impute the missing value multiple times to generate a bigger data set than we originally had. The dataset is then analyzed and the user can make a judgment on the imputed values that should be accepted. The assumption is that we cannot be sure of the value to impute, so we try and have multiple possible values, test the process of imputation for statistical significance, and then take a decision on which value should work best. Simple imputation may be faster to implement, but can be misleading. Let's say that we have daily credit card data for a year. However, in one of the months there are 10 days with missing data. We can explore various ways to impute. One of them could be monthly seasonality during that week, or averages of those days across the various months, average spend in the month prior, or post the missing values, and so on. In all these methodologies, we will be assuming that one of the past trends will be carried on to these ten days of missing values. The MI method enables us to do multiple imputation of the missing value based on the plausible values that the particular case may take. The confidence intervals and the probability coverage of the imputed values, along with the statistical inferences from the process, add credibility to the imputation process. Let's explore the MI procedure and MCMC methodology in the context of our business problem discussed earlier in the chapter.

In this chapter, we have used the half yearly time series containing the counts of customers who have the classic, premium, and platinum accounts. Imagine that the finance team wants some granular data and would ideally like to do their budgeting on a quarterly basis. Some of the information isn't held by the marketing team on a quarterly basis, and also when the data transfer took place, some quality issues arose due to which the finance team is missing data in some quarters. Prior to running any analysis on it, the team wanted to leverage the MCMC method to impute values. In the data set used, we still have in any quarter 37.92 million customers that have been active since 2008.

This is the MI procedure with the MCMC method on quarterly data:

```
Data Base_Qtr;
input date $ cl pr pl @@;
datalines;
2008_Q1 30.69 5.71 1.52 2008_Q2 30.68 5.73 1.51 2008_Q3 30.68 5.72 1.52
2008_Q4 . 5.74 .
2009_Q1 30.76 5.56 1.6 2009_Q2 30.83 5.43 1.66 2009_Q3 . 5.5 . 2009_Q4 30.9
5.3 1.72
2010_Q1 . 5.2 . 2010_Q2 31.1 . . 2010_Q3 31.4 4.6 1.92 2010_Q4 31.05 . .
2011_Q1 31 4.5 2.42 2011_Q2 31.01 4.81 2.1 2011_Q3 30.9 4.9 2.12 2011_Q4 .
5.01 2.21
2012_Q1 30.5 5.2 . 2012_Q2 30.3 5.3 2.32 2012_Q3 30.9 . 1.52 2012_Q4 29.3
6.4 2.22
2013_Q1 . 6.3 . 2013_Q2 29.3 6.5 2.12 2013_Q3 28.3 7 2.62 2013_Q4 . . 1.82
2014_Q1 . 7.8 . 2014_Q2 28.8 8.1 1.02 2014_Q3 . . 1.05 2014_Q4 28.7 8.3
0.92
2015_Q1 28.5 8.4 1.02 2015_Q2 28.6 8.34 0.98 2015_Q3 28.5 . . 2015_Q4 . .
1.15
2016_Q1 28.1 . 1.22 2016_Q2 27.6 9.01 1.31 2016_Q3 27.6 9.1 1.22 2016_Q4 .
9.5 1.92
2017_Q1 26.5 9.5 1.92 2017_Q2 26 . . 2017_Q3 26.1 9.7 2.12 2017_Q4 . 10.3
2.32
;
Run;

Proc MI Data=Base_Qtr seed=313232 nimpute=5 mu0=29.2 7 1.7 out=imputed;
   MCMC chain=single displayinit initial=em(itprint) plots=all;
   Var cl pr pl;
Run;
```

Via the `nimpute` option, we have explicitly stated that we want five imputations of the missing data. The default number of imputations if the option isn't specified is also five. The MCMC chain assumes a multivariate normal distribution for the data. We have used a single chain for imputation. The other option available is multiple chains. We have requested the trace and ACF plots. The `mu0` option helps us specify the means of the three variables we want imputation for. At the end, we will be able to test whether the imputed values are statistically significant when compared to the specified mean.

Expectation maximization (EM) is a technique that finds maximum likelihood estimates for parametric models. The code first summarizes the missing data pattern, as shown in *Figure 4.28*:

Missing Data Patterns								
						Group Means		
Group	cl	pr	pl	Freq	Percent	cl	pr	pl
1	X	X	X	22	55.00	29.475000	6.723182	1.721818
2	X	X	.	1	2.50	30.500000	5.200000	.
3	X	.	X	2	5.00	29.500000	.	1.370000
4	X	.	.	4	10.00	29.162500	.	.
5	.	X	X	3	7.50	.	8.270000	2.150000
6	.	X	.	5	12.50	.	6.108000	.
7	.	.	X	3	7.50	.	.	1.340000

Figure 4.28: Missing data patterns

Out of the 40 data points (we had 20 in *Figure 4.3* when we had half-yearly data), there are 22 cases with non-missing information. The highest proportion of missing cases (12.50%) is where we have missing information for both classic and platinum customer counts. The missing data patterns table provides a helpful overview of the data:

EM (Posterior Mode) Iteration History					
Iteration	-2 Log L	-2 Log Posterior	cl	pr	pl
0	-275.191302	-338.255077	29.379642	6.811634	1.728727
1	-294.520112	-361.918031	29.379641	6.811634	1.728727
2	-314.072897	-385.153015	29.379640	6.811634	1.728727
3	-333.706902	-408.378668	29.379254	6.812047	1.728700
4	-353.367316	-431.605907	29.379049	6.812254	1.728698
5	-373.012100	-454.834889	29.378966	6.812331	1.728702
6	-392.668757	-478.065386	29.378936	6.812358	1.728706
7	-412.326557	-501.297230	29.378926	6.812367	1.728707
8	-431.985534	-524.530223	29.378922	6.812370	1.728708
9	-451.644966	-547.763939	29.378921	6.812371	1.728708

EM (Posterior Mode) Estimates				
TYPE	_NAME_	cl	pr	pl
MEAN		29.378921	6.812371	1.728708
COV	cl	2.660817	-2.697188	0.036371
COV	pr	-2.697188	2.940847	-0.243660
COV	pl	0.036371	-0.243660	0.207289

Figure 4.29: Posterior estimates

While dealing with MCMC, we are working on Bayesian principles. In the Bayesian world, we are not so concerned about the prior estimates but interested to derive the posterior estimates to being our analysis. The prior beliefs or values are updated using our learning and the new posterior estimates are formed. This is what is displayed in *Figure 4.29* where we have the posterior estimates. The actual process of using the MCMC method can now begin. *Figure 4.30* shows the output of the five imputations we requested:

	Initial Parameter Estimates for MCMC				
IMPUTATION	_TYPE_	_NAME_	cl	pr	pl
1	MEAN		29.378921	6.812371	1.728708
1	COV	cl	2.660817	-2.697188	0.036371
1	COV	pr	-2.697188	2.940847	-0.243660
1	COV	pl	0.036371	-0.243660	0.207289

	Initial Parameter Estimates for MCMC				
IMPUTATION	_TYPE_	_NAME_	cl	pr	pl
2	MEAN		29.187913	7.034202	1.697886
2	COV	cl	3.034460	-3.119419	0.084959
2	COV	pr	-3.119419	3.527739	-0.408321
2	COV	pl	0.084959	-0.408321	0.323362

	Initial Parameter Estimates for MCMC				
IMPUTATION	_TYPE_	_NAME_	cl	pr	pl
3	MEAN		29.301575	6.913311	1.705114
3	COV	cl	3.283471	-3.178922	-0.104550
3	COV	pr	-3.178922	3.289191	-0.110269
3	COV	pl	-0.104550	-0.110269	0.214819

	Initial Parameter Estimates for MCMC				
IMPUTATION	_TYPE_	_NAME_	cl	pr	pl
4	MEAN		29.272617	6.982255	1.665128
4	COV	cl	3.028325	-3.077575	0.049251
4	COV	pr	-3.077575	3.344962	-0.267386
4	COV	pl	0.049251	-0.267386	0.218136

	Initial Parameter Estimates for MCMC				
IMPUTATION	_TYPE_	_NAME_	cl	pr	pl
5	MEAN		29.686068	6.493707	1.740226
5	COV	cl	2.637065	-2.399042	-0.238023
5	COV	pr	-2.399042	2.386590	0.012452
5	COV	pl	-0.238023	0.012452	0.225571

Figure 4.30: Imputation output

The variance information displays the between, within, and final variance after imputation as the total variance. The parameter estimates, however, show that the series after imputation doesn't have the same mean as specified in the *Mu0* option in the code (and also displayed as a column in parameter estimates, *Figure 4.31*). The p values are not significant while comparing the specified mean the parameter estimates for the population. But why did this happen? The specified mean is the actual distribution of the past data between 2008 and 2017, when it was compiled on a half-yearly basis. Is the imputation approach wrong or is there something in the data that has been overlooked? See the following table:

Variance Information (5 Imputations)							
	Variance				Relative Increase in Variance	Fraction Missing Information	Relative Efficiency
Variable	Between	Within	Total	DF			
cl	0.009713	0.074831	0.086487	28.045	0.155760	0.142520	0.972286
pr	0.005852	0.080932	0.087955	32.412	0.086769	0.082760	0.983717
pl	0.001236	0.006403	0.007887	23.81	0.231603	0.202036	0.961162

Parameter Estimates (5 Imputations)										
Variable	Mean	Std Error	95% Confidence Limits		DF	Minimum	Maximum	Mu0	t for H0: Mean=Mu0	Pr > |t|
cl	29.452876	0.294087	28.85051	30.05524	28.045	29.329753	29.604468	29.200000	0.86	0.3972
pr	6.717135	0.296571	6.11334	7.32093	32.412	6.592498	6.789329	7.000000	-0.95	0.3473
pl	1.749989	0.088806	1.56662	1.93335	23.81	1.714585	1.800918	1.700000	0.56	0.5788

Figure 4.31: Variance information and parameter estimates

If you have a look back at the data in *Figure 4.3*, you may notice that after 2014 H1 the platinum customer count dipped below the one million mark briefly. After this, in just 2.5 years it went from below a million to 2.32 million by the end of 2017. Premium customer counts also roughly went up by 20 – 25% in a similar period, whereas towards the end of the series the customer counts for classic customers went down. While the trend of the last few years might be more reflective of the trend in the years to come, for imputation of historic data it wouldn't be prudent to take the mean of the whole population as it would be skewed by the big movements in the last 2.5 years. Hence, we ran another imputation model with the specified mean being tested equal to the population of classic, premium, and platinum customers between 2008 and 2014 H1.

Let's look at the results from the new imputation model in *Figure 4.32*. Please note that the posterior estimates have not changed. What is different now are the parameter estimates:

Parameter Estimates (5 Imputations)										
Variable	Mean	Std Error	95% Confidence Limits		DF	Minimum	Maximum	Mu0	t for H0: Mean=Mu0	Pr > |t|
cl	29.452876	0.294087	28.85051	30.05524	28.045	29.329753	29.604468	30.300000	-2.88	0.0075
pr	6.717135	0.296571	6.11334	7.32093	32.412	6.592498	6.789329	5.500000	4.10	0.0003
pl	1.749989	0.088806	1.56662	1.93335	23.81	1.714585	1.800918	2.000000	-2.82	0.0096

Figure 4.32: Variance information and parameter estimates – mean specified 2014 H1

As we can see, now the p values are significant and we can say that the imputed values are acceptable. Note that the output data set imputed has 40 (original rows) * 5 (imputations) = 200 rows of data. We have in the output a column that specifies the imputation count for each row of data. The finance team can choose to use any of the population by selecting the number of the imputation they want to use from the output data set. The choice of the imputation they use can be arbitrarily done as the parameter estimates have shown the imputed values to be statistically significant. Let us take a look at the trace and the ACF plots we requested.

The following graph shows the trace plot for classic account customers:

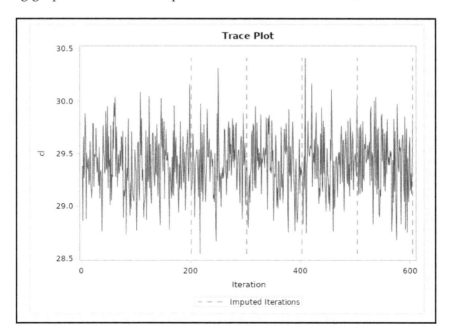

The following graph shows the trace plot for premium account customers:

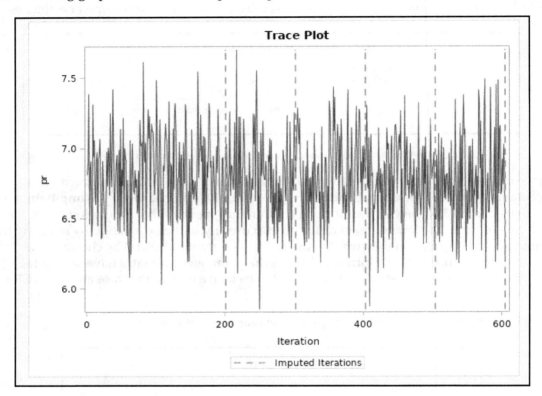

The following graph shows the trace plot for platinum account customers:

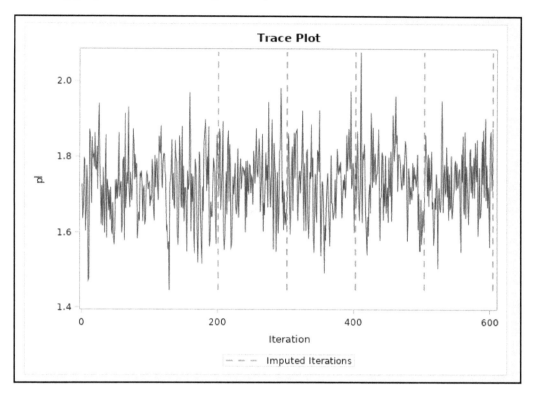

Figure 4.33: Trace plots

The trace plots in *Figure 4.33* help us spot any outliers that might be there due to the imputation process. No outward outliers seem to have been populated as a result of the imputation exercise.

The following graph shows the autocorrelation plot for classic account customers:

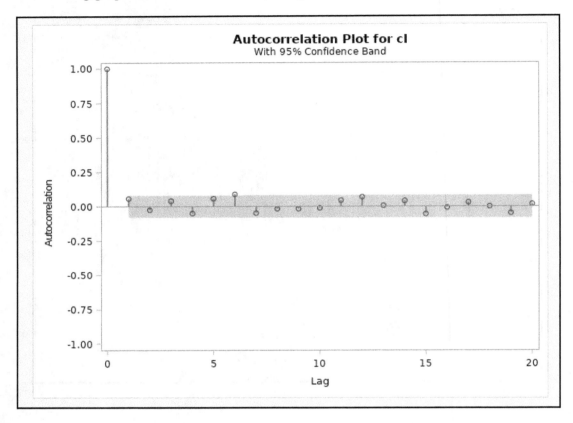

The following graph shows the autocorrelation plot for premium account customers:

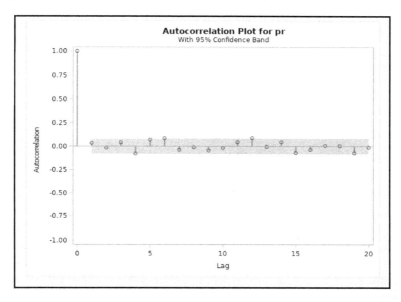

The following graph shows the autocorrelation plot for platinum account customers:

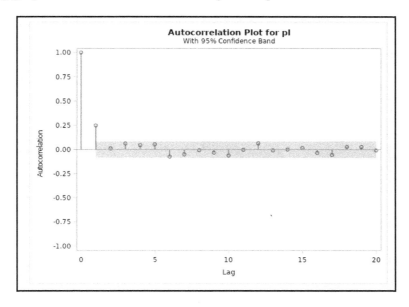

Figure 4.34: ACF plots

The ACF plots show that the after **Lag 1**, for all the account types the series declines rapidly. We can go ahead and use the output from the imputation model.

Summary

In this chapter, we reviewed the following three methodologies: Markov models, ARIMA, and MCMC as part of Proc MI. We also reviewed various terms such as stationarity, trend, autocorrelation, residual plots, and so on.

We have learned that Markov models can be used both for forecasting and imputation. We compared our results to ARIMA process. Using an alternate scenario for the transition matrix, we have shown how easy it is to come up with forecasts based on different assumptions about transition states.

In our business problem, we have tried to help the finance team come up with robust projections about the number of customers they can expect to have over the next two and half years across various customer accounts. The finance team can use this information to estimate the revenue generated. Along with the operating costs and other inputs available to the finance team, they can compute the profitability of the customer accounts. In the next chapter, we will cover econometric modeling for inflation forecasting.

5
Inflation Forecasting for Financial Planning

There isn't a standard way of forecasting inflation in the industry. In the risk-modeling world, the models have to be submitted to a regulatory body to receive the approval for using an advanced modeling approach for credit risk. This has somehow ensured that, across the world, analysts and modelers are using a similar suite of statistical techniques to manage risk. However, in the case of inflation, there isn't much exchange of ideas or a platform available from where we can choose the best modeling technique. Usually, the central bank publishes some inflation figures and these can be used as a benchmark for inflation-forecasting accuracy checks. Most of the models built by organizations are proprietary in nature. Moreover, these organizations are chiefly concerned about benchmarking a model to the central bank inflation index rather than agreeing to and conforming to an industry-level approach to forecasting methodology. In some organizations, modelers prefer to use the past inflation data only to forecast future levels. In other countries, the modelers have preferred to lag some particular variables, as they believe that there is a lag between the driver and inflation growth.

In this chapter, we will introduce new ways to prepare time series data for inflation forecasting. Although the SAS University Edition (the software used for this book) doesn't provide the full suite of SAS ETS procedures in this version of the software, we will try to maximize the use of the available procedures. Let us try and explore the concept of inflation before we try to solve a business problem.

The chapter consists of the following topics:

- Inflation definition and overview
- Reasons for inflation
- Inflation outcomes and the Philips curve
- Leveraging the time ID procedure for data quality checks
- The modeling methodology: the past trend (univariate analysis) and methodology based on predictors (multivariate regression)

What is inflation?

Inflation can be defined as the increase in pricing of products and services and the resultant fall in the purchasing power of money. Measuring inflation is critical for any business. Inflation impacts the input price of goods and services and needs to be taken into account for pricing strategies. It also impacts the purchasing power of consumers and does thereby play a role in revenue generated by businesses. When we talk about measuring inflation, we aren't interested in the price of a single product. The basket of products and services that we usually buy or need is what we measure inflation against.

The most common measure of inflation that we can see being discussed by the central banks, government, and media is **consumer price inflation** (**CPI**). This may be called something slightly different in other countries. It is used to measure goods and services that are frequently purchased by consumers. The central bank or a central institution, such as the **Office for National Statistics** (**ONS**) in the UK, computes the CPI measure on a monthly basis. Rather than measuring inflation on an ad hoc basis, various measures of inflation, such as CPI, are calculated on a monthly basis in the UK. ONS collects data from hundreds of retailers and monitors the price of similar products and services to measure the change in CPI. CPI is formed from various products and categories that are bought frequently by consumers in the UK.

The **Federal Reserve System** (**FED**) also uses a different yardstick to track inflation in the US. It is called the **Personal Consumption Expenditures** (**PCE**) index. It doesn't include the utility sector and food prices and instead focuses on what it terms as the real expenditure that people are incurring. The composition of any such index also needs to be dynamic and must be able to adapt to spending patterns. A communication change in the rental price of landline phones, for example, might have been a significant measure, but this was easily usurped by mobile phones a few decades ago. In the early mobile phone era, the call charges were higher but, later on, the handsets became more expensive while the charges reduced. Any price index should be reviewed to ensure this sort of behavior is captured. Indexes also have weights assigned to various categories. Food bills may have a higher weight than family holidays.

But why does a change in inflation matter?

Let's take the case of a premium biscuit manufacturer in the US. It uses the following key ingredients in manufacturing:

- Flour
- Butter
- Icing sugar
- Vanilla extract
- Milk

Most of the ingredients, apart from vanilla extract, are sourced from the US. However, recently the price of oil has gone up and the transporters have passed on the higher costs to the buyers. As a result, four of the five ingredients have become costly. Also, the main vanilla export regions of Indonesia and Madagascar are facing a decline in vanilla bean production. Even though it is used in the smallest possible quantities in the biscuit, it remains a key ingredient. The consumer of the biscuit is only interested in the price for the finished product. However, the manufacturer is interested in the basket of products that are used as ingredients. For the consumer, CPI may be able to capture the expected increase in the price of a biscuit (assuming that the manufacturer passes the full price burden to the consumer). However, for the manufacturer, CPI may only be a partial measure, as it won't capture the higher import costs. In either case, it would be great to know in which directions the prices are headed. The manufacturer can take better decisions on sourcing and pricing, whereas, in some instances, the consumer, if notified about price hikes, may purchase a higher quantity, reduce consumption, or delay purchasing.

Reasons for inflation

There are numerous factors driving supply-and-demand changes. This, in turn, leads to changes in the inflation level. This can also at times cause deflation. Deflation is when the general prices tend to decrease in a basket or the broader economy. We will explore inflation by looking at **aggregate demand** (**AD**) and **aggregate supply** (**AS**):

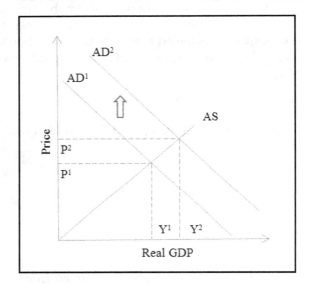

Figure 5.1: AD curve

In *Figure 5.1*, we can see that the aggregate supply is constant. When the aggregate demand in the GDP is at AD^1, the price is P^1. But as the AD increases to AD^2, the price moves to P^2. The percentage change in price is $(P^2-P^1)/P^1$. The intersection of AD^1 and AS resulted in price P^1 and output Y^1. However, the change in demand to AD^2 has resulted in the aggregate output going up to Y^2, but, in turn, the price also has gone up.

This phenomenon of constant supply but increased prices due to higher demand is known as demand-pull inflation. Some of the reasons that could trigger demand-pull inflation are as follows:

- **Increased consumption but inelastic production**: This can happen when the producers are unable to meet the increased demand by raising capacity. Inelastic production means that the producers are unable to increase or decrease production in the short run. In some instances, alternative products aren't available and this leads to increased demand and higher prices if supply remains constant. Consumers may shift to alternative products where possible. If in extreme summer, if the additional stock of cola products is unavailable, some of the consumption might move to fruit-based drinks. In such a scenario, the price increase may be minimal, as there is an alternative product.
- **Monetary policy**: If cheaper credit is made available, then higher borrowing may push house prices. This may further lead more people to buying furniture or renovating their existing or newly bought houses. While, in the case of furniture, the supplies may increase, the overall supply of houses may remain constant even though the builders may be rushing into building more houses in the medium term. This can cause house prices to go up, with a domino effect on related products and services.
- **Government spending**: In some developing economies, there is higher inflation compared to the European or the US economy. Governments in such a scenario have been known to give higher wage rises to government employees to ensure that they can afford a healthy lifestyle. In such a scenario, at times, higher wages, in turn, push demand, thereby increasing inflation rather than cooling it. Government spending in infrastructure or particular areas of the economy can also increase inflation. There is no single mechanism to manage inflation as is obvious from the long deflation cycle of the Japanese economy in spite of various government interventions.
- **Earnings rising above productivity**: This can happen when wages increase, whereas the productivity level in the economy remains the same.

In the **AS** graph in *Figure 5.2*, we can see the effect that a change in supply has on price when demand remains inelastic. Inelastic demand relates to the phenomenon where the demand remains constant irrespective of a supply decrease or increase. The demand for staple foods in a household may remain inelastic in the short run but, in the long run, families may change their food habits by shifting to alternative foods:

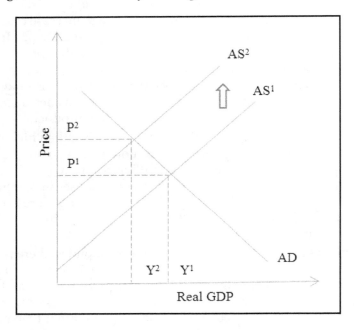

Figure 5.2: AS curve

The **AD** doesn't change but the **AS** reduces from **AS^1** to **AS^2** in *Figure 5.2*. This results in the price increasing from **P^1** to **P^2** and the output shrinking from **Y^1** to **Y^2**. With decreasing supply, **AS**-related inflation is also known as **cost-push inflation**, where, primarily, the price of raw materials and costs go up and this, in turn, has an impact on the price of the goods. The principle reasons for cost-pull inflation are as follows:

- **Increase in wages**: This has been observed in economies or sectors of an economy where the workers may be able to get deals that increase their wages every year above the general wage growth. This can lead to a situation where the cost of supplying the good to the market goes up while the demand remains constant.

- **Raw material price increase**: Cost-push inflation can have a ripple effect through the economy. The raw material price increase of commodities can lead to supply issues of various value-added products that depend on the raw materials.
- **Exchange rate**: A sudden shift in the exchange rate could end up pushing the cost of imported raw inputs. In energy deficient markets, the cost of importing petroleum or natural gas for energy consumption can push up the prices.
- **Monopoly/cartels**: The existence of monopolies or the formation of cartels can ensure that supply is restricted, thereby pushing up the price. While various countries have watchdogs in place to ensure that cartels can be disbanded and punished, mismanagement, or high entry barriers, leads to some sectors with a handful of players. This leads to the development of monopolies.

Inflation outcome and the Philips curve

There are many concepts to explain the effects of inflation. Rather than making a voluminous chapter on economics, let's look at one of them: the Phillips curve. It is a concept that was developed by A.W.Phillips. The concept explains the stable and inverse relationship between inflation and unemployment. The reason for choosing this concept is because this was used by economists and governments for a very long time, starting in the 1960s and 1970s. Economists now tend to disagree with the concept or have developed variations of the concept to show why the Phillips curve may only work in the short run. Over time, the way the economy and the constituents react to inflation changes. Concepts to explain inflation also evolve.

In *Figure 5.3*, we can see the inverse relationship between inflation and unemployment. As inflation remains high, the unemployment rate is low. As inflation decreases, the unemployment rate increases. In the 1960s and 1970s, the governments and central banks started using the premise of this relationship to artificially manage the inflation level depending on whether they wanted the economy to expand or contract. It was a choice being made between acceptable inflation levels and the level of unemployment. On some occasions, the central banks were fixing inflation targets and devising fiscal policy stimulus measures to ensure that their stated equilibrium of inflation and unemployment rate was achieved. The Phillips curve formed the basis of their belief in tweaking fiscal stimulus limits.

The Phillips curve in its original form has lost significance as various examples have shown that the relationship between inflation and unemployment isn't inverse and there are, as some theories suggest, other factors at play:

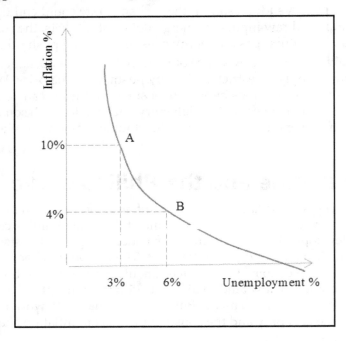

Figure 5.3: Phillips curve

Winners and losers

So far, our focus has been on the negative aspects of inflation. However, not everyone is a loser when inflation fluctuates. Individuals, governments, or corporates who have fixed rate debt products tend to be winners in rising inflation. An individual with a mortgage might see the house price increase during times of high inflation. The fixed rate mortgage product will keep the payments steady. However, if the real estate market shows significant slowdown, then the homeowner may be left with a large debt and hence potentially a negative equity in the house.

Savers with inflation-linked index products are also typical winners. However, fixed rate savers are losers when it comes to high inflation. When their term product matures, the purchasing power of the money will be less than expected due to the high inflation in the years when their money was locked into the product.

Pensioners tend to be on the losing side of high inflation. Their pension payments may have started 10 years ago in a non-inflationary economy. However, any rise in inflation will see their pension payments purchasing power decrease.

Business case for forecasting inflation

A leading bank depended heavily on the central bank's monthly inflation report for various aspects of business planning. The in-house economic team provided a directional statement on whether inflation was expected to increase, decrease, or remain stable. This directional statement preceded the official government numbers by a week. The forecasted direction and lack of information on the expected quantum of change was something that suited the bank in the economic scenario when inflation was stable. Recently, however, the inflation rate has been fluctuating a lot and the bank was keen to have high-quality forecasts of the inflation rate as soon as possible.

The bank had a leading presence in the wholesale and retail market in the country. Some of the management was of the opinion that it would be prudent to assume that their customer base was a fair representation of the country's consumer. In such a scenario, they wanted the modeling team to use the in-house transactional data and, if need be, various other data sources, to create a weekly or a daily available model that could predict the likely change in the inflation rate on a monthly basis. The goal wasn't merely forecasting inflation accurately, but harvesting their in-house data to make available the inflation data in the shortest possible time to various teams in the bank.

Data-gathering exercise

Since the team wanted to leverage internal data, a data quality exercise needed to be conducted. Multiple variables were probably going to be needed to predict CPI. These variables were in turn classified into various categories. The categories were based on areas where the modelers thought the consumers were primarily spending money. The hypothesis was that, by using these categories, they would be able to identify significant categories that predict CPI. The lower the number of categories that would come out as predictors, the less the team would have to invest in ensuring that the data quality remains consistent with implementing the model. The initial list of categories of interest that the team had are as follows:

- Clothing and generic shopping
- Communication (phone, broadband, and so on)
- Eating out (restaurants, takeaways, and so on)

- Education (nursery and school fees)
- Entertainment (TV subscription, iTunes, Google Play Store, Netflix, and so on)
- Furniture and home improvements
- Grocery shopping
- Spending and savings ratio
- Travel, including leisure

To derive these classifications, a considerable effort needed to be spent to ensure that variables that were to be mapped into categories met the data quality requirements. For the entertainment category, the modelers wanted to include spending on the app stores of iPhone and Android handsets. This meant that each such transaction of the customer using various forms of payments needed to be tracked and classified in a data warehouse. Conversations with the IT team revealed that they had started this tracking and classification exercise a few years ago and they even did a historic classification exercise to ensure that data going back to 2012 was available. They believed that the mappings of transactions were correct and the data was of good quality. The modelers decided to have a look at some of the app spend data.

The following code shows the data quality checks:

```
Data Playstore;
   Format Date Date.;
   Input Date : Date. @@;
Datalines;
21JAN12 20FEB12 22MAR12 21APR12 21APR12 13MAY12 21JUN12 20JUL12 21AUG12
22SEP12
15OCT12 16NOV12 21DEC12 21DEC12 20JAN13 19FEB13 19MAR13 18MAY13 17JUN13
18JUL13
17OCT13 18NOV13 17DEC13 01JAN14 02FEB14 03MAR14 04APR14 05MAY14 06JUN14
07AUG14
11SEP14 31OCT14 01NOV14 01DEC14 25FEB15 01MAR15 01APR15 01MAY15 01JUN15
01JUL15
01AUG15 01SEP15 01OCT15 01NOV15 01DEC15 05JAN16 01FEB16 01MAR16 01APR16
01MAY16
01JUN16 01JUL16 01AUG16 01SEP16 01OCT16 01NOV16 01DEC16 05JAN17 01FEB17
01FEB17
01APR17 01MAY17 01JUN17 01JUL17 01AUG17 01SEP17 01NOV17 01DEC17 01FEB18
01MAR18
;

ODS GRAPHICS ON;
```

```
PROC TIMEID Data=Playstore PRINT=All PLOT=All;
    Id Date Interval=MONTH;
Run;
```

They used the procedure, TIMEID, which helps to understand the interval between each observation, the number of duplicate observations, and pointers to any missing observations. It has been assumed that there is a monthly interval between the observations:

The TIMEID Procedure

Input Data Set	
Name	WORK.PLAYSTORE
Label	
Time ID Variable	Date
Time Interval	MONTH

The TIMEID Procedure

Time Component

Value Index	Date	Offset	Span	Interval Count
1	JAN2012	20	.	1
2	FEB2012	19	1	1
3	MAR2012	21	1	1
4	APR2012	20	1	2
5	MAY2012	12	1	1
6	JUN2012	20	1	1
7	JUL2012	19	1	1
8	AUG2012	20	1	1
9	SEP2012	21	1	1
10	OCT2012	14	1	1
11	NOV2012	15	1	1
12	DEC2012	20	1	2
13	JAN2013	19	1	1
14	FEB2013	18	1	1
15	MAR2013	18	1	1
16	MAY2013	17	2	1
17	JUN2013	16	1	1
18	JUL2013	17	1	1
19	OCT2013	16	3	1
20	NOV2013	17	1	1

Figure 5.4: TIMEID procedure–partial results of time component

In *Figure 5.4*, we have the partial results of the time component analysis. As mentioned earlier, we have assumed that the data is at a monthly interval. We have a record for January 21, 2012 and February 20, 2012 in the `Playstore` data. For these days, the offset is the difference in the number of dates in the month to the 1st of each month. This highlights how many days it has taken for the report to be published with the previous month-end data. This can set expectations on how regularly the data feed can be expected. In an ideal scenario, the previous month-end data should be available with the modeler in an aggregate manner on the first of each month. This expectation isn't being met at the start of the time series. As the data-collection process evolves, it seems that, looking at the following table, that the data is being made available on the 1st of each month and the offset value is now **0**. There is still a four-day offset in **JAN2017** when the data wasn't made available on the first. This could be a processing difficulty owing to holidays at the start of the year:

50	JUL2016	0	1	1
51	AUG2016	0	1	1
52	SEP2016	0	1	1
53	OCT2016	0	1	1
54	NOV2016	0	1	1
55	DEC2016	0	1	1
56	JAN2017	4	1	1
57	FEB2017	0	1	2
58	APR2017	0	2	1
59	MAY2017	0	1	1
60	JUN2017	0	1	1
61	JUL2017	0	1	1
62	AUG2017	0	1	1
63	SEP2017	0	1	1
64	NOV2017	0	2	1
65	DEC2017	0	1	1
66	FEB2018	0	2	1
67	MAR2018	0	1	1

Figure 5.5: TIMEID procedure–regular reporting instances

Going back to *Figure 5.4*, we also have the **Span** column. If you look at the **Date MAY2013**, you can see that the value of the **Span** is equal to **2**. This is because there was no data available for **APR2013**. The **Span** highlights the gap in data between **MAR2013** and **MAY2013**. Since we have given the interval as monthly, the query highlights that it has found a gap of two months between **MAR2013** and **MAY2013**. The **Interval Count** column for **APR2012** has a value of **2**. This again points to a data quality issue, as we have two rows of data entered in **APR2012** with a date of 21.

Figure 5.6 illustrates graphs of **Interval Count**, **Offset**, and **Span**:

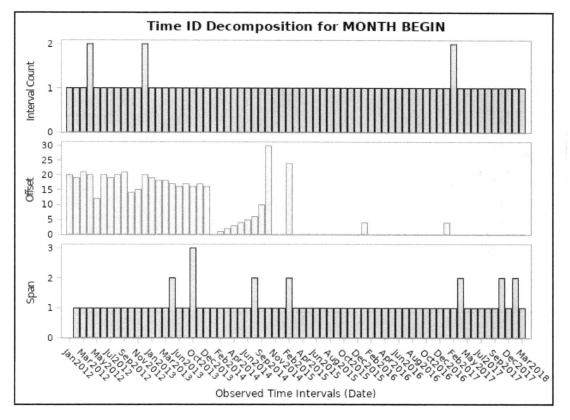

Figure 5.6: TIMEID procedure–data decomposition charts

Figure 5.7 provides further details on duplicated time IDs and the number of offset days when the series is assumed to be monthly:

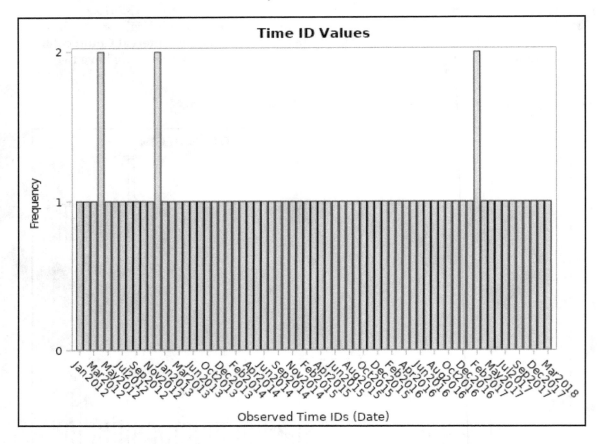

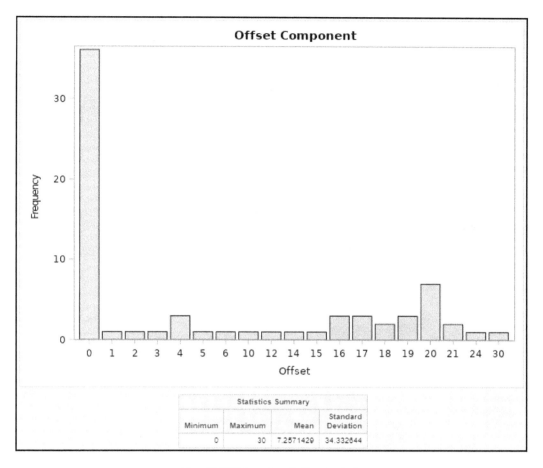

Figure 5.7: TIMEID procedure–offset frequency details

In *Figure 5.8*, we can see that there are seven instances when a month is missing in the series, as this leads to a **Span** of **2**. There is one instance of a **Span** equal to **3**, as data for August and September 2013 is missing:

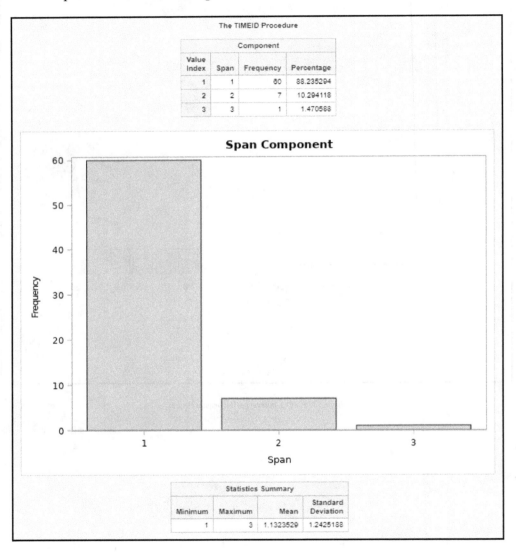

Figure 5.8: TIMEID procedure–span component frequency details

This sort of analysis was done for multiple variables that were used to form the categories of interest for forecasting inflation. Conversations with IT, historic data correction where possible, and imputation of missing values helped resolve most of the data quality issues. After this, the modelers shifted their focus to building the model.

Modeling methodology

Until now, we have discussed various aspects of inflation and some SAS procedures to evaluate the time series component. However, to deal with the business problem at hand, the modeling team needed to come up with a solution. The two approaches that the modeling team wanted to consider are as follows:

- Using a regression model to understand the interaction of various factors on CPI.
- Forecasting CPI for some periods based on the current CPI time series data. This did not involve understanding the interaction with various variables that can influence CPI.

There were pros and cons to both approaches. Whereas the multivariate regression model would help understand what aspect of consumer spending is statistically significant in predicting CPI, it at times isn't the best method to be used for forecasting. Multivariate regression could in this instance lead to a better understanding of the influencer variables and their statistical significance. However, due to the presence of autocorrelation, it may not be the best prediction method. However, the modelers could still use the resultant regression equation to forecast a few periods ahead. Using the second method of leveraging the CPI variable would mean the use of the **Autoregressive Integrated Moving Average (ARIMA)** model or some other similar procedure. Autocorrelation could be dealt with in a robust manner. Both the multivariate regression model and a model that leveraged the CPI variable only were built. Let's examine the outcome of the different modeling approaches.

Multivariate regression model

For this model, 75 months of data from January 2012 to March 2018 was available. From this, only data up until September 2017 was used for modeling. Data from October 2017 to March 2018 was used as a hold-out sample to validate the forecasts generated. Regression modeling was done as part of the effort to build a multivariate model. To refer to details about pros and cons of regression models and other details, please refer to `Chapter 2`, *Forecasting Stock Prices and Portfolio Decisions Using Time Series*.

The modelers built three types of regression models: forward selection, backward selection, and maximizing R. The forward selection model starts with the intercept and then finds the best variable that serves as a predictor. It then continues to add other variables until the specified selection criteria is met. The backward selection model starts with the full model; that is, all the independent variables as predictors. It keeps on removing variables deemed not important enough. The maximizing R model, as the name suggests, tries to maximize R^2 on the introduction of each variable in the model (for details on the R^2 metric, please refer to Chapter 2, *Forecasting Stock Prices and Portfolio Decisions using Time Series*, which introduces regression as a concept). The model starts by having a single variable with the maximum R^2. After the second variable is added, the model analyzes whether adding one variable and dropping one from the existing selection would increase R^2. This process continues while adding the third, fourth, fifth, and so on variables until the model runs out of independent variables. There is a regression type which is called **stepwise regression**. At times, some people confuse stepwise regression with maximizing R. In stepwise regression, the variables are added and removed at each step of the regression. However, the dropping of the worst performing variable is done before looking at the alternative variables that can be added to the model to improve the performance.

The following code is for modeling and validating a dataset:

```
Data Model;
Set Inflation;
;
If Month gt "30Sep2017"d then do;
CPI=.;
End;
Run;
```

The CPI value in the current dataset has been set to null for the period October 17 to March 18, as we are interested in generating forecasts for this period based on the regression model.

In this multivariate regression code, three models are compared:

```
Proc Reg Data=Model Plots=(Criteria SBC);
   Id Month;
   /*Forward selection*/
   Model CPI = Furniture_Home_Improvement Travel_including_Leisure
Eating_out Entertainment Grocery Education            Communication
Clothing_and_shopping
Spend_save_quaterly_ratio
        / Selection=Forward Details=All;
/*Backward selection*/
Model CPI = Furniture_Home_Improvement Travel_including_Leisure
Eating_out Entertainment Grocery Education            Communication
Clothing_and_shopping
Spend_save_quaterly_ratio
        / Selection=Backward Details=All;

   /*Maxr*/
   Model CPI = Furniture_Home_Improvement Travel_including_Leisure
Eating_out Entertainment Grocery Education            Communication
Clothing_and_shopping
Spend_save_quaterly_ratio
        / Selection=Maxr Details=All;
Run;
```

Forward selection model

In *Figure 5.9*, we can see that the number of observations read are 75, but the number of observations used is only 65. This highlights the fact that we have entered null values for CPI for six months when we are interested in generating the forecast. The first variable of the spending to saving ratio calculated on a quarterly basis was entered in the model.

The variable is significant with a p-value of **<0.0001**:

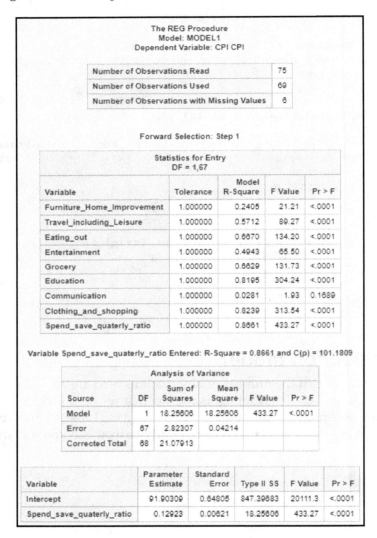

The REG Procedure
Model: MODEL1
Dependent Variable: CPI CPI

Number of Observations Read	75
Number of Observations Used	69
Number of Observations with Missing Values	6

Forward Selection: Step 1

Statistics for Entry DF = 1,67				
Variable	Tolerance	Model R-Square	F Value	Pr > F
Furniture_Home_Improvement	1.000000	0.2405	21.21	<.0001
Travel_including_Leisure	1.000000	0.5712	89.27	<.0001
Eating_out	1.000000	0.6670	134.20	<.0001
Entertainment	1.000000	0.4943	65.50	<.0001
Grocery	1.000000	0.6629	131.73	<.0001
Education	1.000000	0.8195	304.24	<.0001
Communication	1.000000	0.0281	1.93	0.1689
Clothing_and_shopping	1.000000	0.8239	313.54	<.0001
Spend_save_quaterly_ratio	1.000000	0.8661	433.27	<.0001

Variable Spend_save_quaterly_ratio Entered: R-Square = 0.8661 and C(p) = 101.1809

Analysis of Variance					
Source	DF	Sum of Squares	Mean Square	F Value	Pr > F
Model	1	18.25606	18.25606	433.27	<.0001
Error	67	2.82307	0.04214		
Corrected Total	68	21.07913			

Variable	Parameter Estimate	Standard Error	Type II SS	F Value	Pr > F
Intercept	91.90309	0.64805	847.39683	20111.3	<.0001
Spend_save_quaterly_ratio	0.12923	0.00621	18.25606	433.27	<.0001

Figure 5.9: Forward selection regression: step 1

The second variable entered in the model is the category of clothing and shopping spend by the bank's customers. The variable is again deemed significant and has a p-value of **<0.0001** (*Figure 5.10*):

Forward Selection: Step 2

Variable	Tolerance	Model R-Square	F Value	Pr > F
Furniture_Home_Improvement	0.689061	0.8673	0.59	0.4457
Travel_including_Leisure	0.347601	0.8661	0.02	0.8770
Eating_out	0.265277	0.8674	0.68	0.4133
Entertainment	0.355325	0.8716	2.82	0.0980
Grocery	0.228051	0.8661	0.03	0.8715
Education	0.148517	0.8806	8.06	0.0060
Communication	0.944481	0.8689	1.43	0.2362
Clothing_and_shopping	0.240857	0.9050	27.07	<.0001

Statistics for Entry DF = 1,66

Variable Clothing_and_shopping Entered: R-Square = 0.9050 and C(p) = 54.8481

Analysis of Variance

Source	DF	Sum of Squares	Mean Square	F Value	Pr > F
Model	2	19.07714	9.53857	314.46	<.0001
Error	66	2.00199	0.03033		
Corrected Total	68	21.07913			

Variable	Parameter Estimate	Standard Error	Type II SS	F Value	Pr > F
Intercept	85.53920	1.34109	123.40594	4068.34	<.0001
Clothing_and_shopping	0.11089	0.02131	0.82107	27.07	<.0001
Spend_save_quaterly_ratio	0.08058	0.01073	1.70936	56.35	<.0001

Bounds on condition number: 4.1518, 16.607

Figure 5.10: Forward selection regression: step 2

In *Figure 5.11*, we can see that the third variable of entertainment spending is entered and that too is significant with p<0.0001:

Forward Selection: Step 3

	Statistics for Entry DF = 1,65			
Variable	Tolerance	Model R-Square	F Value	Pr > F
Furniture_Home_Improvement	0.481411	0.9342	28.81	<.0001
Travel_including_Leisure	0.198806	0.9311	24.60	<.0001
Eating_out	0.247564	0.9052	0.15	0.7035
Entertainment	0.285849	0.9374	33.57	<.0001
Grocery	0.186638	0.9152	7.83	0.0068
Education	0.068038	0.9063	0.91	0.3428
Communication	0.940321	0.9066	1.13	0.2920

Variable Entertainment Entered: R-Square = 0.9374 and C(p) = 16.7114

Analysis of Variance

Source	DF	Sum of Squares	Mean Square	F Value	Pr > F
Model	3	19.75898	6.58633	324.29	<.0001
Error	65	1.32016	0.02031		
Corrected Total	68	21.07913			

Variable	Parameter Estimate	Standard Error	Type II SS	F Value	Pr > F
Intercept	83.43388	1.15596	105.80571	5209.52	<.0001
Entertainment	-0.04118	0.00711	0.68184	33.57	<.0001
Clothing_and_shopping	0.16070	0.01944	1.38735	68.31	<.0001
Spend_save_quaterly_ratio	0.09622	0.00919	2.22716	109.66	<.0001

Bounds on condition number: 5.161, 39.611

Figure 5.11: Forward selection regression: step 3

In *Figure 5.12*, we can see that the fourth variable of entertainment spending is entered and that too is significant with p<0.0001:

Forward Selection: Step 4

Statistics for Entry DF = 1,64				
Variable	Tolerance	Model R-Square	F Value	Pr > F
Furniture_Home_Improvement	0.127589	0.9384	1.08	0.3026
Travel_including_Leisure	0.050971	0.9375	0.16	0.6873
Eating_out	0.239789	0.9377	0.32	0.5757
Grocery	0.101851	0.9381	0.77	0.3833
Education	0.036368	0.9513	18.38	<.0001
Communication	0.938853	0.9385	1.15	0.2885

Variable Education Entered: R-Square = 0.9513 and C(p) = 1.3699

Analysis of Variance					
Source	DF	Sum of Squares	Mean Square	F Value	Pr > F
Model	4	20.05357	5.01339	312.86	<.0001
Error	64	1.02556	0.01602		
Corrected Total	68	21.07913			

Variable	Parameter Estimate	Standard Error	Type II SS	F Value	Pr > F
Intercept	84.33993	1.04830	103.72301	6472.84	<.0001
Entertainment	-0.06644	0.00863	0.94870	59.20	<.0001
Education	0.11236	0.02620	0.29460	18.38	<.0001
Clothing_and_shopping	0.09246	0.02349	0.24830	15.50	0.0002
Spend_save_quaterly_ratio	0.06974	0.01024	0.74399	46.43	<.0001

Bounds on condition number: 27.497, 202.93

Figure 5.12: Forward selection regression: step 4

In the final step *Figure 5.13* of the forward selection model, as shown in the following diagram, we can review the statistics for entry of the five variables that did not make it in the summary of the forward selection model. These variables were deemed insignificant and after introducing four variables in the model, there were no other variables that were retained:

Forward Selection: Step 5				
Statistics for Entry DF = 1,63				
Variable	Tolerance	Model R-Square	F Value	Pr > F
Furniture_Home_Improvement	0.105777	0.9517	0.44	0.5117
Travel_including_Leisure	0.050890	0.9516	0.39	0.5330
Eating_out	0.239778	0.9516	0.37	0.5477
Grocery	0.096775	0.9513	0.00	0.9734
Communication	0.918195	0.9516	0.33	0.5701

No other variable met the 0.5000 significance level for entry into the model.

	Summary of Forward Selection								
Step	Variable Entered	Label	Number Vars In	Partial R-Square	Model R-Square	C(p)	F Value	Pr > F
1	Spend_save_quaterly_ratio	Spend_save_quaterly_ratio	1	0.8661	0.8661	101.181	433.27	<.0001
2	Clothing_and_shopping	Clothing_and_shopping	2	0.0390	0.9050	54.8481	27.07	<.0001
3	Entertainment	Entertainment	3	0.0323	0.9374	16.7114	33.57	<.0001
4	Education	Education	4	0.0140	0.9513	1.3699	18.38	<.0001

Figure 5.13: Forward selection regression: step 5–model summary

We have also requested plots to summarize the fit criteria for CPI. *Figure 5.14* in step 4, we achieved the highest R^2, adjusted R^2, lowest C(p), AIC, BIC, and SBC metrics. We have spoken about the rest of the diagnostic terms earlier, except Mallows Cp. It is a function of the sum of squared errors and, in general, a model with lower C(p) is preferred when comparing models:

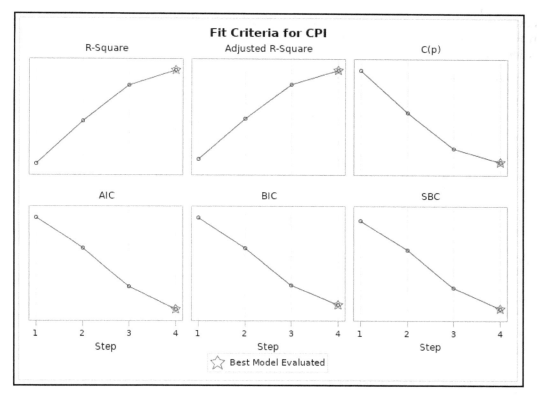

Figure 5.14: Forward selection regression–fit criteria

Another important chart that is produced is the Cook's D for CPI. The statistics can also be evaluated using the observed versus predicted CPI value table that is produced as part of the model output. Large values of studentized residuals indicate observations that will influence the model significantly if the observation is deleted. For these observations, there can be a higher residual value (that is, a higher difference between observed versus predicted when compared to other observations). Cook's D is helpful in identifying extreme/outlier observations. A studentized residual gt 2 and a Cook's D value gt 0.2 should be investigated. The CPI value for January 2012 seems to have been considered as an important observation by the studentized residual and Cook's D metric.

If you look at residuals for any of the observations highlighted by blue bars in *Figure 5.15*, you will realize that they have the highest absolute residual values in the observed versus predicted table:

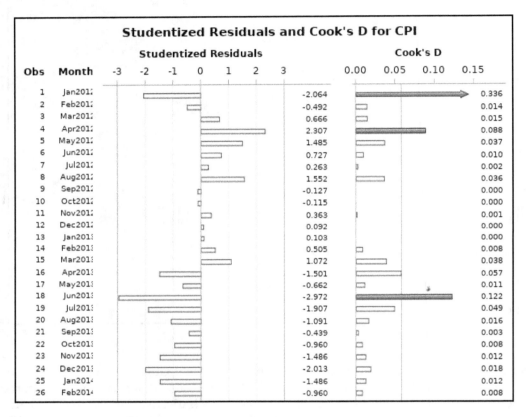

Figure 5.15: Forward selection partial output–studentized residuals and Cook's D

Backward selection

In the backward selection model, our step 0, as shown in the following diagram, includes all the variables that have been included as independent variables. We have calculated the parameter estimates, the F values, and tested for statistical significance of the variable:

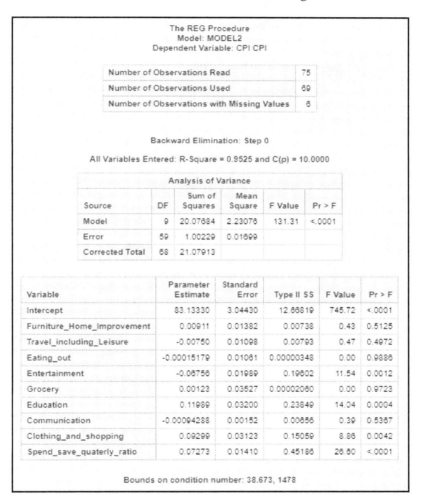

The REG Procedure
Model: MODEL2
Dependent Variable: CPI CPI

Number of Observations Read	75
Number of Observations Used	69
Number of Observations with Missing Values	6

Backward Elimination: Step 0

All Variables Entered: R-Square = 0.9525 and C(p) = 10.0000

Analysis of Variance

Source	DF	Sum of Squares	Mean Square	F Value	Pr > F
Model	9	20.07684	2.23076	131.31	<.0001
Error	59	1.00229	0.01699		
Corrected Total	68	21.07913			

Variable	Parameter Estimate	Standard Error	Type II SS	F Value	Pr > F
Intercept	83.13330	3.04430	12.66819	745.72	<.0001
Furniture_Home_Improvement	0.00911	0.01382	0.00738	0.43	0.5125
Travel_including_Leisure	-0.00750	0.01098	0.00793	0.47	0.4972
Eating_out	-0.00015179	0.01061	0.00000348	0.00	0.9886
Entertainment	-0.06756	0.01989	0.19602	11.54	0.0012
Grocery	0.00123	0.03527	0.00002060	0.00	0.9723
Education	0.11989	0.03200	0.23849	14.04	0.0004
Communication	-0.00094288	0.00152	0.00656	0.39	0.5367
Clothing_and_shopping	0.09299	0.03123	0.15059	8.86	0.0042
Spend_save_quaterly_ratio	0.07273	0.01410	0.45186	26.60	<.0001

Bounds on condition number: 38.673, 1478

Figure 5.16: Backward selection: step 0

The **Eating_out** variable has the highest p-value in the *Figure 5.17* statistics for removal section. In the next section of the output, the **Eating_out** variable is dropped from the model. New parameter estimates, F values, and test of significance values are generated for the model, as shown in the following diagram:

Backward Elimination: Step 1

Statistics for Removal DF = 1,59				
Variable	Partial R-Square	Model R-Square	F Value	Pr > F
Furniture_Home_Improvement	0.0004	0.9521	0.43	0.5125
Travel_including_Leisure	0.0004	0.9521	0.47	0.4972
Eating_out	0.0000	0.9525	0.00	0.9886
Entertainment	0.0093	0.9432	11.54	0.0012
Grocery	0.0000	0.9525	0.00	0.9723
Education	0.0113	0.9411	14.04	0.0004
Communication	0.0003	0.9521	0.39	0.5367
Clothing_and_shopping	0.0071	0.9453	8.86	0.0042
Spend_save_quaterly_ratio	0.0214	0.9310	26.60	<.0001

Variable Eating_out Removed: R-Square = 0.9525 and C(p) = 8.0002

Analysis of Variance					
Source	DF	Sum of Squares	Mean Square	F Value	Pr > F
Model	8	20.07684	2.50960	150.23	<.0001
Error	60	1.00229	0.01670		
Corrected Total	68	21.07913			

Variable	Parameter Estimate	Standard Error	Type II SS	F Value	Pr > F
Intercept	83.14480	2.91172	13.62114	815.40	<.0001
Furniture_Home_Improvement	0.00901	0.01205	0.00934	0.56	0.4576
Travel_including_Leisure	-0.00741	0.00878	0.01188	0.71	0.4024
Entertainment	-0.06759	0.01959	0.19883	11.90	0.0010
Grocery	0.00130	0.03461	0.00002364	0.00	0.9701
Education	0.11976	0.03049	0.25767	15.42	0.0002
Communication	-0.00094349	0.00150	0.00657	0.39	0.5328
Clothing_and_shopping	0.09292	0.03056	0.15446	9.25	0.0035
Spend_save_quaterly_ratio	0.07263	0.01205	0.60671	36.32	<.0001

Bounds on condition number: 35.718, 1083.5

Figure 5.17: Backward selection: step 1

In *Figure 5.18*, we can see that **Grocery** has the highest *p*-value before being dropped out of the model. As you can see, we started with a full selection of variables but in the backward selection process, we are continuously eliminating the insignificant variables. This process continues until we reach step 6, which generates the summary of the backward selection model:

Backward Elimination: Step 2

Statistics for Removal DF = 1,60				
Variable	Partial R-Square	Model R-Square	F Value	Pr > F
Furniture_Home_Improvement	0.0004	0.9520	0.56	0.4576
Travel_including_Leisure	0.0006	0.9519	0.71	0.4024
Entertainment	0.0094	0.9430	11.90	0.0010
Grocery	0.0000	0.9524	0.00	0.9701
Education	0.0122	0.9402	15.42	0.0002
Communication	0.0003	0.9521	0.39	0.5328
Clothing_and_shopping	0.0073	0.9451	9.25	0.0035
Spend_save_quaterly_ratio	0.0288	0.9237	36.32	<.0001

Variable Grocery Removed: R-Square = 0.9524 and C(p) = 6.0016

Analysis of Variance					
Source	DF	Sum of Squares	Mean Square	F Value	Pr > F
Model	7	20.07682	2.86812	174.55	<.0001
Error	61	1.00231	0.01643		
Corrected Total	68	21.07913			

Variable	Parameter Estimate	Standard Error	Type II SS	F Value	Pr > F
Intercept	83.23078	1.78902	35.56396	2164.39	<.0001
Furniture_Home_Improvement	0.00901	0.01195	0.00933	0.57	0.4539
Travel_including_Leisure	-0.00739	0.00869	0.01186	0.72	0.3988
Entertainment	-0.06744	0.01901	0.20669	12.58	0.0008
Education	0.11998	0.02969	0.26828	16.33	0.0002
Communication	-0.00094741	0.00149	0.00666	0.41	0.5267
Clothing_and_shopping	0.09286	0.03027	0.15465	9.41	0.0032
Spend_save_quaterly_ratio	0.07274	0.01155	0.65162	39.66	<.0001

Bounds on condition number: 34.431, 850.97

Figure 5.18: Backward selection: step 2

In the final step, as shown in *Figure 5.19*, we can see the variables **Entertainment**, **Education**, **Clothing_and_shopping**, and **Spend_save_quarterly_ratio** have been retained in the model. Incidentally, these are the same variables retained by the forward selection model: Let us see if the maximize R model produces a different set of statistically significant variables for predicting CPI.

Backward Elimination: Step 6

Statistics for Removal DF = 1,64				
Variable	Partial R-Square	Model R-Square	F Value	Pr > F
Entertainment	0.0450	0.9063	59.20	<.0001
Education	0.0140	0.9374	18.38	<.0001
Clothing_and_shopping	0.0118	0.9396	15.50	0.0002
Spend_save_quaterly_ratio	0.0353	0.9161	46.43	<.0001

All variables left in the model are significant at the 0.1000 level.

Summary of Backward Elimination								
Step	Variable Removed	Label	Number Vars In	Partial R-Square	Model R-Square	C(p)	F Value	Pr > F
1	Eating_out	Eating_out	8	0.0000	0.9525	8.0002	0.00	0.9886
2	Grocery	Grocery	7	0.0000	0.9524	6.0016	0.00	0.9701
3	Communication	Communication	6	0.0003	0.9521	4.3937	0.41	0.5267
4	Travel_including_Leisure	Travel_including_Leisure	5	0.0005	0.9517	2.9554	0.59	0.4467
5	Furniture_Home_Improvement	Furniture_Home_Improvement	4	0.0003	0.9513	1.3699	0.44	0.5117

Figure 5.19: Backward selection: step 6

Maximize R

In the maximize R model, the first variable selected leads to the highest R^2 value when entered initially in the model. As shown in *Figure 20*, in the case of our model, the first variable entered is **Spend_save_quarterly_ratio**. The variable is statistically significant. After this, the **Clothing_and_shopping** variable is entered. At this stage, the R^2 value further increases. The model declares that the best two variable combination in the model has been found:

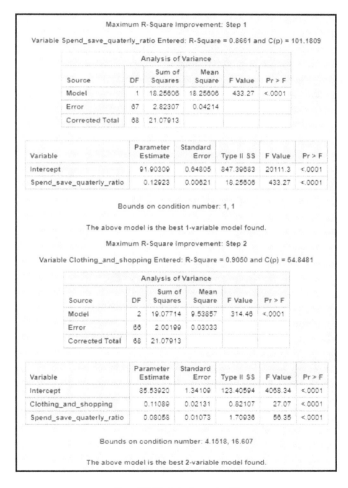

Figure 5.20: Maximize R: steps 1 and 2

In *Figure 5.21*, we see the attempt by the model to find the best possible three variable model. The **Entertainment** variable is entered in step 3. However, step 4, rather than just seeing an entry of the **Education** variable, we also see the exit of the **Clothing_and_shopping** variable that was introduced in the model in step 2. The model determines that the best three variable model should contain the **Spend_and_save_quarterly_ratio**, **Entertainment**, and **Education** variables:

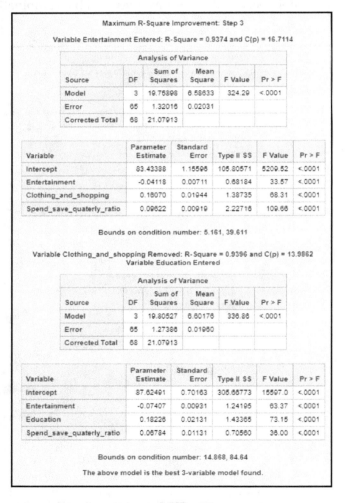

Maximum R-Square Improvement: Step 3

Variable Entertainment Entered: R-Square = 0.9374 and C(p) = 16.7114

Analysis of Variance

Source	DF	Sum of Squares	Mean Square	F Value	Pr > F
Model	3	19.76898	6.58633	324.29	<.0001
Error	65	1.32016	0.02031		
Corrected Total	68	21.07913			

Variable	Parameter Estimate	Standard Error	Type II SS	F Value	Pr > F
Intercept	83.43388	1.15596	105.80571	5209.52	<.0001
Entertainment	-0.04118	0.00711	0.68184	33.57	<.0001
Clothing_and_shopping	0.16070	0.01944	1.38735	68.31	<.0001
Spend_save_quaterly_ratio	0.09622	0.00919	2.22716	109.66	<.0001

Bounds on condition number: 5.161, 39.611

Variable Clothing_and_shopping Removed: R-Square = 0.9396 and C(p) = 13.9862
Variable Education Entered

Analysis of Variance

Source	DF	Sum of Squares	Mean Square	F Value	Pr > F
Model	3	19.80527	6.60176	336.86	<.0001
Error	65	1.27386	0.01960		
Corrected Total	68	21.07913			

Variable	Parameter Estimate	Standard Error	Type II SS	F Value	Pr > F
Intercept	87.62491	0.70163	305.66773	15597.0	<.0001
Entertainment	-0.07407	0.00931	1.24195	63.37	<.0001
Education	0.18226	0.02131	1.43365	73.15	<.0001
Spend_save_quaterly_ratio	0.06784	0.01131	0.70560	36.00	<.0001

Bounds on condition number: 14.868, 84.64

The above model is the best 3-variable model found.

Figure 5.21: Maximize R: steps 3 and 4

In step 5 in *Figure 5.22*, we end up with the same variables in the model as we did with the forward and backward selection models. However, in step 6, we have an additional variable, but all the variables are still significant. Until now this is the first time that we have had a five variable model with none of the variables insignificant. The R^2 achieved is the highest in step 6. However, do notice that the C(p) value has gone down by the addition of the **Furniture_home_improvement** variable in step 6:

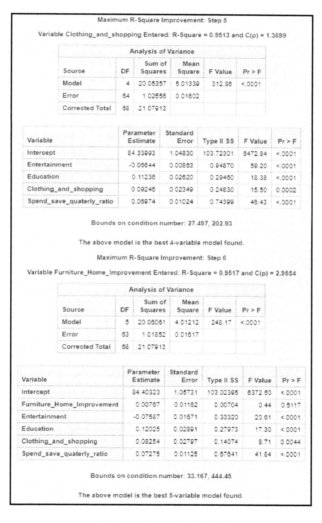

Figure 5.22: Maximize R: steps 5 and 6

The model continues to include variables until all of them have been included. Step 10 is the last step for the maximize R model. However, as we can see in *Figure 5.23*, we are left with a model that has many statistically insignificant variables and a high C(p) when compared to models in steps 5 or 6 of the maximize R^2 model:

Maximum R-Square Improvement: Step 10

Variable Eating_out Entered: R-Square = 0.9525 and C(p) = 10.0000

		Analysis of Variance			
Source	DF	Sum of Squares	Mean Square	F Value	Pr > F
Model	9	20.07684	2.23076	131.31	<.0001
Error	59	1.00229	0.01699		
Corrected Total	68	21.07913			

Variable	Parameter Estimate	Standard Error	Type II SS	F Value	Pr > F
Intercept	83.13330	3.04430	12.66819	745.72	<.0001
Furniture_Home_Improvement	0.00911	0.01382	0.00738	0.43	0.5125
Travel_including_Leisure	-0.00750	0.01098	0.00793	0.47	0.4972
Eating_out	-0.00015179	0.01061	0.00000348	0.00	0.9886
Entertainment	-0.06756	0.01989	0.19602	11.54	0.0012
Grocery	0.00123	0.03527	0.00002060	0.00	0.9723
Education	0.11989	0.03200	0.23849	14.04	0.0004
Communication	-0.00094288	0.00152	0.00656	0.39	0.5367
Clothing_and_shopping	0.09299	0.03123	0.15059	8.86	0.0042
Spend_save_quaterly_ratio	0.07273	0.01410	0.45186	26.60	<.0001

Bounds on condition number: 38.673, 1478

The above model is the best 9-variable model found.

No further improvement in R-Square is possible.

Figure 5.23: Maximize R: step 10

The studentized residuals and Cook's D chart, shown in *Figure 5.24*, did point out to an outlier present in **May2015**, which seems to be the result of some data storage issue. On checking the modeling dataset, it was observed that the **May2015** value for the **Communication** variable is 18. This is an outlier, as the **Apr2015** and **Jun2015** values are 108 and 109, respectively:

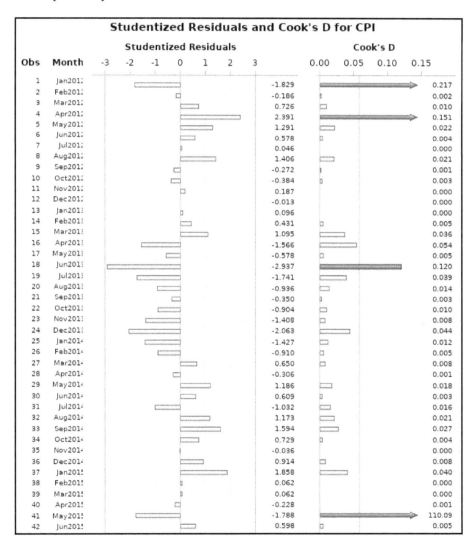

Figure 5.24: Maximize R^2 partial output–studentized residuals and Cook's D

Until now, we have compared three models in the multivariate regression section. Apart from the **furniture_home_improvement** variable being present in step 6 of the maximize R model, all the statistically significant variables are the same across the three models. Let us look at another modeling methodology before we compare the forecasts from the models.

Univariate model

For the model that primarily uses only CPI data series, we will use a procedure in SAS called the **Unobserved Components Model (UCM)**. While we are calling it a univariate model, we will end up using some components of the CPI time series as independent variables. Remember, we aren't using the nine internal variables that are available to us as part of the business problem. Those nine variables have been used in the multivariate regression model. The components we will be using are the irregular, trend, and seasonal components. We will also leverage some of the plots that can be produced as part of the UCM procedure.

The following is a univariate model code, using `Proc UCM`:

```
Proc UCM Data=Model;
    Id Month Interval=Month;
    Model CPI;
    Irregular;
    Level;
    Slope Var = 0 Noest;
    Season Length = 12 Type = Trig;
    Estimate Back = 6 Plot = (loess panel cusum wn);
    Forecast Back = 0 Lead = 24 Print = Forecasts Plot=(forecasts decomp);
Run;
```

The trend has been specified using the level and the slope options. In *Figure 5.25*, we can see the preliminary estimates of the free parameters:

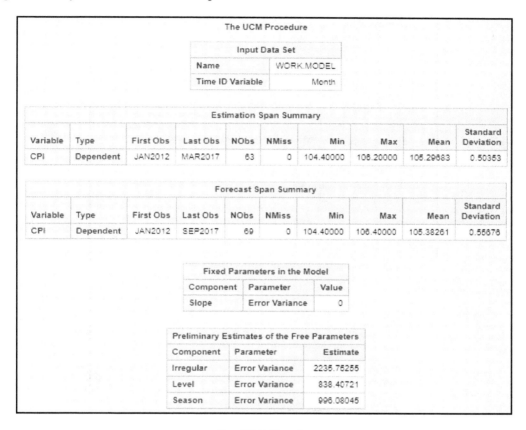

The UCM Procedure

Input Data Set	
Name	WORK.MODEL
Time ID Variable	Month

Estimation Span Summary

Variable	Type	First Obs	Last Obs	NObs	NMiss	Min	Max	Mean	Standard Deviation
CPI	Dependent	JAN2012	MAR2017	63	0	104.40000	106.20000	105.29683	0.50353

Forecast Span Summary

Variable	Type	First Obs	Last Obs	NObs	NMiss	Min	Max	Mean	Standard Deviation
CPI	Dependent	JAN2012	SEP2017	69	0	104.40000	106.40000	105.38261	0.55676

Fixed Parameters in the Model

Component	Parameter	Value
Slope	Error Variance	0

Preliminary Estimates of the Free Parameters

Component	Parameter	Estimate
Irregular	Error Variance	2235.75255
Level	Error Variance	838.40721
Season	Error Variance	996.08045

Figure 5.25: UCM procedure

As seen in *Figure 5.26*, both the **Level** and **Slope** (part of the trend component) are significant components in the model:

Final Estimates of the Free Parameters					
Component	Parameter	Estimate	Approx Std Error	t Value	Approx Pr > |t|
Irregular	Error Variance	5.94778E-10	6.58962E-7	0.00	0.9993
Level	Error Variance	0.00513	0.0010253	5.00	<.0001
Season	Error Variance	1.25548E-12	2.07609E-9	0.00	0.9995

Fit Statistics Based on Residuals	
Mean Squared Error	0.00852
Root Mean Squared Error	0.09228
Mean Absolute Percentage Error	0.07073
Maximum Percent Error	0.19139
R-Square	0.96825
Adjusted R-Square	0.96690
Random Walk R-Square	-0.71148
Amemiya's Adjusted R-Square	0.96420
Number of non-missing residuals used for computing the fit statistics = 50	

Significance Analysis of Components (Based on the Final State)			
Component	DF	Chi-Square	Pr > ChiSq
Irregular	1	0.00	0.9999
Level	1	1.177E7	<.0001
Slope	1	4.68	0.0305
Season	11	15.69	0.1530

Figure 5.26: UCM procedure–final estimates

Let us evaluate the residual diagnostics, shown in *Figure 5.27*. In the histogram, the residuals seem to be normally distributed. In the Q-Q plot, the residuals are closer to the line and hence seem to be normally distributed. The ACF and PACF don't exhibit any violation of the whiteness assumption:

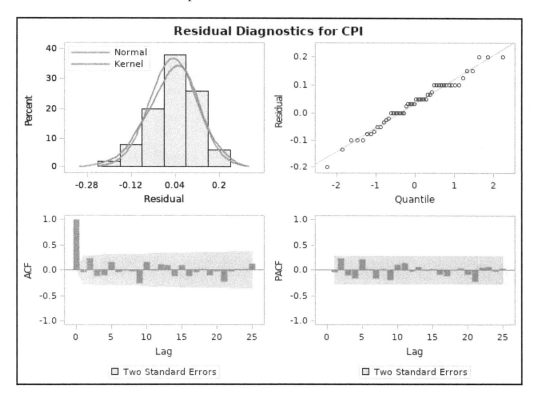

Figure 5.27: UCM procedure–residual diagnostics

In *Figure 5.28*, showing the residual white noise test, the first three lags correspond to the three components we have included in the model. As a standard, the white noise test is not done for the number of lags that equal the number of components used in the model. While the fourth lag is within the 0.05 p-value, from the fifth lag onwards, we can see that the residuals have a p-value greater than 0.05. Hence, no violation of the whiteness can be observed in the model:

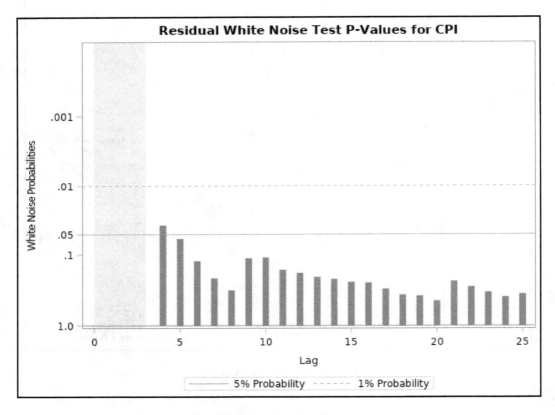

Figure 5.28: UCM procedure–residual white noise test

There is a structural break in cumulative residuals, as seen in *Figure 5.29*. For a period of almost two years, the cumulative residuals are above the 95% confidence limit:

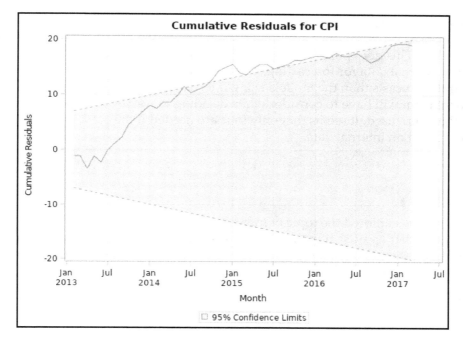

Figure 5.29: UCM procedure–cumulative residuals

We have tried to solve the business problem using the multivariate regression and the UCM model approach. Let us compare the forecasts generated for our validation period:

Forecasted Month	Forward Selection	Backward Selection	Maximize R	UCM	Observed Values
Oct 2017	106.4077	106.4077	106.3580	106.46	106.4
Nov 2017	106.4077	106.4077	106.3592	106.48	106.5
Dec 2017	106.3413	106.3413	106.2917	106.48	106.6
Jan 2018	106.2715	106.2715	106.2025	106.46	106.6
Feb 2018	106.2051	106.2051	106.1272	106.46	106.6
Mar 2018	106.2051	106.2051	106.1198	106.476667	106.7

Figure 5.30: Model forecasts versus observed

From the preceding table, we can observe that, in absolute terms, the UCM forecasts are closer to the observed values and also directionally right more number of times compared to other models. This does pose a dilemma for the bank's management. They are keen to leverage the internal data for forecasting. The publicly available CPI data seems to produce more accurate forecasts than the models using internal data. This is an aspect that the management team will have to consider while deciding to use internal data. From the nine variables that were used, it seems that only four are needed if the bank does go ahead and use models based on internal data.

Summary

In this chapter, we explored the topic of inflation in detail and the driving factors for inflation. We further learned about inflation outcomes and the Philips curve using real-life examples. We further discussed various aspects of inflation and simultaneously covered different models, such as multivariate regression, Maximize R, and the univariate model.

6
Managing Customer Loyalty Using Time Series Data

In `Chapter 1`, *Time Series Modeling in the Financial Industry,* we briefly touched upon the myth that every time we spoke about time series data and forecasting behavior. While this is true most of the time, it isn't valid on a lot of occasions. It was mentioned that time series data can be used for benchmarking, quality control, pattern recognition, and even estimating the effect of one variable on the observed values of another variable. Survival analysis focuses on estimating time to an event. In `Chapter 2`, *Forecasting Stock Prices and Portfolio Decisions using Time Series Data,* while discussing ARIMA, we saw that the model primarily depends on the time component and didn't focus much on the influencer variables. Survival analysis, just like multivariate regression, can also help emphasize the role of other influencer variables. The methodology isn't used to forecast solely on the basis of time components such as seasonality and trends of a single variable. We will focus on nuances of survival modeling a bit later in the chapter. Survival analysis uses the time series data to forecast when an event might happen. The event could be related to any of the following:

- The probability of a machine to stop functioning in the next 20 years
- A customer not renewing their internet broadband contract at the end of its fixed term
- The likelihood of a patient consuming tobacco regularly dying early, compared to a patient with relatively healthy habits
- The likelihood of a customer defaulting on his payments at a future date

The Kaplan-Meier estimator, the Nelson-Aalen estimator, Cox regression, parametric, and non-parametric models are some of the key aspects of survival analysis that we will explore in detail. We will also try and understand the basics of probability density function, cumulative density function, hazard ratio, survival curve, and the importance of censoring.

So, how can we define survival analysis? It is a broad range of statistical methods used to determine the time to an event. Let's plot the survival and hazard curve of a sample dataset. The dataset shows the lifespan of an engine in years:

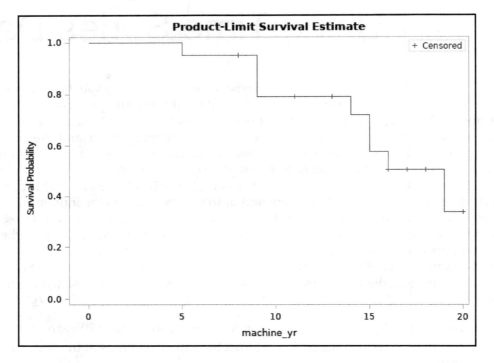

The product-limit survival estimate chart plots the time of the machine's life span on the X-axis and the survival probability on the Y-axis. It shows that for a period up to five years and between 8 and 13 years of the machine's lifespan, the survival rate remains consistent. However, before the 10th, 15th, and 20th anniversary of the machine, the survival rates quickly drop:

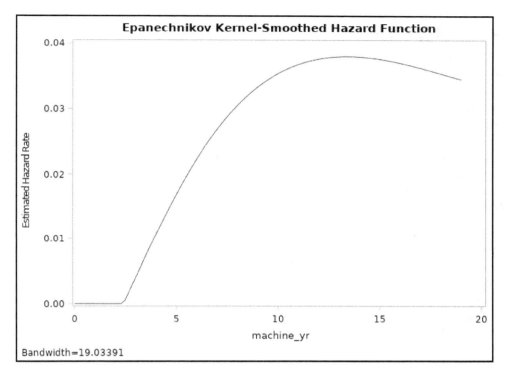

Figure 6.1: Survival function and hazard rate sample data illustration

The hazard rate chart shows the rate of failures (*Y*-axis) at each anniversary point (*X*-axis) assuming that the machine hasn't already failed. Once a machine reaches it's 14th anniversary, the hazard rate after raising until now, starts falling. It shows that if a machine is able to survive the 14th anniversary, then the chances of it not surviving start falling. The lowest hazard rate is at the five-year interval, where one of the machines first stops performing.

By using the survival and hazard rate chart, we have been able to decipher the survival probability of a machine at various stages of its lifespan and also to see the hazard rate at any given point. You may have already noticed the word censoring appearing on the chart. Let's take a step back and see why survival analysis is better suited for some business problems and then explore the various aspects and terminologies used in survival models.

Advantages of survival modeling

In our illustration, the business problem could be defined as the need to understand the probability of a machine being operational across its lifespan. Did all the machines fail at some point in the period of evaluation? No. The data spans 20 years and we have 55% of the instances when the machines haven't stopped functioning in the given time span. So how can we find the survival rate or hazard rate of machines when they haven't stopped functioning? Well, we could use the data of the machines that did stop functioning. We could maybe look at the common characteristics (such as the manufacturer, functional area the machine has been deployed for, the location of the plant where it has been installed, servicing history, and so on) of the failed and the functioning machines and extrapolate the knowledge gained from analyzing failed machines to the functioning ones.

This opens up the possibility of using multiple regression (which was covered in `Chapter 2`, *Forecasting Stock Prices and Portfolio Decisions using Time Series Data*, while looking at portfolio investment decisions) to find the drivers that led to 45% of the machines not lasting until their 20th anniversary. One of the fundamental requirements to use regression is that our data is normally distributed. One of the implicit assumptions in such a scenario would be that all the machines in the data were operationalized at the same time and given a chance to perform for the tenure of 20 years. Notwithstanding this assumption, there could be some issues in achieving normal distribution of the variable. If the machines didn't get operationalized at the same time, there would be issues in inferring the output from the model. What happens when all the failed machines got installed at year four? Did something go particularly wrong at this point? What if the machines were all installed in no particular order in the 20-year period and that some of the functioning machines were installed in the last few years of the observation period? Survival modeling is adept at dealing with data when there is a challenge in identifying the start or the end period of data constituents.

Another advantage of survival analysis is to incorporate the effects of covariates. Not all survival modeling techniques can incorporate the effects of covariates or what we termed as independent variables while introducing multivariate regression in `Chapter 2`, *Forecasting Stock Prices and Portfolio Decisions using Time Series Data*. The inclusion of covariates adds an important explanatory part to survival analysis.

It is also possible to compare survival curves between various strata or groups. For instance, if we had five different brands of machines, we could plot different survival curves for each brand. This gives us the flexibility of comparing across groups. In the other predictor models, we will have to construct different models for each of the groups to be able to perform inter-group comparison.

Multivariate regression is unable to inform on how likely a machine is going to be functional or what is the risk of a machine being non-functional at a given time. Using multivariate regression, we can just model the drivers and their importance in determining failure but that won't give us the time element information. Even if we built a logistic regression model with a binary outcome of 1 (functioning) and 0 (machine not functioning), we will not be able to deal with instances when the non-functioning has happened due to external decisions. The logistic model will assume that every instance of 0 is bad and that the machine has failed. In survival modeling, we don't begin with an assumption that every instance of a machine non-functioning is solely due to a mechanical failure. There could be other reasons, such as over-production, which may have decided to pull the plug and reduce the number of operational machines. The survival analysis models deal with this issue by censoring.

But what is censoring a variable? Let's go back to the definition of probability. Probability is the chance of an event occurring. What could be an event? The tossing of a coin can have two events-heads or tails. If we are interested in quantifying the chance of getting heads in the tossing of the coin, we need to perform the tossing a certain n number of times. Let's say, we toss the coin 100 times and observe that the event heads was observed for 55 times. So we can say the probability of observing heads is 55/100 or 0.55 or the probability of not observing heads is 45/100 or 0.45. The 0.45 probability of heads can also be explained as 1 - 0.55. In determining the probability of a 0.55, we used both the chance of something happening and not occurring at all.

Similarly, in the probability of machine failure, we either have machines functioning or those that aren't. The final outcome is assumed to be the non-functioning of a machine at some point in time. What is unknown is when the functioning machines will stop. In the coin toss illustration, the outcome was heads or not heads (tails). There was never a possibility of the outcome tails turning into heads at a later stage. Hence, the observed experimentation tosses couldn't be predicted. Whereas, in the machine data, we have to assume that the active machines are going to stop at some point and this assumption has to be built in before we can try and understand what point they may stop. When an event hasn't occurred for a part of the population and we want to call out such data points, we censor them. Against each machine ID, we can simply add a new variable called censored with values 1 and 0. Value 1 can be coded for each active machine and 0 for the non-functional machine. It would be a flawed survival analysis model if none of the machines in the database churned.

This would mean that we are trying to model the good (active) behavior of machines without any negative event information. In this instance, we have done a right-censoring where the expected life cycle of the machines is expected to be same. An instance of a left-censoring data could be when we expect a particular machine to have a shorter lifespan compared to the observed. This could be if we don't know when the machine stopped working but we can assume that the observed functioning time is greater than the actual time.

When we censor machine A, it will be called **right censoring**, as it has survived the study period of five years and we don't have an actual time to failure. In the instance of machine B, we are doing left censoring, as we don't know the exact time when it stopped functioning. We only know that at the two-year mark, the machine was recorded as being non-functional. The censoring in such cases is known as left censoring. There is also a type of censoring called interval censoring. In the case of machine C, it was functioning when observed at the two-year mark but had stopped working somewhere before the three-year mark recorded on the data system. In this case, we don't know at which point during the interval of the two observed points the machine stop functioning:

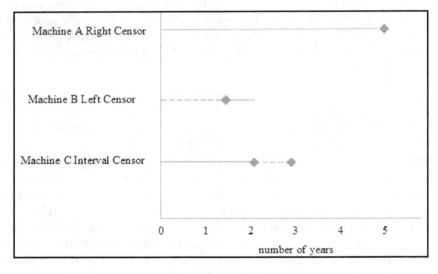

Figure 6.2: Types of censoring

Any censoring can only work if we assume that the underlying subjects in the study have an equal survival probability. Irrespective of the time that they entered the study, it is assumed that the subject still has a chance of experiencing the event. If we are undertaking a clinical trial, we assume that subject x who enters the trial in the last two years of the drug study will have an equal survival probability when compared to the subjects who entered the trial at its inception. Also, it assumed that subject x has a chance to experience the event even though it has entered the trials at a later stage. Subject x does require censoring, as it entered the trial at a later stage and has still not encountered an event.

Key aspects of survival analysis

Now we will discuss parametric versus non-parametric tests.

The main type of survival analysis methodologies can be classified as parametric or non-parametric. Across statistical analysis, users would come across both these types of tests and models. While non-parametric approaches have their benefits, in practice parametric tests are used more in the financial world.

Parametric tests assume that the data follows some distribution. For instance, this is one of the critical conditions of regression. Parametric tests in some instances have a greater statistical significance. They can also perform quite well if the spread of two or more groups being compared is quite different. If survival times of two or more industry groups are quite different then a parametric test might be more useful for comparison. The biggest drawback of the parametric test is the assumption that you know the distribution. Further constraints occur when the assumption needs to conform to a specific type.

Non-parametric tests are popular as there is no conformity condition regarding the distribution. This means that there is less overhead associated with using data for these tests. Treating outliers to achieve normality or ensuring that there is enough number of observations to have a particular distribution are all requirements that aren't associated with non-parametric tests. Non-parametric tests also work well with ranked or ordinal data.

In some instances, when the data size is small, an analyst may be waiting for the right amount of data to be captured before parametric tests are done. If the analyst feels that the right amount of data is available, the analyst should exercise caution when testing for normality. A normality test might not generate the right answer as the power of the normality test may be low. Hence, when transitioning from non-parametric to parametric tests, the analyst has to exercise caution.

Let's now move on to the key procedures for survival analysis.

The Kaplan-Meier estimator is conducted using `PROC LIFTEST` in SAS. This is a non-parametric procedure for estimating the survivor function, comparing survival curves of groups, and testing the relationship between survival time and other covariates. For fitting a parametric procedure, we can use `PROC LIFEREG`. There is also a type of procedure known as semi-parametric. The Cox model is fitted using `PROC PHREG`. The Cox model also allows for studying the relationship between the survival time and other influencer variables. It is worth noting that `PROC PHREG` doesn't allow the use of left or interval censored observations, whereas `PROC LIFEREG` can use such variables. We will study the pros and cons of these procedures in further detail later in the chapter.

Data structure

Both `PROC LIFETEST` and `PROC PHREG` will allow the analyst to take into account the variables that explain the survival time. However, there is a difference in how input data can be structured for the latter procedure. Both these procedures will take into account instances where each subject will have one row of data. This is the major deviation from most of the time series datasets we have observed in this book. Most of the data have subjects with multiple rows, with each row signifying a point in time. The periodicity is constant between each row of the subject. However, the survival data is constructed by aggregating the data at a subject level. `PROC PHREG` does allow the use of multiple rows per each subject. However, the periodicity doesn't need to be constant between each subject or similar to the time gap between multiple observations of another subject. Also, not all subjects need to have multiple rows.

The multiple row situation arises in survival analysis when the same subject has influencer variables which have different values across time:

Obs	Custid	Tenure	AUM	Risk_Appetite	Fund_Performance	Inv_Potential	Inv_Involvement	Complex_Prod	Complaints	Region	Censor
1	10018	5	2	1	3	1	1	1	1	Yorkshire and Humber	1
2	10025	6	3	3	2	1	1	1	1	Yorkshire and Humber	0
3	10047	15	2	1	1	1	2	1	1	N Ireland	0
4	10050	20	1	3	3	3	3	0	0	N East	1
5	10120	18	2	2	1	2	1	0	1	N West	1
6	10166	2	1	1	1	2	1	0	0	Yorkshire and Humber	0
7	10170	14	3	1	3	2	3	0	1	G London	0
8	10190	14	2	1	1	3	2	0	0	W Midlands	1
9	10191	20	1	3	1	3	3	1	1	E England	1
10	10225	7	1	1	2	1	3	1	1	G London	1
11	10226	10	2	1	1	2	1	0	0	S East	1
12	10276	9	2	2	1	1	2	1	0	S West	1
13	10283	16	2	1	3	1	2	1	0	G London	1
14	10294	7	2	1	2	1	1	1	0	Yorkshire and Humber	0
15	10434	6	2	2	1	1	2	1	1	Yorkshire and Humber	0
16	10436	6	3	2	1	1	1	0	1	Wales	0

Figure 6.3: Typical survival analysis data structure

Business problem

A brokerage firm has just been acquired by a large fund manager who wanted access to the client base of the firm. The purchase of the brokerage firm was done after due diligence. However, before reaching out to the newly acquired client base the fund manager wanted to analyze the client database in detail. The aim of the analysis was to identify the clients who met the following criteria:

- Have been with the firm for a long time
- Are probably going to stay for a long time
- Are at risk of churn
- Continue to have **assets under management** (**AUM**) with the brokerage, and the reasons for this

The fund-managers team decided to use survival analysis and ended up building a non-parametric, parametric, and a semi-parametric model to try and provide answers. Let's look into each of the procedures and their output. The analysis was broken down into the following steps:

1. Data preparation and exploration.
2. Non-parametric procedure analysis.
3. Parametric procedure analysis.
4. Semi-parametric procedure analysis.

Data preparation and exploration

The time series data of the customers was aggregated to one single row per customer ID. Some of the business questions raised needed the exclusion of some variables that could possibly explain the client behavior through their life cycle. The variables that were identified for analysis were the following:

- **Customer ID**: This was used as an ID variable and not for analysis.
- **Tenure**: The number of years the customer has been with the brokerage firm. Right censoring was done in 31 instances where the customer is still active after being with the firm for 20 years.
- **AUM**: Assets under £0.5 million are classed as 1, between £0.5 and £1 million as 2, 2 to £5 million as 3, and above £5 million as 4.
- **Risk appetite**: As part of its compliance process and to better understand the customer's investment needs, the brokerage had assigned a low risk (1), medium risk (2), and a high risk (3) strategy value to the customer's risk appetite.
- **Fund performance**: At the end of the day, the customers were interested in growing their capital invested via the brokerage.
- **Investment potential**: This is the level of investment that the client can have. The client may have already invested this money elsewhere. The fund manager was interested in the investment potential that the brokerage customers offered and this was one of the reasons for the takeover. It had a value 1 (£1 – £5 m), 2 (£5 – £10 m), and 3 (£10 million+).

- **Investment involvement**: This is a variable that is linked to compliance requirements mandated by certain oversight bodies, such as the **Financial Conduct Authority** (**FCA**) in the UK. Clients have varying levels of preference regarding how much time they want to spend actively managing their investments. Also, not all clients have prior investment experience and their level of understanding of the financial instruments available may be limited. In such cases, the brokerage firm has a responsibility to either offer advice or ensure that the client has sought advice independently prior to investing. The variable is classed as 1, 2, and 3 for clients with low, medium, and high involvement, respectively.
- **Complex product**: This is classed as 1 if the customer holds complex products and 0 in other cases. Some of the complex products may involve higher investment criteria, may require more understanding of how they are structured, or might be customized offerings.
- **Complaints**: Unfortunately, like any business, the brokerage firm had received complaints in the past. The fund managers were busy trying to understand the nature of these complaints and resolve them. Instances where clients had complained have the value 1.
- **Region**: All these customers were UK based and the values represented the geographic location where they were primarily based.
- **Censor**: Right censoring was done in the instances where clients were still active.

PROC UNIVARIATE and PROC CORR were run to get a better understanding of the dataset, survival_analysis.

This was PROC UNIVARIATE normal distribution code:

```
PROC UNIVARIATE Data = survival_analysis Normal Plot;
    Var tenure;
    Cdfplot tenure;
RUN;
```

The `UNIVARIATE` procedure has output four statistical tests to check the assumption that the data is normally distributed. The Shapiro-Wilk, Kolmogorov-Smirnov, Cramer-von Mises, and Anderson-Darling tests are produced as part of the tests for normality. The Shapiro-Wilk test is relevant in this case as the sample size is less than 2,000. The test rejects the hypothesis that the data is normally distributed:

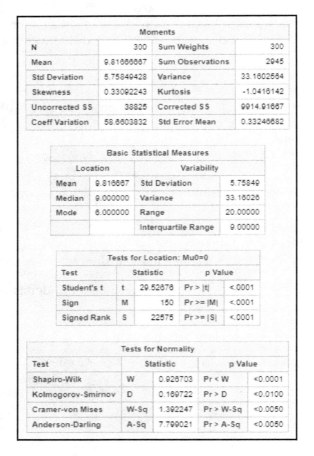

Moments			
N	300	Sum Weights	300
Mean	9.81666667	Sum Observations	2945
Std Deviation	5.75849428	Variance	33.1602564
Skewness	0.33092243	Kurtosis	-1.0416142
Uncorrected SS	38825	Corrected SS	9914.91667
Coeff Variation	58.6603832	Std Error Mean	0.33246682

Basic Statistical Measures			
Location		Variability	
Mean	9.816667	Std Deviation	5.75849
Median	9.000000	Variance	33.16026
Mode	6.000000	Range	20.00000
		Interquartile Range	9.00000

Tests for Location: Mu0=0				
Test		Statistic	p Value	
Student's t	t	29.52676	Pr > |t|	<.0001
Sign	M	150	Pr >= |M|	<.0001
Signed Rank	S	22575	Pr >= |S|	<.0001

Tests for Normality				
Test		Statistic	p Value	
Shapiro-Wilk	W	0.926703	Pr < W	<0.0001
Kolmogorov-Smirnov	D	0.169722	Pr > D	<0.0100
Cramer-von Mises	W-Sq	1.392247	Pr > W-Sq	<0.0050
Anderson-Darling	A-Sq	7.799021	Pr > A-Sq	<0.0050

Figure 6.4: PROC UNIVARIATE - data exploration

In *Figure 6.4*, the extreme observations highlight the fact that some of the clients have left the brokerage within the first year. Whereas, there are instances when some of the clients have left the brokerages in the past year after having been a customer for 20 years. The recent departures after a long stay may potentially be linked to the takeover of the brokerage by the fund manager.

This was an aspect that needed to be looked in to. Without analyzing further, the analyst wasn't keen to remove or transform any extreme observations from the study:

Extreme Observations			
Lowest		Highest	
Value	Obs	Value	Obs
1	247	20	269
1	245	20	281
1	207	20	286
1	205	20	289
1	199	21	74

The preceding diagram highlights the fact that the mean and median values are quite close. The quantiles plot highlights that the tenure is fairly distributed across the quantiles line. Ideally, the skewness should be close to 0. The skewness for tenure is 0.33092243 in our case. The kurtosis should ideally be close to 3 but it is - 1.0416142. The negative kurtosis highlights a lighter tail and is also known as **platykurtic distribution**:

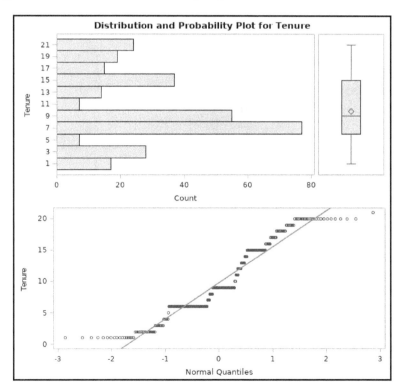

We also requested for a **cumulative distribution (cdf)** plot for tenure. The chart plotted includes both censored and non-censored data. Let's look at the cdf plot for the uncensored data:

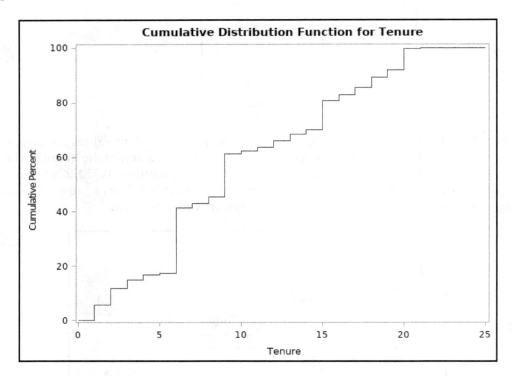

The PROC UNIVARIATE normal distribution code for uncensored is as follows:

```
PROC UNIVARIATE Data = survival_analysis (where=(censor=0));
    Var tenure;
    Cdfplot tenure;
RUN;
```

The CDF plots in *Figure 6.4* and *Figure 6.5* are different as the population in the latter is a subset and only includes the uncensored data. The uncensored data has already experienced the event of churn. The CDF plot highlights the chances of a client churning. The biggest increase in churn is happening at the 6th, 9th, and 15th anniversaries of the clients:

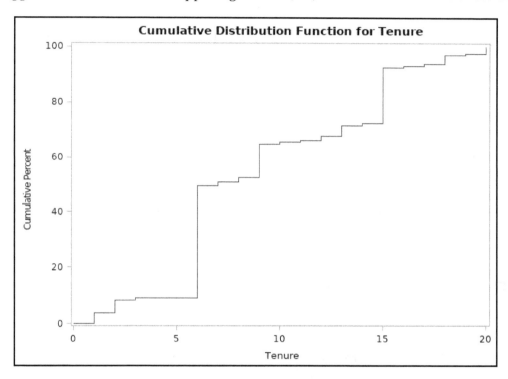

Figure 6.5: CDF of uncensored data

Let's analyze the data further using survival analysis procedures.

The following is the correlation analysis:

```
PROC CORR Data = survival_analysis;
    Var Risk_appetite Fund_performance Inv_potential Inv_involvement AUM
Complex_prod Complaints;
RUN;
```

All variables have a low correlation with other variables. None of the variables have a correlation value of more than 0.4:

	Risk_Appetite	Fund_Performance	Inv_Potential	Inv_Involvement	AUM	Complex_Prod	Complaints
Risk_Appetite Risk Appetite	1.00000	0.01994 0.7309	0.14472 0.0121	-0.01345 0.8165	0.06264 0.2795	-0.00551 0.9242	-0.07306 0.2070
Fund_Performance Fund Performance	0.01994 0.7309	1.00000	0.38475 <.0001	0.23188 <.0001	0.12430 0.0314	0.00758 0.8960	-0.15005 0.0092
Inv_Potential Inv Potential	0.14472 0.0121	0.38475 <.0001	1.00000	0.31415 <.0001	0.17964 0.0018	-0.34222 <.0001	-0.10040 0.0825
Inv_Involvement Inv Involvement	-0.01345 0.8165	0.23188 <.0001	0.31415 <.0001	1.00000	0.05550 0.3380	-0.19712 0.0006	-0.00333 0.9542
AUM AUM	0.06264 0.2795	0.12430 0.0314	0.17964 0.0018	0.05550 0.3380	1.00000	-0.00904 0.8761	-0.03256 0.5742
Complex_Prod Complex Prod	-0.00551 0.9242	0.00758 0.8960	-0.34222 <.0001	-0.19712 0.0006	-0.00904 0.8761	1.00000	-0.00053 0.9927
Complaints Complaints	-0.07306 0.2070	-0.15005 0.0092	-0.10040 0.0825	-0.00333 0.9542	-0.03256 0.5742	-0.00053 0.9927	1.00000

Pearson Correlation Coefficients, N = 300
Prob > |r| under H0: Rho=0

Figure 6.6: Correlation table

Non-parametric procedure analysis

Let's now discuss plotting the survival curve.

PROC LIFETEST has been used to analyze the survival plot and observe the percentage of the population that has censored data. The procedure produces a graph of the Kaplan-Meier estimator of the survival function.

Here is the code for a non-parametric procedure survival chart:

```
PROC LIFETEST Data=Survival_Analysis Plots=survival;
   Time tenure*censor(1);
Run;
```

The CDF plot in *Figure 6.5* is quite similar to the survival plot in *Figure 6.7*. The survival function, *S(t)* is derived after subtraction of the CDF from 1:

S(t) = 1 - CDF

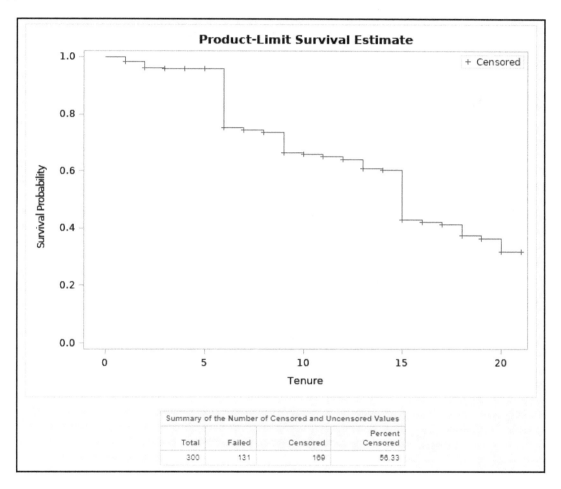

Figure 6.7: Survival plot using non-parametric procedure

The survival function states the probability of survival past time *t*. In the case of the brokerage firm's clients, the survival probability reduces sharply at the 6th and the 15th client anniversaries. There is only a 75% chance of a client surviving after the 6th anniversary. This reduces down to 66% after the 9th anniversary but continues to be around 60% till the 14th anniversary. Only after this point, at the fifteenth anniversary, does the survival probability again decrease significantly and becomes 43%.

Clients have a 31% chance of still being there with the brokerage firm after the 21st year. The survival rate table has been created by modifying the output dataset that can be saved as part of the PROC LIFETEST analysis. To save an output dataset, use the outs option. You can also view the lower and the upper confidence limits of the survival time.

Out of the 300 clients included in the study, 131 have churned, whereas 169 are active clients.

Survival curve for groups

We earlier spoke about comparing groups using non-parametric procedures. One of the hypotheses that the business wants to test is whether the risk appetite influences the tenure that the client has. Let's test this using a Strata option.

Here is the code for non-parametric procedure survival by Strata:

```
PROC LIFETEST Data=Survival_Analysis Plots=survival (strata=panel);
    Time tenure*censor(1);
    Strata risk_appetite;
Run;
```

The clients with medium risk have the lowest percent censored population (43.80) across the strata. The highest percent of the censored population (68.92) is for the customers with the riskiest appetite:

Summary of the Number of Censored and Uncensored Values					
Stratum	Risk_Appetite	Total	Failed	Censored	Percent Censored
1	1	105	40	65	61.90
2	2	121	68	53	43.80
3	3	74	23	51	68.92
Total		300	131	169	56.33

Figure 6.8: Survival plot strata

At the 20th anniversary, the survival chance of the low (risk appetite=1), medium (risk appetite = 2), and high-risk customers (risk appetite = 3) is around 20%, 12%, and 56%, respectively. This means the higher the customer's risk-taking appetite, the more chances are that they will survive with the brokerage. This insight needs to be further assessed for the reasons that drive this customer behavior. Some of the hypotheses supporting this insight could be that a high-risk customer is getting more returns, tends to have more funds to invest, or this client set is getting more attention and consequently has retained the faith in the brokerage:

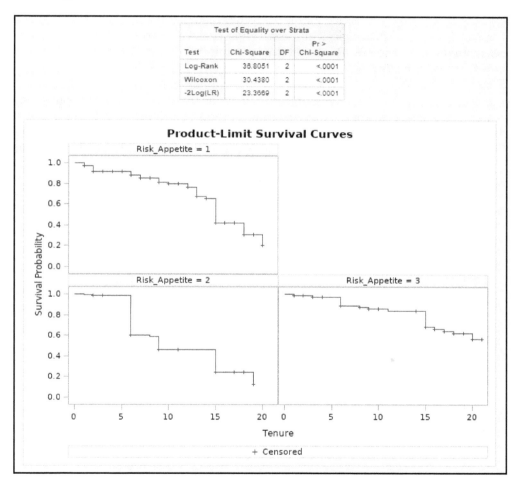

But are these three strata statistically similar? To answer this, we can look at the **Test of Equality over Strata** output in *Figure 6.8*. The rank tests for a homogeneity highlight that the three `Strata` are significantly different when evaluating the survival time of clients. Hence, the hypothesis that the business had about the risk appetite influencing the tenure of clients seems validated.

The test of equality over the strata needs to take into perspective the implication of using the Log-Rank, Wilcoxon, and the -2Log(LR) test. Let's assume a scenario where not all three of them are statistically significant. The -2Log(LR) test assumes that the survival curve is exponentially distributed and since that is seldom a case that the analyst experiences, its use is limited. If the later differences in the survival curve are more important for the business problem, then the Log-Rank test is a better judge. If the earlier differences are important then use the Wilcoxon test. If the survival curves of the strata cross at any point, then either of the Log-Rank and Wilcoxon tests is unreliable. But the survival curves in *Figure 6.8* don't cross. Well, we have populated them as three separate panel outputs. We need to do a quick check where all three graphs are populated together. If you have 10 strata, this graph will get messy but a quick visual inspection with all the strata on one graph is helpful. The alternative is to go through the survival estimate output diagram:

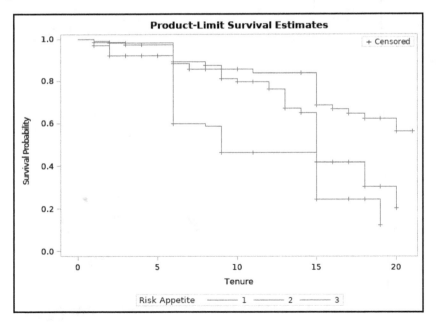

Figure 6.9: Survival plot cross

As we can see from *Figure 6.9*, our survival plots at a strata level cross between the 5 and 10-year tenure. While choosing graphs, the analyst has to be careful about the repercussions of viewing data in a particular manner. The output also means that the Log-Rank test and the Wilcoxon test aren't reliable.

Survival curve and covariates

Here is the code for the non-parametric procedure survival and covariates:

```
PROC LIFETEST Data=Survival_Analysis Plots=(h,ls,lls) Atrisk
Outs=Survival_Table;
    Time tenure*censor(1);
    ID custid;
    Test Risk_appetite Fund_performance Inv_potential Inv_involvement AUM
Complex_prod Complaints;
Run;
```

This produces the negative log graph, among others:

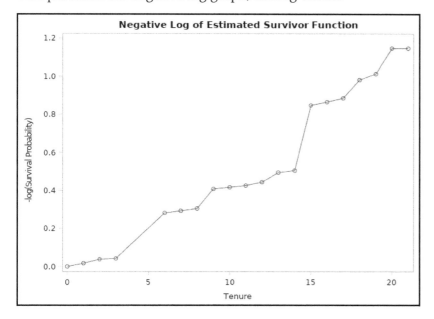

Figure 6.10: Kaplan-Meier survival estimator with covariates

In *Figure 6.10*, the negative log of the estimated survivor function passes through the origin and looks a fit case of exponential distribution:

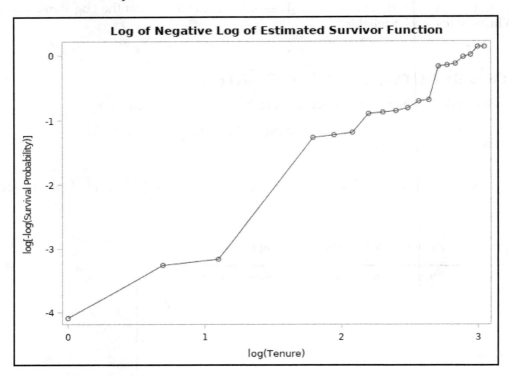

The cumulative hazard is rising exponentially over time. In the `LIFEREG` procedure, we will be testing the shape of the distribution for the model specification.

The hazard rate follows an interesting pattern. The hazard rate keeps on increasing until the 9th year and then actually decreases for a while before spiking up close to the maximum tenure being observed in the data:

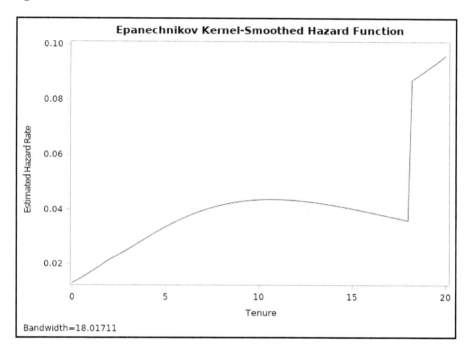

If we look at the univariate chi-squares for the Wilcoxon test, we can see that the variable fund performance has the highest chi-square followed by complex products and investment involvement:

Summary of the Number of Censored and Uncensored Values			
Total	Failed	Censored	Percent Censored
300	131	169	56.33

Rank Tests for the Association of Tenure with Covariates

	Univariate Chi-Squares for the Wilcoxon Test				
Variable	Test Statistic	Standard Error	Chi-Square	Pr > Chi-Square	Label
Risk_Appetite	12.6805	6.3827	3.9470	0.0470	Risk Appetite
Fund_Performance	36.9483	7.4449	24.6305	<.0001	Fund Performance
Inv_Potential	12.7693	7.3068	3.0540	0.0805	Inv Potential
Inv_Involvement	19.3816	6.5754	8.6884	0.0032	Inv Involvement
AUM	3.4461	8.1878	0.1771	0.6738	AUM
Complex_Prod	13.7158	3.7514	13.3675	0.0003	Complex Prod
Complaints	-5.0054	2.9819	2.8177	0.0932	Complaints

These variables are entered in the order of the highest chi-square values in the stepwise model highlighted in the table labeled forward step-wise sequence of chi-squares for the Wilcoxon test. All three variables, fund performance, complex product, and investment involvement, have a strong association with tenure and the association is statistically significant ($p<0.05$):

Covariance Matrix for the Wilcoxon Statistics							
Variable	Risk_Appetite	Fund_Performance	Inv_Potential	Inv_Involvement	AUM	Complex_Prod	Complaints
Risk_Appetite	40.7389	4.0848	6.4707	0.1200	1.4449	-0.4395	-1.8707
Fund_Performance	4.0848	55.4263	24.6492	15.2051	8.0213	-0.7802	-2.7327
Inv_Potential	6.4707	24.6492	53.3900	18.8559	6.4341	-8.9374	-1.4090
Inv_Involvement	0.1200	15.2051	18.8559	43.2354	0.8597	-5.7203	0.0107
AUM	1.4449	8.0213	6.4341	0.8597	87.0406	1.1356	0.5597
Complex_Prod	-0.4395	-0.7802	-8.9374	-5.7203	1.1356	14.0732	-0.4183
Complaints	-1.8707	-2.7327	-1.4090	0.0107	0.5597	-0.4183	8.8915

Forward Stepwise Sequence of Chi-Squares for the Wilcoxon Test						
Variable	DF	Chi-Square	Pr > Chi-Square	Chi-Square Increment	Pr > Increment	Label
Fund_Performance	1	24.6305	<.0001	24.6305	<.0001	Fund Performance
Complex_Prod	2	39.0423	<.0001	14.4118	0.0001	Complex Prod
Inv_Involvement	3	44.9929	<.0001	5.9506	0.0147	Inv Involvement
Risk_Appetite	4	47.8839	<.0001	2.8910	0.0891	Risk Appetite
Complaints	5	48.6108	<.0001	0.7269	0.3939	Complaints
AUM	6	48.7261	<.0001	0.1153	0.7342	AUM
Inv_Potential	7	48.7290	<.0001	0.00282	0.9577	Inv Potential

In the forward stepwise sequence of the log-rank test, the same three sets of variables are also significant:

Univariate Chi-Squares for the Log-Rank Test					
Variable	Test Statistic	Standard Error	Chi-Square	Pr > Chi-Square	Label
Risk_Appetite	21.3570	9.1875	5.4036	0.0201	Risk Appetite
Fund_Performance	49.9318	10.1059	24.4121	<.0001	Fund Performance
Inv_Potential	17.7009	10.1381	3.0484	0.0808	Inv Potential
Inv_Involvement	25.8945	8.6846	8.8903	0.0029	Inv Involvement
AUM	6.7746	11.4894	0.3477	0.5554	AUM
Complex_Prod	17.4102	4.7170	13.6234	0.0002	Complex Prod
Complaints	-6.6492	3.6648	3.2918	0.0696	Complaints

Covariance Matrix for the Log-Rank Statistics							
Variable	Risk_Appetite	Fund_Performance	Inv_Potential	Inv_Involvement	AUM	Complex_Prod	Complaints
Risk_Appetite	84.410	14.499	18.786	0.710	8.538	-1.694	-3.574
Fund_Performance	14.499	102.129	42.852	22.129	19.304	-1.216	-7.263
Inv_Potential	18.786	42.852	102.782	26.607	11.328	-14.530	-1.803
Inv_Involvement	0.710	22.129	26.607	75.422	2.049	-7.148	-0.330
AUM	8.538	19.304	11.328	2.049	132.007	1.693	-2.065
Complex_Prod	-1.694	-1.216	-14.530	-7.148	1.693	22.250	-0.931
Complaints	-3.574	-7.263	-1.803	-0.330	-2.065	-0.931	13.431

Forward Stepwise Sequence of Chi-Squares for the Log-Rank Test						
Variable	DF	Chi-Square	Pr > Chi-Square	Chi-Square Increment	Pr > Increment	Label
Fund_Performance	1	24.4121	<.0001	24.4121	<.0001	Fund Performance
Complex_Prod	2	38.9911	<.0001	14.5790	0.0001	Complex Prod
Inv_Involvement	3	45.2167	<.0001	6.2256	0.0126	Inv Involvement
Risk_Appetite	4	48.4817	<.0001	3.2650	0.0708	Risk Appetite
Complaints	5	48.8079	<.0001	0.3261	0.5679	Complaints
AUM	6	49.0028	<.0001	0.1949	0.6588	AUM
Inv_Potential	7	49.0598	<.0001	0.0570	0.8113	Inv Potential

Figure 6.10: Kaplan Meier Survival Estimator with Covariates

Parametric procedure analysis

The parametric procedure that we are going to use to analyze the same business problem is PROC LIFEREG. This is a procedure that isn't as popular a procedure as LIFETEST or PHREG but still is an important one. As we discussed earlier, the Cox methodology cannot handle left and interval censored data. We also highlighted that the time-dependent covariates cannot be handled by PROC PHREG. In such cases, we will end up with multiple rows per subject when the covariates change values across time. If the survival function is known, then PROC LIFEREG can produce more accurate estimates. Let's try and explore the procedure using variations of the distribution types.

Here is the code for the `PROC LIFEREG` Weibull distribution:

```
PROC LIFEREG Data=Survival_Analysis;
    Model tenure*censor(1)= /distribution=weibull;
    probplot;
    Output out=new cdf=prob;
run;
```

The default distribution in `PROC LIFEREG` is the Weibull. In the preceding code, we could have avoided explicitly mentioning it. One of the metrics that we will see often in this chapter is the likelihood statistic. Likelihood can be loosely termed as the probability of observing the parameters associated with the model. A more accurate definition of likelihood is that it is a function of the parameters of the model. Different measures of likelihood may be presented in the book. The maximum likelihood function in the model requests the quantities of the model parameters that help maximize the likelihood function of the data. We use the log-likelihood function, which is simply the sum of the log **probability density function** (**PDF**) evaluated at the data values. On most occasions, you will encounter a negative log likelihood. However, a positive log likelihood value isn't necessarily incorrect. The log- likelihood will depend on the density observed while plotting a variable and its resultant log value. In a normal distribution with an extremely small standard deviation, we will observe that the density will predominantly be values around zero since the distribution is normal and the deviation is small. In such instances, the log values will be positive. However, the whole point of the calculation of likelihood in the model is that it is a function of the parameter estimates. To create this function, for each fitted value, the likelihood is computed. Some of these fitted values will not be normally distributed and will lie away from the central tendency measures. Hence, taking a log of these values may result in negative values.

The log likelihood values are most useful when comparing models and, as a rule of thumb, we should be trying to select models with a larger log likelihood:

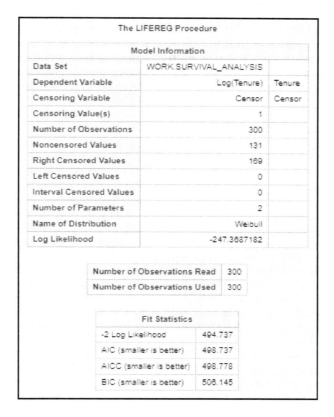

The LIFEREG Procedure

Model Information		
Data Set	WORK.SURVIVAL_ANALYSIS	
Dependent Variable	Log(Tenure)	Tenure
Censoring Variable	Censor	Censor
Censoring Value(s)	1	
Number of Observations	300	
Noncensored Values	131	
Right Censored Values	169	
Left Censored Values	0	
Interval Censored Values	0	
Number of Parameters	2	
Name of Distribution	Weibull	
Log Likelihood	-247.3687182	

Number of Observations Read	300
Number of Observations Used	300

Fit Statistics	
-2 Log Likelihood	494.737
AIC (smaller is better)	498.737
AICC (smaller is better)	498.778
BIC (smaller is better)	506.145

Figure 6.11: PROC LIFEREG Weibull distribution

The AIC and BIC fit statistics were briefly mentioned in `Chapter 2`, *Forecasting Stock Prices and Portfolio Decisions using Time Series*, while building ARIMA models. Both these statistics are information criteria (IC) that help us understand the difference between the fitted and the actual model. AICC is also an IC, which is derived by penalizing the AIC for additional parameters. There is a risk of overfitting if AIC is used and hence AICC published by the fit statistics can be considered more reliable while trying to avoid an overfitted model. The AICC IC uses a sample size in its calculation. With a lower sample size, AICC can be significantly different than AIC but, as the sample size increases, the values may converge.

What should a modeler do when AIC is lower for a model but BIC is lower for an alternate model? Both are IC statistics but don't point to the same things. While AIC tries to find the true model, the BIC statistics use the parameters from the true models. BIC penalizes free parameters more strongly. However, it's best to select a model with both AIC and BIC as the lowest values. Where available (or computed), AICC should be preferred over AIC (especially in smaller sample sizes):

Fit Statistics (Unlogged Response)	
-2 Log Likelihood	1030.876
Weibull AIC (smaller is better)	1034.876
Weibull AICC (smaller is better)	1034.917
Weibull BIC (smaller is better)	1042.284

Algorithm converged.

Analysis of Maximum Likelihood Parameter Estimates

Parameter	DF	Estimate	Standard Error	95% Confidence Limits		Chi-Square	Pr > ChiSq
Intercept	1	2.8773	0.0537	2.7720	2.9825	2871.52	<.0001
Scale	1	0.5794	0.0412	0.5040	0.6661		
Weibull Scale	1	17.7654	0.9539	15.9908	19.7369		
Weibull Shape	1	1.7258	0.1228	1.5012	1.9840		

Weibull is the most common failure distribution used in reliability analysis. For us, the most important feature of Weibull distribution should be the shape (also known as the slope of Weibull) parameter. When it is less than 1, it denotes that the failure rate is decreasing over time. When the value of the shape is closer to 1, then the failure rate is constant over time and when this value is greater than 1 it means that the failure rate increases over time.

In the Weibull plot, we can see that the fitted values are predominantly lying within the upper and lower confidence limits. However, at the six-year tenure mark, we observe a lot of values lying outside the confidence limits:

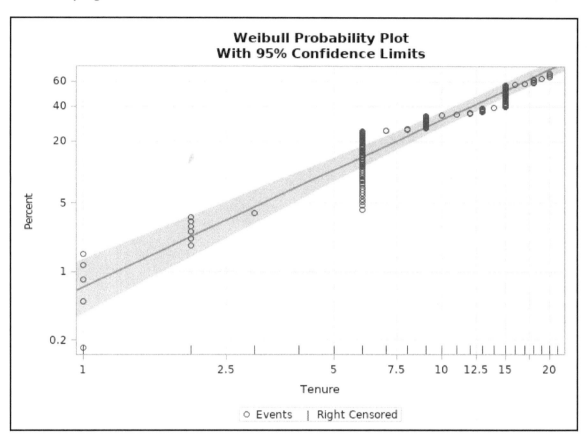

Let's now run the same procedure with exponential distribution.

Here is the code for the PROC LIFEREG exponential distribution:

```
PROC LIFEREG Data=Survival_Analysis;
    Model tenure*censor(1)= /distribution=exponential;
    probplot;
    Output out=new cdf=prob;
Run;
```

In the model with an exponential distribution (*Figure 6.12*), the log-likelihood has decreased and AIC, AICC, and BIC have increased when compared to the Weibull distribution model output in *Figure 6.11*:

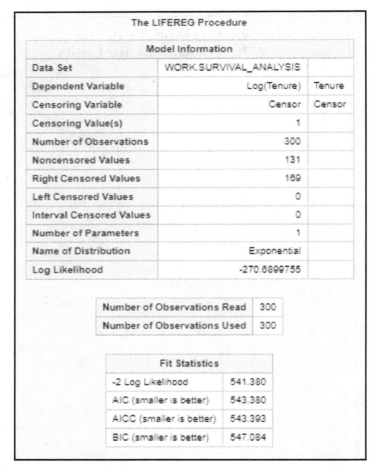

The LIFEREG Procedure

Model Information		
Data Set	WORK.SURVIVAL_ANALYSIS	
Dependent Variable	Log(Tenure)	Tenure
Censoring Variable	Censor	Censor
Censoring Value(s)	1	
Number of Observations	300	
Noncensored Values	131	
Right Censored Values	169	
Left Censored Values	0	
Interval Censored Values	0	
Number of Parameters	1	
Name of Distribution	Exponential	
Log Likelihood	-270.6899755	

Number of Observations Read	300
Number of Observations Used	300

Fit Statistics	
-2 Log Likelihood	541.380
AIC (smaller is better)	543.380
AICC (smaller is better)	543.393
BIC (smaller is better)	547.084

Figure 6.12: PROC LIFEREG exponential distribution

From the following diagram, we can compare the shape and scale estimate between *Figure 6.12* and *Figure 6.11*:

Fit Statistics (Unlogged Response)	
-2 Log Likelihood	1077.519
Exponential AIC (smaller is better)	1079.519
Exponential AICC (smaller is better)	1079.532
Exponential BIC (smaller is better)	1083.222

Algorithm converged.

Analysis of Maximum Likelihood Parameter Estimates							
Parameter	DF	Estimate	Standard Error	95% Confidence Limits		Chi-Square	Pr > ChiSq
Intercept	1	3.1127	0.0874	2.9414	3.2839	1269.22	<.0001
Scale	0	1.0000	0.0000	1.0000	1.0000		
Weibull Scale	1	22.4809	1.9642	18.9428	26.6799		
Weibull Shape	0	1.0000	0.0000	1.0000	1.0000		

Lagrange Multiplier Statistics		
Parameter	Chi-Square	Pr > ChiSq
Scale	368.1538	<.0001

Also, compared to the Weibull distribution plot where we only had issues with values at the six-year tenure, the exponential distribution values at the first and second-year anniversaries also don't fall within the confidence limits:

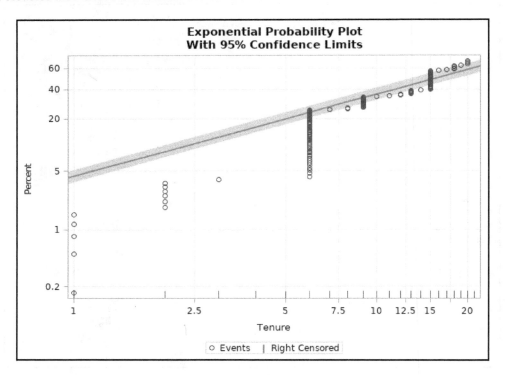

Given these concerns, the distribution that will be used in PROC LIFEREG is the Weibull. While analyzing the survival probability using PROC LIFETEST (*Figure 6.10*), we found that fund performance, complex product, and investment involvement have a strong association with tenure and the association is statistically significant ($p<0.05$). Let's review the PROC LIFEREG results after taking into account the covariates based on the Weibull distribution.

Here is the code for the PROC LIFEREG Weibull distribution with covariates:

```
PROC LIFEREG Data=Survival_Analysis;
    Model tenure*censor(1)= Risk_appetite Fund_performance Inv_potential
Inv_involvement AUM Complex_prod Complaints/distribution=weibull;
    Probplot;
    Output out=new cdf=prob;
Run;
```

Compared to the instance in *Figure 6.11*, when no covariates were used, in *Figure 6.13* we see that the log-likelihood value has increased and the AIC and BIC values have decreased compared to the earlier model:

The LIFEREG Procedure

Model Information		
Data Set	WORK.SURVIVAL_ANALYSIS	
Dependent Variable	Log(Tenure)	Tenure
Censoring Variable	Censor	Censor
Censoring Value(s)	1	
Number of Observations	300	
Noncensored Values	131	
Right Censored Values	169	
Left Censored Values	0	
Interval Censored Values	0	
Number of Parameters	9	
Name of Distribution	Weibull	
Log Likelihood	-221.8754708	

Number of Observations Read	300
Number of Observations Used	300

Fit Statistics	
-2 Log Likelihood	443.751
AIC (smaller is better)	461.751
AICC (smaller is better)	462.372
BIC (smaller is better)	495.085

Figure 6.13: PROC LIFEREG Weibull distribution with covariates

Similar to our observation after running PROC LIFETEST, we can see that fund performance, complex product, and investment potential are the three variables that are statistically significant:

Analysis of Maximum Likelihood Parameter Estimates							
Parameter	DF	Estimate	Standard Error	95% Confidence Limits		Chi-Square	Pr > ChiSq
Intercept	1	1.6526	0.2311	1.1996	2.1057	51.12	<.0001
Risk_Appetite	1	0.0973	0.0597	-0.0198	0.2144	2.65	0.1033
Fund_Performance	1	0.2390	0.0716	0.0986	0.3793	11.13	0.0008
Inv_Potential	1	0.0337	0.0712	-0.1058	0.1732	0.22	0.6356
Inv_Involvement	1	0.1609	0.0721	0.0196	0.3023	4.98	0.0257
AUM	1	-0.0350	0.0537	-0.1402	0.0703	0.42	0.5150
Complex_Prod	1	0.4376	0.1133	0.2156	0.6597	14.92	0.0001
Complaints	1	-0.0367	0.1354	-0.3021	0.2287	0.07	0.7863
Scale	1	0.5543	0.0394	0.4822	0.6372		
Weibull Shape	1	1.8041	0.1282	1.5694	2.0738		

The models built using the LIFEREG procedure have used the frequentist method. There is an additional option in LIFEREG to use the Bayesian method. But what is the difference between the frequentist and the Bayesian methodology?

Before finalizing a model, the modeler may build multiple draft models using the same underlying methodology. In each run of the draft model, the modeler may tweak some aspects of data, diagnostic tests, variables used, and so on, to try to build the final model. The final model may be run only once in its lifetime or could be run hundreds of times depending on the nature and requirement of the modeling output. In the frequentist method, we will assume that if the model is run 100 times, and 95% of the time (the usual confidence limit that most models are accepted at) it will produce the same results as desired. But what if we are more keen on the confidence of producing the desired results in that one run of the model that we are more keen on? If each run or a particular run of the model is very important for the business, then a Bayesian method should be considered. This methodology assumes that there is a prior probability. However, any prior estimation of values may ignore certain possible scenarios where the actual value may differ significantly from the prior estimated. In such a scenario, the frequentist approach becomes more reliable. A frequentist believes that data is a repeatable random sample, whereas the Bayesian assigns probability on what it observes. In the classical toss of a coin experiment, the frequentist and Bayesian will probably end up assigning the probability of the next toss coming as heads as 50%. What will differ is how they reach this answer. The frequentist will say that out of the 100 observed tosses, there is a 50% chance of either achieving heads or tails. Hence, this is a repeatable experiment and my probability has come from the data observed.

The Bayesian would say that there are only two outcomes in the instance of the toss of a coin and since there is no bias involved and I can say that the probability of achieving a head is 50%. So, while both approaches may lead to the same answer, the difference is between assigning probability via the observed data or via some prior probability assumption. We will now run a Bayesian analysis using PROC LIFEREG. Note that the elements in output of *Figure 6.14* are quite different. The aim of the Bayesian analysis is to produce estimates of the regression coefficients:

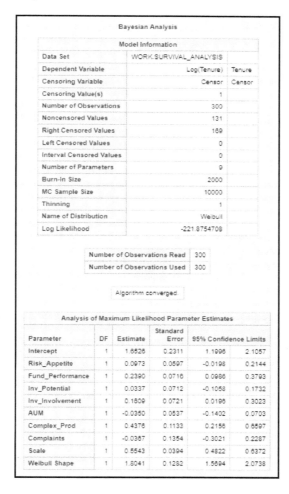

Figure 6.14: PROC LIFEREG Bayesian analysis

In our example of survival times being assessed by the fund manager, the MLE parameter estimates for the PROC LIFEREG frequentist (*Figure 6.13*) and the Bayesian approach (*Figure 6.14*) have the same value across variables. The main difference is that in the frequentist approach, there is a P value associated that helps establish the significance level, whereas in the Bayesian output, we have a confidence limit:

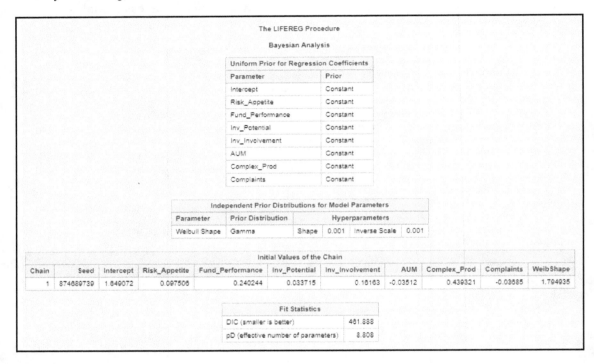

While no explicit values of the prior probabilities have been entered in the code, the model has used the constant values for each variable and the same have been output in the **Initial Values of the Chain**. Before we start using the model, we should ensure that the model has converged. This is displayed in the output as well as the notes section of the session:

Posterior Correlation Matrix									
Parameter	Intercept	Risk_Appetite	Fund_Performance	Inv_Potential	Inv_Involvement	AUM	Complex_Prod	Complaints	WeibShape
Intercept	1.0000	-.4267	-.1093	-.3113	-.4127	-.3298	-.4665	-.2881	0.2177
Risk_Appetite	-.4267	1.0000	-.0469	-.0835	0.0397	-.0256	-.0171	0.1164	-.0529
Fund_Performance	-.1093	-.0469	1.0000	-.3385	-.1273	-.2140	-.0787	0.1201	-.2786
Inv_Potential	-.3113	-.0835	-.3385	1.0000	-.1341	-.0191	0.3386	-.0218	-.0030
Inv_Involvement	-.4127	0.0397	-.1273	-.1341	1.0000	-.0534	0.0979	0.0638	-.1293
AUM	-.3298	-.0256	-.2140	-.0191	-.0534	1.0000	-.0473	0.0094	0.0492
Complex_Prod	-.4665	-.0171	-.0787	0.3386	0.0979	-.0473	1.0000	0.1532	-.2153
Complaints	-.2881	0.1164	0.1201	-.0218	0.0638	0.0094	0.1532	1.0000	-.0007
WeibShape	0.2177	-.0529	-.2786	-.0030	-.1293	0.0492	-.2153	-.0007	1.0000

The posterior correlation matrix shows that none of the variables are strongly correlated. The posterior autocorrelations show a sudden reduction between Lag 1 and Lag 5 for all the variables.

In this instance, a low autocorrelation means that we don't need to wait a long time for the model to converge Please refer to the notes in `Chapter 2`, *Forecasting Stock Prices and Portfolio Decisions using Time Series,* to see a detailed discussion on autocorrelations and lags.

The LIFEREG Procedure

Bayesian Analysis

Posterior Autocorrelations				
Parameter	Lag 1	Lag 5	Lag 10	Lag 50
Intercept	0.1694	0.0203	0.0092	0.0177
Risk_Appetite	0.0597	0.0013	0.0013	-0.0021
Fund_Performance	0.4277	0.0081	-0.0002	0.0017
Inv_Potential	0.3856	-0.0048	0.0021	0.0025
Inv_Involvement	0.2514	0.0085	-0.0150	-0.0052
AUM	0.1872	0.0022	-0.0105	0.0035
Complex_Prod	0.2756	0.0037	-0.0037	0.0152
Complaints	0.5010	0.0594	-0.0132	0.0020
WeibShape	0.2747	0.0178	0.0012	0.0074

Geweke Diagnostics		
Parameter	z	Pr > |z|
Intercept	1.8932	0.0583
Risk_Appetite	-0.6224	0.5337
Fund_Performance	-1.0738	0.2829
Inv_Potential	-0.1164	0.9073
Inv_Involvement	-0.2338	0.8151
AUM	-1.4728	0.1408
Complex_Prod	-1.0482	0.2946
Complaints	-1.2882	0.1977
WeibShape	1.5412	0.1233

The Geweke test statistic takes two proportions of the Markov chain and compares their means to test if the two parts of the chain are from the same distribution. The Z-score is calculated to test the difference of means. If the first proportion (usually 0.10 of the chain) and second proportion (usually 0.50 of the chain) have similar means, it means that the chain has achieved stationarity. Large absolute Z- scores indicate rejection. As a rule of thumb, any value greater than 2 would be of concern:

Effective Sample Sizes			
Parameter	ESS	Autocorrelation Time	Efficiency
Intercept	6949.8	1.4389	0.6950
Risk_Appetite	8933.2	1.1194	0.8933
Fund_Performance	4277.0	2.3381	0.4277
Inv_Potential	4990.6	2.0038	0.4991
Inv_Involvement	6614.8	1.5118	0.6615
AUM	7132.6	1.4020	0.7133
Complex_Prod	5618.4	1.7799	0.5618
Complaints	3098.2	3.2276	0.3098
Weib Shape	5243.3	1.9072	0.5243

Furthermore, the Bayesian method also outputs the trace, autocorrelation, and density plot for each variable. In our model, these plots give no indication that the Markov chains have not converged. The trace diagrams indicate that a longer burn in period is not required. We can say that chains are mixing well, as across variables the distribution of points is not changing as the chain progresses. For instance, for risk appetite, the distribution seems to be centered at 0.1 and moves between +0.2 and -0.2 (that is, 0.3 and -0.1) as the chain progresses:

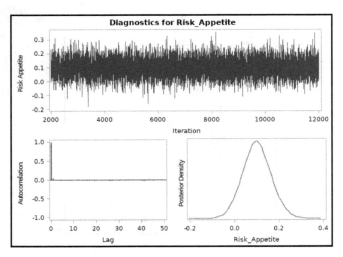

The following shows the diagnostics for fund performance:

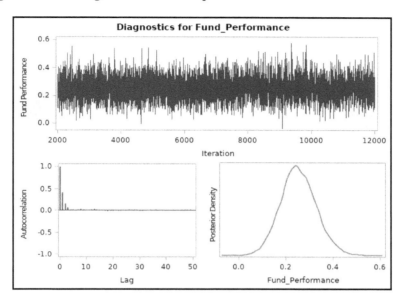

The following shows the diagnostics for investment involvement:

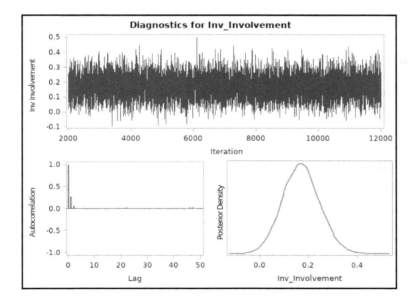

The following shows the diagnostics for complex product:

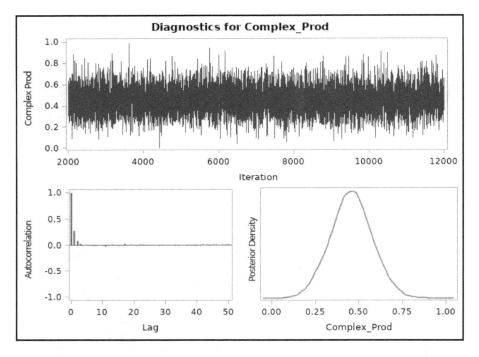

We have mentioned the concept of Markov chains. This is a probabilistic process that predicts the future state based on the current. If we were to plot the behavior of a customer in the run up to customer churn, it may showcase that the customer has gone through multiple experiences with the organization. These multiple experiences can be defined as life stages or states. The more the number of states that are recorded, the higher the complexity in tracking the change of customer from one state to another prior to churn. Let's consider an example with two states and then one with eight states.

In the first example, the customer who churns only ever experiences a satisfied or dissatisfied state. If the customer is in the satisfied state at time *t*, there is a chance that there could be movement to the dissatisfied state at time *t+1*. At time *t+2*, the customer could move back to the satisfied state or stay in the dissatisfied state. If at time *t+3*, the customer moves back to the satisfied state, again there is a chance that the customer could stay in the same state or move out of it to the dissatisfied state. Tracking this movement to *t+100* time will give us a observations where the customer state may be continuously changing. The current state can help us describe the probability of moving to the next state. The observations we record take the form of a chain of events.

But what happens when we have eight states? These states can be defined as a customer opening newer products with the organization, experiencing high credit, lower credit balance, actively engaged, passively engaged with the organization, providing positive feedback, complaining about services, and, finally, the last state being renewing the annual contract with the organization. There are eight states now and the customer at any given state could be deciding to stay in a current state or move to a new state. Instead of 100 such observations, if the customer had a million such movements recorded as a chain of events, interpreting this movement would become complex. Even computing any meaningful insights would become tough.

This is where the concept of Markov chains evolved. While the concept may sound overtly confusing, think of it as a chain of events over time when a subject moves from one state to another and we are interested in predicting the probability of movement based on the previous state.

Semi-parametric procedure analysis

Earlier, we introduced the concept of the semi-parametric model and the advantages of using PROC PHREG. Let's conduct a semi-parametric analysis on our survival data. We will use the stepwise methodology (selection option) to introduce the covariates in the model and give inclusion (slentry option) and exclusion criteria (slstay option) to control which covariate can enter the model and on what basis the covariate should be retained in the model. We also add an assess statement to test the proportional hazard (PH option) and linearity assumption (resample option) for the Cox regression model.

Here is the code for the PROC PHREG stepwise regression:

```
PROC PHREG Data=Survival_Analysis Plots=survival;
    Model tenure*censor(1)=Risk_appetite Fund_performance Inv_potential
Inv_involvement AUM Complex_prod Complaints
                                    / Selection=stepwise Slentry=0.25
Slstay=0.15 Details;
    Assess var = (Risk_appetite Fund_performance Inv_potential
Inv_involvement AUM        Complex_prod Complaints)  PH / Resample;

RUN;
```

The initial part of the analysis output lists information about the data and the analysis of effects eligible for entry:

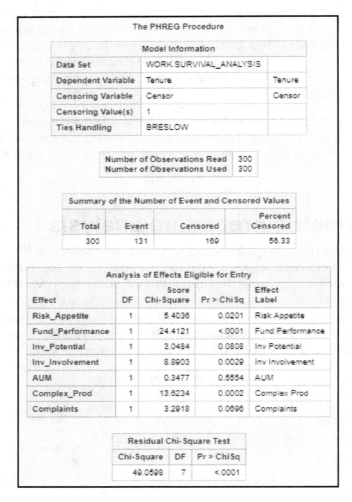

The PHREG Procedure

Model Information		
Data Set	WORK.SURVIVAL_ANALYSIS	
Dependent Variable	Tenure	Tenure
Censoring Variable	Censor	Censor
Censoring Value(s)	1	
Ties Handling	BRESLOW	

Number of Observations Read	300
Number of Observations Used	300

Summary of the Number of Event and Censored Values			
Total	Event	Censored	Percent Censored
300	131	169	56.33

Analysis of Effects Eligible for Entry				
Effect	DF	Score Chi-Square	Pr > ChiSq	Effect Label
Risk_Appetite	1	5.4036	0.0201	Risk Appetite
Fund_Performance	1	24.4121	<.0001	Fund Performance
Inv_Potential	1	3.0484	0.0808	Inv Potential
Inv_Involvement	1	8.8903	0.0029	Inv Involvement
AUM	1	0.3477	0.5554	AUM
Complex_Prod	1	13.6234	0.0002	Complex Prod
Complaints	1	3.2918	0.0696	Complaints

Residual Chi-Square Test		
Chi-Square	DF	Pr > ChiSq
49.0598	7	<.0001

Figure 6.15: PROC PHREG semi-parametric analysis

After this, the stepwise process is initiated and variables are entered into the model according to the descending chi-square scores:

Step 1. Effect Fund_Performance is entered. The model contains the following effects:

Fund_Performance

Convergence Status

Convergence criterion (GCONV=1E-8) satisfied

Model Fit Statistics

Criterion	Without Covariates	With Covariates
-2 LOG L	1323.959	1299.034
AIC	1323.959	1301.034
SBC	1323.959	1303.909

Testing Global Null Hypothesis: BETA=0

Test	Chi-Square	DF	Pr > ChiSq
Likelihood Ratio	24.9255	1	<.0001
Score	24.4121	1	<.0001
Wald	23.0332	1	<.0001

Analysis of Maximum Likelihood Estimates

Parameter	DF	Parameter Estimate	Standard Error	Chi-Square	Pr > ChiSq	Hazard Ratio	Label
Fund_Performance	1	-0.51172	0.10662	23.0332	<.0001	0.599	Fund Performance

Analysis of Effects Eligible for Entry

Effect	DF	Score Chi-Square	Pr > ChiSq	Effect Label
Risk_Appetite	1	2.7017	0.1002	Risk Appetite
Inv_Potential	1	0.1441	0.7042	Inv Potential
Inv_Involvement	1	3.1591	0.0755	Inv Involvement
AUM	1	0.1223	0.7266	AUM
Complex_Prod	1	14.5333	0.0001	Complex Prod
Complaints	1	0.5591	0.4546	Complaints

Residual Chi-Square Test

Chi-Square	DF	Pr > ChiSq
23.4874	6	0.0006

The key outputs of the model are the results from the last step of the model (step 4), the summary of stepwise selection, and the survival chart in *Figure 6.15*. There is one more output that we requested as part of the assess statement. The output that checks for proportional hazard and linearity assumption for all the variables selected in the summary of the stepwise selection is met. The proportional hazard assumption states that the hazard ratio must be relatively constant while comparing strata or variables. Whereas the linearity assumption states that the relationship between the dependent and the independent variables should be significant.

In the analysis of the MLE section in step 4, we can see that the hazard ratio of the variable risk appetite has a p-value of 0.0783, which is not statistically significant at the 0.05 level. The hazard ratios for all other variables in step 4 are significant. Furthermore, while checking for the plot of proportional hazards for risk appetite versus the standardized score process, we can see that around the two and 12-year tenure the observed path deviates from the spread of the simulations. The deviation doesn't seem to be the norm and hence, rather than take a judgment using the plot, we will use the output from the assess statement.

The supremum test for functional form highlights that the linearity assumption isn't met for risk appetite, investment involvement, and complex product variables. All the values are significant at the p<0.05 level. The supremum test for proportional hazard assumptions shows that while all the variables met the assumption, risk appetite barely passed it, as it has a significance just outside the p<0.05 mark.

Since the linearity assumption doesn't hold true for three of the four statistically significant covariates in the model, we cannot use the model in the current form. We should look to transform the current covariates that have failed the linearity assumption or we should drop them while building the model:

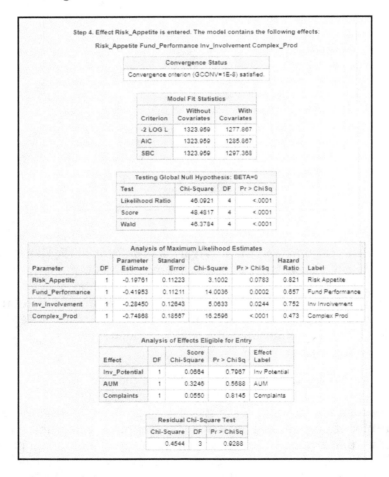

Step 4. Effect Risk_Appetite is entered. The model contains the following effects:

Risk_Appetite Fund_Performance Inv_Involvement Complex_Prod

Convergence Status
Convergence criterion (GCONV=1E-8) satisfied.

Model Fit Statistics		
Criterion	Without Covariates	With Covariates
-2 LOG L	1323.959	1277.867
AIC	1323.959	1285.867
SBC	1323.959	1297.368

Testing Global Null Hypothesis: BETA=0			
Test	Chi-Square	DF	Pr > ChiSq
Likelihood Ratio	46.0921	4	<.0001
Score	48.4817	4	<.0001
Wald	46.3784	4	<.0001

Analysis of Maximum Likelihood Estimates							
Parameter	DF	Parameter Estimate	Standard Error	Chi-Square	Pr > ChiSq	Hazard Ratio	Label
Risk_Appetite	1	-0.19761	0.11223	3.1002	0.0783	0.821	Risk Appetite
Fund_Performance	1	-0.41953	0.11211	14.0036	0.0002	0.657	Fund Performance
Inv_Involvement	1	-0.28450	0.12643	5.0633	0.0244	0.752	Inv Involvement
Complex_Prod	1	-0.74868	0.18567	16.2596	<.0001	0.473	Complex Prod

Analysis of Effects Eligible for Entry				
Effect	DF	Score Chi-Square	Pr > ChiSq	Effect Label
Inv_Potential	1	0.0664	0.7967	Inv Potential
AUM	1	0.3246	0.5688	AUM
Complaints	1	0.0550	0.8145	Complaints

Residual Chi-Square Test		
Chi-Square	DF	Pr > ChiSq
0.4544	3	0.9288

The following is a summary of the stepwise selection method:

	Effect			Number	Score	Wald		Effect
Step	Entered	Removed	DF	In	Chi-Square	Chi-Square	Pr > ChiSq	Label
1	Fund_Performance		1	1	24.4121		<.0001	Fund Performance
2	Complex_Prod		1	2	14.5333		0.0001	Complex Prod
3	Inv_Involvement		1	3	5.0234		0.0250	Inv Involvement
4	Risk_Appetite		1	4	3.1181		0.0774	Risk Appetite

Summary of Stepwise Selection

While checking for the plot of proportional hazards for risk appetite versus the standardized score process, we can see that around the two and 12-year tenure the observed path deviates from the spread of the simulations. The deviation doesn't seem to be the norm and hence, rather than making a judgment using the plot, we will use the output from the assess statement to check the usefulness of the model:

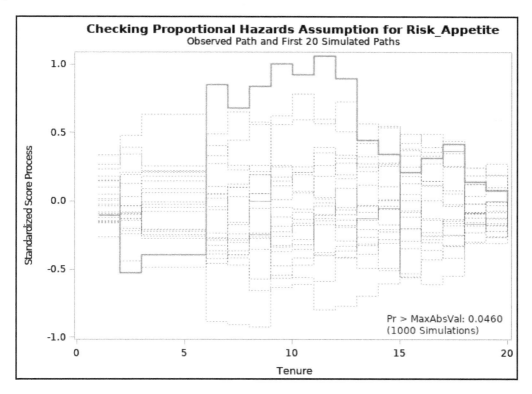

Checking Proportional Hazards Assumption for Risk_Appetite
Observed Path and First 20 Simulated Paths

Pr > MaxAbsVal: 0.0460
(1000 Simulations)

The following diagram shows the proportional hazards assumption for investment involvement. The spread of simulated paths is more consistent than in the case of risk appetite:

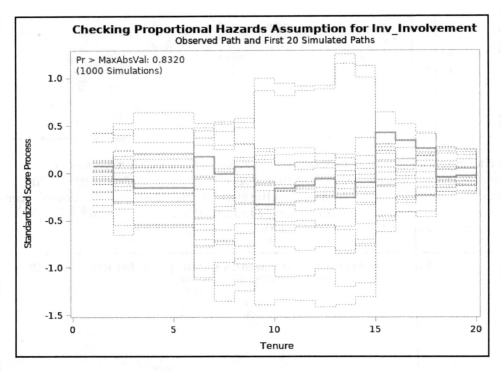

Again, in the case of complex products, the spread of simulated paths is more consistent than in the case of risk appetite:

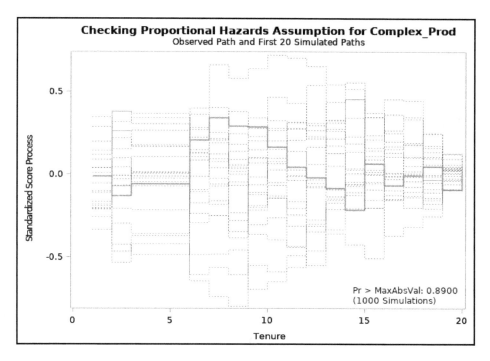

The supremum test for functional form highlights that the linearity assumption isn't met for risk appetite, investment involvement, and complex product variables, as all the values are significant at the p<0.05 level:

Supremum Test for Functional Form				
Variable	Maximum Absolute Value	Replications	Seed	Pr > MaxAbsVal
Risk_Appetite	11.2957	1000	240078360	<.0001
Fund_Performance	2.2044	1000	240078360	0.3530
Inv_Involvement	8.1274	1000	240078360	0.0010
Complex_Prod	0.0000	1000	240078360	<.0001

The supremum test for proportional hazard assumptions shows that while all the variables met the assumption, risk appetite barely passed it, as it has a significance just outside the p<0.05 mark:

Supremum Test for Proportionals Hazards Assumption				
Variable	Maximum Absolute Value	Replications	Seed	Pr > MaxAbsVal
Risk_Appetite	1.0622	1000	240078360	0.0460
Fund_Performance	0.6833	1000	240078360	0.3470
Inv_Involvement	0.4299	1000	240078360	0.8320
Complex_Prod	0.3422	1000	240078360	0.8900

Figure 6.15 PROC PHREG semi-parametric analysis

Summary

In our business case, we realized that our fund manager wanted to identify clients who met the following criteria:

- Have been with the firm for a long time
- Are probably going to stay for a long time
- Are at risk of churn
- Continue to have AUM with the brokerage, and the reasons for this

Survival analysis models were run to try to understand how some of the business questions could be answered. Prior to that, we tried to gain an understanding of what survival analysis modeling is, the advantages it presents over other modeling types, and the various forms of the analysis techniques, namely parametric, semi-parametric, and non-parametric approaches. We also highlighted the differences between the frequentist and the Bayesian approach using PROC LIFEREG. The concept of Markov chains was also introduced in the chapter as part of the discussion on Cox models. To use these techniques, we discussed the need and the way to build censoring variables.

From a modeling output perspective, it is clear that the Cox proportional hazard parametric model has shown that some of the variables used in the other survival analysis approaches aren't fit for use in the current form. We would have to transform some of these variables (please see the output of *Figure 6.15* for detailed discussions). Results from the non-parametric (PROC LIFETEST) and the parametric (PROC LIFEREG) procedure are quite similar and we can use either of the two models. However, as we discussed, there are differences in both these analytical techniques.

Looking at the data, we can answer the business question: who are the customers that have been with the brokerage organization for a long time? We now know the survival probability of our customers across their tenure. Using various covariates, we have been able to establish which among these are important and the degree of their influence on tenure, which is the key business metric we were trying to evaluate. These two pieces of information can help us identify the customers who may stay for a long time and identify those who are at immediate risk (based on their position on the survival curve). We now know the important covariates. We can evaluate each customer based on the role these covariates have played over the years. These can act as discriminatory factors and help understand why some customers continue to have AUM with the firm whereas others don't. Hence, using the survival technique, we can answer multiple questions that the business case posed.

In the next chapter, we will explore how financial institutions leverage market basket analysis and segment their customers using clustering techniques.

7
Transforming Time Series – Market Basket and Clustering

In the first chapter, we defined time series and spoke about their merits. In this chapter, we will expand our understanding of time series data and whether it can be transformed to extract more insights by conducting a couple of other analysis methodologies not yet introduced in this book. We will leverage market basket analysis and segmentation using clustering to solve business problems. Both methodologies help generate insights from products and services that customers have bought.

We will be covering the following topics:

- The role of market basket analysis and segmentation via clustering
- A market basket business problem, data preparation, assumptions, and analysis
- A segmentation business problem

Market basket analysis

Remember, a successful analyst must not be guided by the methodology but instead think about the business problem, and only thereafter about the methodology that could provide the answers. Most practitioners of analysis/modeling think of the time series methodology as one where the final modeling dataset has a variable with a date or date-time stamp. But there could be other instances where time-stamped data might be transformed to conduct an analysis. Remember, transforming does not mean that the time element isn't important to the analysis methodology or insights generated. We will use this transformation for both **market basket analysis (MBA)** and clustering in this chapter. Let's look at data transformation in MBA to provide some context.

MBA's goal is to find common purchase items across customer's basket. It is also at times referred to as affinity or association analysis. This analysis is widely used in the retail sector but has found its takers in other domains as well. The most widespread example used to introduce this methodology is of a supermarket that discovered a shopping pattern. In their data analysis, they found that male customers who bought diapers were also likely to buy beer. While this is an odd combination, the retailer decided to use this insight to manage their shelf space and ended up placing beer close to diapers. This analysis also supports sequential mapping. We can not only try to ascertain which products are common in customers' baskets, we can also ascertain in which order they were purchased. Financial institutions can also benefit from this sort of analysis.

In the following example, we have the product purchase history of two customers in time series format. Both customers have been using various products and services. MBA can be conducted using the `Transaction date` variable. However, look at the transformed data without the date variable. Each row represents the purchase history of the customer. Let's try and use the transformed data in the chapter to conduct MBA:

Custid	Transaction date	Product
1	Jan 5, 2016	Credit Card
1	Feb 8, 2016	Personal Loan
2	Apr 1, 2016	Current Account
2	Aug 29, 2016	Savings Account
1	Sep 4, 2016	Insurance
2	Sep 30, 2016	Mortgage
1	Nov 5 2016	Mortgage
1	Jan 13, 2017	Savings Account
1	Apr 7, 2017	Current Account
2	Apr 7, 2017	Credit Card

The preceding data has been transformed into a wider dataset. We have also removed the `Transaction date` variable:

Custid	Product 1	Product 2	Product 3	Product 4	Product 5	Product 6
1	Credit Card	Personal Loan	Insurance	Mortgage	Savings Account	Current Account
2	Current Account	Savings Account	Mortgage	Credit Card		

Figure 7.1: Original and transformed data for MBA

Segmentation and clustering

Segmentation is the process by which data is bundled together in segments or clusters. If there are a million customer records, and let's say we want to know what is common among those customers, to do this, we will start aggregating a few customer records or bunching some customers together based on similarities in their profiles. What we are essentially doing is forming close-knit clusters of customers. If all these customers were similar, then it would make the whole process easy. We would end up with one cluster and we could describe it easily. But this seldom happens. There are always some demographic or transactional properties by which we want to segregate customers. This is important as we want to customize our offerings to various clusters of customers. Remember the general rule of marketing: no two customers are the same in their intrinsic needs and wants. One thing to note is that clustering isn't the only way to conduct segmentation; it is merely one of the most popular analytical choices to conduct segmentation.

MBA business problem

A retail bank wanted to understand the products and services that it should try to cross-sell to its customers. The number of new customers joining the bank had reduced due to a general economic slowdown, primarily caused by fewer customers switching providers. Management decided that effective cross-selling was the key to increasing revenues. In the past, there had been continuous attempts at cross-selling. Most of these attempts were supported by some form of analysis, but the success rate of the customer campaigns to cross-sell had been lower than expected. Management wanted to take a comprehensive approach, and rely on multiple strategies and methodologies, if necessary, to drive cross-selling. To understand customer purchase behavior, MBA was proposed as one of the analysis methodologies.

By conducting the analysis, management wanted to explore the affinity between products. Once identified, the aim would be to cross-sell products with a high affinity to the existing purchase baskets of customers. Another option could be to incentivize the customer to purchase products with lower affinity. The incentives could range from preferential rates, cash-backs, freebies, and so on. Currently, the bank sold the following products and services:

Products offered	Type
Business Current Account	Deposit/lending dependent on overdraft facility
Buy to Let Mortgage	Lending – for non-primary homes owned
Credit Card	Lending
Currency Services	Foreign exchange service
Insurance	Insurance
Lockers	Safe deposit service
Personal Current Account	Deposit/lending dependent on overdraft facility
Personal Loans	Lending
Premium Current Account	Deposit/lending dependent on overdraft facility; fee paying account
Residential Mortgage	Lending
Savings Account	Deposit
Trading Account	Deposit

Figure 7.2: Product and service offerings of retail bank

Data preparation for MBA

The time series data was transformed to ensure that each row of data represented the customer's purchase basket. A sample of 500 active customers was selected for the analysis. The definition of active stipulated that the customer had used at least one product or service in the last 12 months and had at least one open product at the time of selection. Only customers with multiple products/services were chosen for the analysis.

The following is a snapshot of the customer data used for modeling:

Custid	Pr1	Pr2	Pr3	Pr4	Pr5
1	Residential_Mortgage	Insurance	Personal_Current_Account	Savings_Account	Premium_Current_Account
2	Personal_Current_Account	Credit_Card	Premium_Current_Account		
3	Locker	Residential_Mortgage	Insurance	Credit_Card	Currency_Services
4	Personal_Current_Account	Trading_Account	Business_Current_Account	Insurance	Credit_Card
5	Savings_Account	Personal_Current_Account	Credit_Card	Insurance	Personal_Loans
6	Savings_Account	Residential_Mortgage	Personal_Current_Account	Credit_Card	Insurance
7	Personal_Current_Account	Personal_Loans	Credit_Card	Savings_Account	BTL_Mortgage
8	Locker	Business_Current_Account	Trading_Account		
9	Business_Current_Account	Currency_Services	Trading_Account	Credit_Card	BTL_Mortgage
10	Personal_Current_Account	Savings_Account	Credit_Card	BTL_Mortgage	Locker

Figure 7.3: Snapshot of modeling data

Assumptions for MBA

Like most analysis, insights generated should be used after a conceptual understanding of how the analysis has been generated. The sequence plays an important role in the analysis. If, for instance, we conclude that customers with a personal current account are more likely to open a savings account, we are implying a sequence. This is easier to infer in a two-product set size. However, for a three-product set size, the insight statement might be misleading. When a customer has a personal current account and savings account, the customer is likely to take out insurance. In this instance, the **right-hand side (RHS)** of the rule is the savings account. The **left-hand side (LHS)** rule is a combination of the two products. If we assume that a personal current account is the first condition to adhere to in the rule, we could be wrong. Some procedures/macros (pre-written in SAS or frequently used by analysts) ignore the sequencing of the products or services. In the preceding instance, when a sequence is ignored, the rule might simply state that as long as the two products from the LHS of the rule are present in a customer's basket, the customer is likely to avail themselves of the third product from the RHS of the rule. In the analysis presented in this chapter, the sequence has been taken into consideration.

MBA could suffer from how products and services have been traditionally sold in an organization. A salesperson might say *all my customers are readers of the Daily Telegraph*. Well, this might be the case if the product was only advertised in the Daily Telegraph. There could be an inherent bias in the way the products and services are advertised and sold, and this could manifest itself in the insights generated. For instance, external regulations or bank policies may stipulate that to trade stocks and cryptocurrency using a trading account, a customer will have to open a current account with the same bank. In this instance, a rule stating that a basket with a trading account is likely to have a current account at some point in time is meaningless.

Most marketers will dismiss the insight that having a current account is likely to lead to the opening of a savings account. There could be some baskets that generate insights that could be meaningless from an execution perspective. As with any other analysis, the analyst should be aware of false positives and should always discuss with the relevant teams to ensure insights are relevant.

The MBA code using inbuilt procedures is fairly short in SAS. However, it isn't available in most SAS versions and definitely not in the SAS University Edition, which has been widely used in this book. Taking this as an opportunity, the detailed code will be shared in this chapter. The code uses commonly available SAS procedures and functionalities to explain the steps involved in executing the analysis and extracting meaningful insights. The code refrains from using complex programming steps, and hence should be fairly easy to understand for users with limited SAS knowledge. Some readers may find that the code can be shortened by using complex joins and arrays. However, for the benefit of all readers, the code has been simplified.

Analysis of a set size of two

To keep matters simple, let's try and study the affinity between two products/services. This can also be phrased as having a set size of two. The data that we have has customers with up to eight products/services in their baskets. Hence, we could have up to a set size of eight. Currently, the data we have resembles a wide state, as represented in *Figure 7.3*. We will transpose this data, find the count of various products/services, and create some `macro` variables to store information. The `macro` variables will primarily hold the count of products and services, and the total number of customers, and a couple of others will aid us in executing the `macro`.

Here is the data transformation and `macro` variable initiation:

```
Proc transpose data=wide out=long (rename=(col1=PRODUCTS) drop=_label_);
By custid;
Var pr1-pr8;
run;

proc sql;
    create table product_customer_count as
    select products, count(distinct(custid)) as ANALYSIS_UNIT_FREQ
    from long
    where products ne ""
    group by 1
    ;
quit;
```

```
proc sql noprint;
    select count(distinct(products)) into: product_count
from long
where products ne "";
select count(distinct(custid)) into: population from long;
select distinct products into :product_1-:product_%trim(&product_count)
from product_customer_count where products ne "" ;

select distinct analysis_unit_freq into :analysis_unit_freq_1-
:analysis_unit_freq_%trim(&product_count) from product_customer_count where
products ne ""order by products;
quit;
```

After the creation of the `macro` variables, a `macro`, `product_tot`, has been written to find the number of instances where products co-occur in the same basket. The loop runs 12 times (the count of products and services the bank has) and produces an equal number of tables. In the following code, the `%put` statement shows that when `i=1`, the LHS product is **Buy to Let Mortgage**.

Here is the common basket count (frequency co-occur):

```
%macro product_tot;
%do i = 1 %to &product_count;
Proc sql;
    create table product_tot_&i as
    select products, count(distinct(custid)) as FREQ_CO_OCCUR
    from
    (select custid, products
    from long
    where custid in (select custid from long where products
eq"&&product_&i"))
    where products ne ""
    group by 1
    order by 1
    ;
quit;
%end;
%mend;
%product_tot;

%put product is &product_1;

%put product is &product_1;
product is BTL_Mortgage
```

In *Figure 7.4*, we have a count of baskets in which the LHS and the RHS products are found together. We can ignore the first row, or the LHS and RHS products will be the same. However, for the second row, we can say that there are 94 customers who have a **Buy to Let Mortgage** product and this is followed by the opening of a `Business_Current_Account` at some stage:

Obs	PRODUCTS	FREQ_CO_OCCUR
1	BTL_Mortgage	157
2	Business_Current_Account	94
3	Credit_Card	147
4	Currency_Services	9
5	Insurance	97
6	Locker	84
7	Personal_Current_Account	60
8	Personal_Loans	53
9	Premium_Current_Account	46
10	Residential_Mortgage	43
11	Savings_Account	110
12	Trading_Account	17

Figure 7.4: Illustration - frequency co-occur

After counting the common baskets for products, let's try and add few metrics to understand the results. The following code adds the metrics and helps us choose the product affinities that are meaningful. The metrics `macro` calculates the `SUPPORT`, `CONFIDENCE`, `LIFT`, `EXPECTED_CONFIDENCE`, `CHISQ`, and `P`-value.

Here are the metrics and relevant affinities:

```
%macro metrics;
%do i = 1 %to &product_count;
Proc sql;
    create table metric_&i as
select distinct "&&product_&i" as LHAND, a.PRODUCTS as RHAND,
a.ANALYSIS_UNIT_FREQ, b.freq_co_occur,
(b.FREQ_CO_OCCUR/&&analysis_unit_freq_&i)*100 as CONFIDENCE format 5.2,
(b.FREQ_CO_OCCUR/&population)*100 as SUPPORT format 5.2,
(a.ANALYSIS_UNIT_FREQ/&population)*100 as EXPECTED_CONFIDENCE format 5.2,
calculated CONFIDENCE/calculated EXPECTED_CONFIDENCE as LIFT format 5.2,
(FREQ_CO_OCCUR*(calculated LIFT-1)**2)*((calculated
SUPPORT/100)*(calculated CONFIDENCE/100))
        /
((calculated CONFIDENCE/100 - calculated SUPPORT/100)*(calculated LIFT -
```

```
calculated CONFIDENCE/100)) as CHISQ format 5.2,
    1 - Probchi(calculated CHISQ,1) as P format 5.4
  from product_customer_count as a left join product_tot_&i as b
  on a.products=b.products
  order by calculated P
  ;
quit;
%end;
%mend;
%metrics;

Proc sql noprint;
Select memname into :datasets separated by' '
From dictionary.tables
Where libname = "WORK" and memname like "METRIC%";
quit;

data summary;
format LHAND $50.;
set &datasets;
if LHAND ne RHAND;
run;

data relevant (drop=analysis_unit_freq);
set summary;
if freq_co_occur ge 50;
if P le 0.05;
if confidence ge 60;
if lift gt 1;
run;

proc sort data=relevant;
by descending lift;
run;
```

So, what are SUPPORT, CONFIDENCE, LIFT, and EXPECTED_CONFIDENCE? Let's look at the output in *Figure 7.5* to understand these metrics. Earlier on, we mentioned that there are 500 customers. This is the population that we are dealing with. Before we move on to the metrics, notice the LHS and RHS columns. In the first row, we can see that when we have Premium_Current_Account in a customer's basket on the LHS, in 93 instances out of 500 the customer subsequently took out a personal loan. Dividing 93 by 500 (the population of baskets analyzed) gives us the support of the rule (18.60). These two products co-occur 93 times in customer baskets. Premium_Current_Account is found in customers' purchase baskets 132 times.

Hence, the confidence of observing the rule, if `Premium_Current_Account` then `Personal_Loans`, is *(93/132)*100* which is equal to 70.45%. `EXPECTED_CONFIDENCE` is simply the frequency of baskets with `Personal_Loans` divided by the population (that is, *(218/500)*100=43.60%)*. `LIFT` is calculated by dividing `CONFIDENCE` by `EXPECTED_CONFIDENCE` *(70.45/43.60=1.62):*

Obs	LHS	RHS	FREQ_CO_OCCUR	CONFIDENCE	SUPPORT	EXPECTED_CONFIDENCE	LIFT	CHISQ	P
1	Premium_Current_Account	Personal_Loans	93	70.45	18.60	43.60	1.62	9.78	.0018
2	Premium_Current_Account	Business_Current_Account	93	70.45	18.60	44.40	1.59	9.17	.0025
3	Premium_Current_Account	Locker	106	80.30	21.20	52.40	1.53	11.87	.0006
4	Personal_Loans	Personal_Current_Account	158	72.48	31.60	57.60	1.26	11.07	.0009
5	Savings_Account	Personal_Current_Account	244	71.98	48.80	57.60	1.25	43.48	.0000
6	Personal_Current_Account	Savings_Account	244	84.72	48.80	67.60	1.25	43.48	.0000
7	Business_Current_Account	Locker	145	65.32	29.00	52.40	1.25	7.74	.0054
8	Savings_Account	Locker	208	61.36	41.60	52.40	1.17	14.09	.0002
9	Locker	Savings_Account	208	79.39	41.60	67.60	1.17	14.09	.0002
10	Savings_Account	Credit_Card	321	94.69	64.20	91.40	1.04	9.31	.0023
11	Credit_Card	Savings_Account	321	70.24	64.20	67.60	1.04	9.31	.0023

Figure 7.5: Set size of 2 relevant insights

Later in the chapter, you will see the inbuilt procedures that are available in some SAS versions. Those procedures produce the `SUPPORT`, `CONFIDENCE`, `EXPECTED_CONFIDENCE`, and `LIFT` metrics. As mentioned in the assumptions about MBA, the code we are using is fairly detailed. However, it gives an opportunity to understand how the metrics are calculated. The code has been further enhanced to include the test of significance. While simulating the model, you can find the denominator values of `CONFIDENCE` and `EXPECTED_CONFIDENCE` in the table called `product_customer_count`.

The `summary` dataset produced a lot of two-way relationships between the products. We have placed some restrictions on the previous code to generate the `relevant` dataset. This was done to only output the insights of potential interest in *Figure 7.5*. Only rules where the products and services co-occur at least 10% of the time in the population were considered. All the rules generated are statistically significant. They all have a minimum confidence of 60%, which is an arbitrary measure that we have added to help focus on key rules.

Lastly, all the rules have a `LIFT` greater than 1. From an insight implementation perspective, we can further condense the list of 11 insights of interest to 4 (*Figure 7.6*):

Obs	LHS	RHS	FREQ_CO_OCCUR	CONFIDENCE	SUPPORT	EXPECTED_CONFIDENCE	LIFT	CHISQ	P
1	Premium_Current_Account	Personal_Loans	93	70.45	18.60	43.60	1.62	9.78	.0018
2	Premium_Current_Account	Business_Current_Account	93	70.45	18.60	44.40	1.59	9.17	.0025
3	Premium_Current_Account	Looker	106	80.30	21.20	52.40	1.53	11.87	.0006
4	Business_Current_Account	Looker	145	65.32	29.00	52.40	1.25	7.74	.0054

Figure 7.6: Set size of 2 insight implementation perspective

We did know about the relationship between savings accounts, current accounts, and credit cards. The metrics related to them only further strengthened our belief in the relationship between them. It helped us quantify the strength of the relationship but it didn't qualify as an insight that we would be eager to implement. However, if you now look at the remaining relationships in *Figure 7.6*, you can see insights that the campaign managers might be delighted to implement. `Premium_Current_Account` is a product of interest for the bank as it is a fee paying current account. It is interesting to note that these customers went on to open other higher-margin products and services. `Personal_Loans` have the highest `LIFT` in this list. `LIFT` is a measure of the strength of the relationship between `Premium_Current_Account` and `Personal_Loans`. `LIFT` values greater than 1 indicate that customers opening `Premium_Current_Account` are more likely to have `Personal_Loans` than customers without a `Premium_Current_Account`. `SUPPORT` merely states how many times the rule has been observed.

A campaign manager can use the preceding rules to cross-sell RHS products and services to customers. Remember, we don't know from this analysis the time taken by 93 customers to apply for a personal loan after opening a `Premium_Current_Account`. But since we know about the strength of this relationship, we can try and sell `Personal_Loans` to customers who don't yet have this product. We can also try and reduce the time that a customer might take to buy both these products. This is helpful as, even though we expect 43.60% (our `EXPECTED_CONFIDENCE`) of customers to buy both products, we can help reduce the time between the opening of these products.

For simplicity's sake, we have only looked at a set size of two. However, the inbuilt SAS procedure produces output for product relationships with a set size of more than two.

The following is code that produces a three-way MBA.

Here is the data transformation for a set size of three:

```
data one;
    input id $ product1 $50.;
datalines;
1 BTL_Mortgage|
2 Business_Current_Account|
3 Credit_Card|
4 Currency_Services|
5 Insurance|
6 Locker|
7 Personal_Current_Account|
8 Personal_Loans|
9 Premium_Current_Account|
10 Residential_Mortgage|
11 Savings_Account|
12 Trading_Account|
;
data two;
    input id $ product2 $50.;
datalines;
1 BTL_Mortgage|
2 Business_Current_Account|
3 Credit_Card|
4 Currency_Services|
5 Insurance|
6 Locker|
7 Personal_Current_Account|
8 Personal_Loans|
9 Premium_Current_Account|
10 Residential_Mortgage|
11 Savings_Account|
12 Trading_Account|
;
data three;
    input id $ product3 $50.;
datalines;
1 BTL_Mortgage
2 Business_Current_Account
3 Credit_Card
4 Currency_Services
5 Insurance
6 Locker
7 Personal_Current_Account
8 Personal_Loans
9 Premium_Current_Account
10 Residential_Mortgage
11 Savings_Account
```

```
12 Trading_Account
;
run;

data stage1;
set one;
   do i = 1 to n;
       set two point=i nobs=n;
   output;
 end;
run;

data stage2;
set stage1;
   do i = 1 to n;
       set three point=i nobs=n;
   output;
 end;
run;

data matrix (drop = lhand1 lhand2);
set stage2 (drop = id);
if product1 ne product2;
if product1 ne product3;
if product2 ne product3;
combo=compress(product1||product2||product3);
lhand1=scan(combo,1);
lhand2=scan(combo,2);
lhand=compress(lhand1||"|"||lhand2);
run;
```

In the preceding code, we have created a dataset matrix with all of the possible three-way sequences that can exist between the product and services offered by the bank. After this, we will run a `macro` to find out the number of instances of each combination in the data.

Here is the pattern finding for a set size of three:

```
Proc sql noprint;
   Select count(distinct(combo)) into:combo_count from matrix;
   Select distinct combo into:combo_1 -:combo_%trim(&combo_count) from
matrix;
   select count(distinct(lhand)) into:lhand_count from matrix;
   select distinct lhand into:lhand_1 -:lhand_%trim(&lhand_count) from
matrix;
quit;
%put lhand count is &lhand_count;
```

```
%macro combo_find;
%do i = 1 %to &combo_count;
Proc sql;
   create table combos_main_&i as
   select a.*,
compress(pr1||"|"||pr2||"|"||pr3||"|"||pr4||"|"||pr5||"|"||pr6||"|"||pr7||"
|"||pr8) as combo, "&&combo_&i" as pattern_found,
   case when calculated combo contains "&&combo_&i" then 1 else 0 end as
combo_count
   from wide as a
   ;
   create table combos_sum_&I as
   select pattern_found, sum(combo_count) as freq_co_occur
   from combos_main_&i
   group by 1
   having freq_co_occur ge 1
   order by calculated freq_co_occur desc
   ;
quit;
%end;
%mend;
%combo_find;

%macro lhand_find;
%do i = 1 %to &lhand_count;
Proc sql;
   create table lhand_main_&i as
   select a.*,
compress(pr1||"|"||pr2||"|"||pr3||"|"||pr4||"|"||pr5||"|"||pr6||"|"||pr7||"
|"||pr8) as combo,
   "&&lhand_&i" as lhand,
   case when calculated combo contains "&&lhand_&i" then 1 else 0 end as
lhand_count
   from wide as a
   ;
   create table lhand_sum_&i as
   select lhand, sum(lhand_count) as lhand_co_occur
   from lhand_main_&i
   group by 1
   having lhand_co_occur ge 1
   order by calculated lhand_co_occur desc
   ;
quit;
%end;
%mend;
%lhand_find;
```

Once the product combination pattern has been found, we will calculate the metrics related to various rules that have been generated.

Here are the metrics for a set size of three:

```
Proc sql noprint;
    Select memname into:combosets separated by ' '
    From dictionary.tables
    where libname eq "WORK" and memname like "COMBOS_SUM_%"
    ;
quit;

data combos_main (drop = lhand1 lhand2);
format pattern_found $200.;
set &combosets;
lhand1=scan(pattern_found,1);
lhand2=scan(pattern_found,2);
lhand=compress(lhand1||"|"||lhand2);
rhand=scan(pattern_found,-1);
run;

proc sort data=combos_main;
by descending freq_co_occur;
run;

proc sql noprint;
    select memname into:lhandsets separated by ' '
    from dictionary.tables
    where libname eq "WORK" and memname like "LHAND_SUM_%"
    ;
quit;

data lhand_main;
format lhand $200.;
set &lhandsets;
run;

proc sql;
    create table metric_three_way as
    select distinct a.LHAND as LHS, a.RHAND as RHS, c.lhand_co_occur as
ANALYSIS_UNIT_FREQ, a.freq_co_occur, (a.FREQ_CO_OCCUR/c.lhand_co_occur)*100
as CONFIDENCE format 5.2,
    (a.FREQ_CO_OCCUR/&population)*100 as SUPPORT format 5.2,
(d.analysis_unit_freq/&population)*100 as EXPECTED_CONFIDENCE format 5.2,
    calculated CONFIDENCE/calculated EXPECTED_CONFIDENCE as LIFT format 5.2,
(a.FREQ_CO_OCCUR*(calculated LIFT-1)**2)*((calculated
SUPPORT/100)*(calculated CONFIDENCE/100))
```

```
        /
        ((calculated CONFIDENCE/100 - calculated SUPPORT/100)*(calculated
LIFT - calculated CONFIDENCE/100)) as CHISQ format 5.2,
        1 - Probchi(calculated CHISQ,1) as P format 5.4
    From combos_main as a left join product_customer_count as b
    On a.lhand=b.products
    left join lhand_main as c
    on a.lhand=c.lhand
    left join product_customer_count as d
    on a.rhand=d.products
    order by calculated P, calculated confidence desc, calculated
expected_confidence desc
    ;
quit;
```

Similar conditions to the one used for a set size of two have been applied. However, you will notice that the threshold for accepting CONFIDENCE and the frequency of co-occurrence has been reduced. In a three-way set size, there is less likelihood of observing a higher co-occurring frequency than a two-way set size.

Here are the relevant rules for a set size of three:

```
Data relevant_three_way;
Set metric_three_way;
if P le 0.05;
if confidence ge 40;
if lift gt 1;
if freq_co_occur ge 15;
run;

proc sort data=relevant_three_way;
by descending lift;
run;
```

Our relevant_three_way dataset contains no observations as the WHERE conditions are not met. The metric_three_way dataset contains 162 distinct sequences of a set size of three. *Figure 7.7* contains a partial output with 10 different rules. The standard SAS inbuilt procedures don't take into account the sequence in a set size of three or larger. This is an important differentiation to consider while evaluating the metric values of metric_three_way. In the preceding table, there are only six rules that are statistically significant.

None of these rules have a LIFT greater than 1. This means that these insights aren't meaningful. Does this mean there are no relevant rules where more than two products and services are involved?

Obs	LHS	RHS	ANALYSIS_UNIT_FREQ	freq_co_occur	CONFIDENCE	SUPPORT	EXPECTED_CONFIDENCE	LIFT	CHISQ	P
1	Personal_Current_Account|Savings_Account	Credit_Card	121	56	46.28	11.20	91.40	0.51	46.30	.0000
2	Insurance|Business_Current_Account	Credit_Card	57	11	19.30	2.20	91.40	0.21	9.36	.0022
3	Residential_Mortgage|Insurance	Credit_Card	71	47	66.20	9.40	91.40	0.72	6.29	.0122
4	Locker|Savings_Account	Credit_Card	55	31	56.36	6.20	91.40	0.62	5.98	.0144
5	Insurance|Trading_Account	Credit_Card	42	12	28.57	2.40	91.40	0.31	5.53	.0187
6	BTL_Mortgage|Insurance	Credit_Card	46	22	47.83	4.40	91.40	0.52	5.38	.0203
7	Business_Current_Account|Locker	Savings_Account	91	13	14.29	2.60	67.80	0.21	3.79	.0514
8	Personal_Loans|Insurance	Credit_Card	45	4	8.89	0.80	91.40	0.10	3.43	.0642
9	Premium_Current_Account|Business_Current_Account	Locker	40	40	100.0	8.00	52.40	1.91	3.16	.0755
10	Savings_Account|Residential_Mortgage	Credit_Card	39	22	56.41	4.40	91.40	0.62	2.90	.0886

Figure 7.7: Partial output of metrics for a set size of three

EXPECTED_CONFIDENCE is heavily influencing the LIFT and P values. In a three-product rule, adding the significance values distorts the analysis output. The significance values are an addition that we included in the analysis to focus on some key results. *Figure 7.8* contains the insights from the three set sizes after the removal of the restrictions placed on the significance measures. LIFT greater than 1 and only baskets with at least 25 occurrences of the rule have been included in the output:

Obs	LHS	RHS	ANALYSIS_UNIT_FREQ	freq_co_occur	CONFIDENCE	SUPPORT	EXPECTED_CONFIDENCE	LIFT
1	Premium_Current_Account|Business_Current_Account	Locker	40	40	100.0	8.00	52.40	1.91
2	Personal_Loans|Premium_Current_Account	Business_Current_Account	51	40	78.43	8.00	44.40	1.77
3	Insurance|Personal_Current_Account	Savings_Account	55	51	92.73	10.20	67.80	1.37
4	Savings_Account|Credit_Card	BTL_Mortgage	117	50	42.74	10.00	31.40	1.36
5	Locker|Insurance	Business_Current_Account	42	29	69.05	5.80	44.40	1.56
6	Insurance|Business_Current_Account	Personal_Loans	57	29	50.88	5.80	43.80	1.17
7	Savings_Account|Personal_Current_Account	Credit_Card	43	41	95.35	8.20	91.40	1.04
8	Credit_Card|BTL_Mortgage	Business_Current_Account	52	26	50.00	5.20	44.40	1.13

Figure 7.8: Partial output of relevant set size of three

The following code can be used by non-SAS University Edition users who have access to the full procedures offered by SAS. As discussed earlier, the code uses inbuilt procedures to find the rules.

Here is the MBA code for full SAS access users:

```
Proc dmdb batch data=long out=dmassoc dmdbcat=catseq;
    id custid;
    class products;
run;

proc assoc data=long dmdbcat=catseqout=output items=8 support=15;
```

```
    cust custid;
    target products;
 run;

 proc rulegen in=output out=datarule minconf=75;
 run;

 proc sort  data=datarule;
    by descending lift;
 run;
```

A segmentation business problem

Sam, Jwels, and Darius are partners at a hedge fund that deals with the mining, e-commerce, and aviation sectors. Sam started the fund 10 years ago when he left his employer, the leading commodities fund in London. Vogue was set up with a handful of clients and Sam initially worked on wafer-thin margins to increase his clients and **assets under management (AUM)**. Darius and Jwels joined later on in the first few years of the fund being set up, and brought both e-commerce and aviation expertise to Vogue. The last ten years have been exciting for Vogue. Profits have grown by double digits, apart from in 2008 and 2009. Some of their key clients lost big at that time, either with Vogue or elsewhere. This meant that Sam had to get in new partners and focus on retaining and growing his client base at the same time. Vogue had only started in 2006, and then the global economic crisis of 2007-2008 ensured that the partners spent sleepless nights building a solid client base with sizeable AUM.

The market had started to notice them earlier on. However, now the mergers and acquisitions were picking up pace. Vogue had many suitors in the past. Some of these were existing clients and others were simply friends of friends. The prospect of selling out in any form hadn't been on the agenda for the partners. Things had changed though; they now commanded the attention of a highly successful fund owner who could, via his investment in Vogue, offer them the scale and diversity of sectors that would see Vogue leapfrog its peers. A dinner meeting was fixed and the three partners, along with a few presentations, arrived at the venue. They gave a couple of slick presentations that highlighted the financials and the quality of the AUM. This was followed up with a talk on how they perceived they could use further investments to grow.

All this was well received, but one question left them feeling uncomfortable by the end of the discussion. The question was less about the financials and more about the nature of their clients. The investor wanted to know who the customers of Vogue were. The partners gave a lot of details and were quite convinced about the quality of their answers. Sadly, the investor wasn't. He felt that their customer mix was too diverse and it was difficult to define who Vogue's typical customer was. He wanted a clear answer on the customer profile, as he felt that the growth strategy needed to be based on the current customer profile. On further reflection, the partners felt that perhaps they had muddled things with their view of the customer profile. These customers were acquired over a period when there were big changes in the world markets and when the acquisition strategy for Vogue kept evolving. The inclusion of two new partners further diversified the portfolio. Some initial clients were lost to the financial crisis, some to poor fund performance, and others to client servicing. They didn't know how best to describe their existing customer base in a concise and simple way.

The trio had a couple of weeks before the next round of meetings with the investor, where he was going to bring along a couple of his senior execs. This, they hoped, would give them time to put together a more robust case for funding. They already had £618 million AUM and hoped to grow it to £1 billion in the next 5 years with further investment in Vogue. The company had already come a long way. The analysts from the office of the **Chief Financial Officer (CFO)** had begun compiling financial data and projections for the next round of discussions. They were incorporating the investor's queries into the expected presentation. Sam was still concerned about what he deemed to be the softer but material issue of his customer's profile.

He realized that these things matter. Even the name of the firm hadn't been a big draw for hardened investors. The name was a break from the industry's past and although he had gone ahead with the risk, he never underestimated the pros and cons of the name. Having decided to take no further chances, he had called upon a former PhD student, one of the earliest employees at Vogue and now a professor at a leading London business school, to help.

Prof. Cox had been given a brief description of the problem by Sam in an email earlier. Jwel and Darius were CC'd in the email. Sam made no mention of the investor or his anxiousness to answer the question about customer profiling. All he said was that Vogue wanted to better understand its customer's profile and use this as a basis to target prospects. Prof Cox realized that this was a segmentation and profiling issue. Vogue probably didn't understand what its various customer segments were and how they differed. The former could be understood by building a segmentation model and the latter by profiling how these segments differed.

The trio were a group of financial and IT whiz kids so were quite familiar with data, coding, and algorithms. However, they weren't trained marketers. They probably couldn't structure their thoughts coherently when tasked with deciding on a marketing strategy using behavioral and transaction data. Prof Cox invited them over to the campus and started using her office whiteboard to explain some concepts. She agreed with Sam's initial assessment of why Vogue probably didn't understand its customer profile fully. She said that most businesses need to do a segmentation exercise at some point in their life cycle. Established businesses have to do this on a periodic basis. The economic situation changes, customer behaviors change, and they also end up growing through M&As. All this necessitates the need for segmentation.

Segmentation overview

But what is segmentation? It is the process by which data is bundled together in segments or clusters. If there are a million customer records, and let's say we want to know what is common among those customers, to do this, we will start aggregating a few customer records or bunching some customers together based on similarities in their profiles. What we are essentially doing is forming close-knit clusters of customers. If all these customers were similar, then it would make the whole process easy. We would end up with one cluster, and we could describe it easily. But this seldom happens. There are always some demographic or transactional properties by which we want to segregate customers. This is important, as we want to customize our offerings to various clusters of customers. Remember the general rule of marketing: no two customers are the same in their intrinsic needs and wants. One thing to note is that clustering isn't the only way to conduct segmentation; it is merely one of the most popular analytical choices. Let's look at the following example to understand what clustering is about.

Here is a clustering illustration:

```
data class;
    input id female tall grade;
datalines;
1 1 1 3
2 0 3 1
3 0 3 1
4 0 1 1
5 1 2 4
6 1 2 4
;
run;

proc cluster data=class method=centroid out=tree;
```

```
    id id;
    var Female Tall Grade;
  run;
```

The following table has six records and three variables, apart from the `id` variable. The `female` variable has the value 1 for females and 0 for males. The variables `tall` and `grade` have different values for height and scores in a test. Higher values represent a greater height or grade secured. We have a hypothesis that instead of describing the pupils of this class data in six different ways, we can perform segmentation and cluster them into three different segments.

Obs	id	female	tall	grade
1	1	1	1	3
2	2	0	3	1
3	3	0	3	1
4	4	0	1	1
5	5	1	2	4
6	6	1	2	4

The cluster chart in *Figure 7.9* shows how various individuals have been put into similar clusters. Individuals 1, 5, and 6 are in cluster A, individuals 2 and 3 are in cluster B, and individual 4 is like a separate cluster, C. Leaving statistics aside for a moment, is there any logic in this clustering? Cluster A can be described as having females only, with the highest grades in the class and with two thirds of its constituents of medium height. Cluster B can be described as males, who are the tallest in the class and have the lowest grades. Customer 4, or cluster C, seems to be quite different from cluster B, even though both have male constituents. Cluster C has a constituent who is a male, is short, and has the lowest possible grade. If we wanted a two-segment solution, then perhaps clusters B and C could be joined together.

However, in a three-segment solution, customer 4 is perhaps best suited for cluster C:

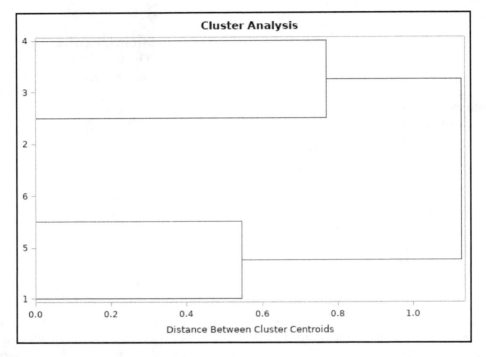

Figure 7.9: Clustering illustration

Clustering methodologies

There are many ways to conduct segmentation. There are various methodologies that one can use to influence how small, big, or distinct the cluster constituents are from each other. Without delving much into the methodology, let's first look at what we mean by the distance between clusters and how it impacts on the results. In *Figure 7.10*, we have four imaginary lines, **L1-L4**, which we will use to understand the distance between clusters. The *x*-axis shows the customer IDs and the *y*-axis shows the distance between cluster centroids. The higher the distance, the further the clusters are from each other. At **L1**, we can see that we don't have a relationship between dissimilar customers. Customers **5** and **6** and **2, 3** have matching values and hence they are paired together, but they don't form a cluster with any other (duplicate/non-matching), customers.

At **L2**, we have one cluster where customers **5, 6** have been paired with customer **1**. Customer **1** is shorter than **5** and **6** and has a lower grade. Customer **1** is a female and that is the one attribute that matches exactly with customers **5** and **6**. By moving from **L1** to **L2**, we have increased the distance between clusters. If we further increase the distance and reach **L3**, we can see that we have one more cluster where customers **2** and **3** have been paired with customer **4**. When we reach **L4**, we are left with only one cluster. This cluster is a combination of clusters formed at **L2** and **L3**. At **L4**, we are at the highest distance between cluster centroids. In essence, if you look at this tree-like view from the top, you are going to see one big cluster encompassing all of the clusters within it. It's only when you look down from the top of the tree that you find a different number of clusters. If you look at the bottom of the tree, you find no clusters because you end up seeing all the observations individually:

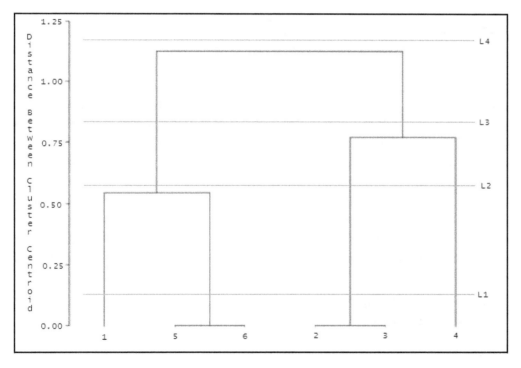

Figure 7.10: Cluster modeling illustration

This is an example of hierarchical clustering. In this form of clustering, we create a tree-like structure (also called a dendrogram) where we start from the bottom when modeling. At the bottom of the X-axis, all the observations are there in their individual clusters. As we move towards the top of the tree, the observations start getting clubbed together based on their similarity or dissimilarity with other observations. The interpretation of the tree may be easier if we start from the top. In non-hierarchical clustering, we begin with a seed (starting point) and estimate how far observations are. Based on the distance, we start clubbing observations together and form clusters. The seed influences the clustering results in a significant way and there are various methodologies that can help identify the seed. However, because of the complexity of identifying the seed and its influence on the output, non-hierarchical clustering isn't as popular as hierarchical clustering.

Segmentation suitability in the current scenario

Prof Cox asked the trio what the output they desired from the segmentation exercise was. They said that it would be best if the data provided the clue. "Fair enough point", said the professor. Segmentation is a discovery exercise rather than a prediction exercise. She asked her question in a different way. Of the following, what is it that you wish to achieve?

1. Understanding how many different types of Vogue customer exist
2. How these customer types are different from each another
3. This segmentation of both existing and past customers
4. Clustering based on a combination of demographic, psychographic, and transactional behavior
5. A manageable number of clusters that don't leave the business with too few or too many clusters

The trio replied in the affirmative to all the preceding objectives. Prof Cox said that she hoped that they realized that the objectives deal with discovering what the data has to say rather than prediction. Segmentation doesn't begin with prediction. Yes, the business usually has a hypothesis about what they believe will go together in a cluster. The hypothesis can be validated using segmentation.

In fact, one of the uses of segmentation is the prediction of customer behavior. Complicated as it may sound, let's think about what Vogue and the investor can do with segmentation. They can:

1. Profile segments
2. Estimate the size of segments
3. Calculate key business metrics such as sales, profitability, and loyalty across various segments
4. Find segments that are growing
5. See how customer profiles are changing based on how segments have evolved over time

After conducting the analysis, Vogue can build a strategy around what their ideal prospect is. Which segment will this prospect belong to once converted as a customer? What are the key needs and wants of the prospect (based on the segment that the prospect's profile matches) that the business can cater to? How successful has the business been in previously attracting similarly profiled prospects? What is the size of each segment going to increase to if the prospect to customer conversion rate of Vogue is applied to the prospect pool? These are all goals that can be met, as segmentation aids the prediction of certain business scenarios. Hence, even though segmentation doesn't start with prediction, one of its goals can be predicting business outcomes.

After having gained a basic understanding of the methodology, the trio felt comfortable with how Prof Cox was intending to help out Vogue. Vogue had data protection agreements in place with Prof Cox and her team. They informed her that someone from their data governance team would be in touch and provide them usernames and passwords to give them access to their remote servers. She and her team would be provided with their own data storage and processing space that would be partitioned off from the rest of the Vogue server operations to maintain client confidentiality and ensure business as usual for Vogue's operations.

Segmentation modeling

When Prof Cox got the data, she realized that it contained details of both past and current customers. She decided to get rid of the past customers. Vogue shouldn't be so keen on spending their energy on seeing how segments have evolved over time. She remembered her early days at the company, where the simple mantra was to get almost any client no matter what their profile was. As long as they had money to invest and passed the regulatory requirement checks, Vogue was more than happy to take them on board. Yes, the trio might be interested in seeing the segmentation comparison over time, but then their immediate task as she understood it was to present the current profiling to the board and their team to draw up a marketing strategy. She ran some descriptive statistics on the data and she found that there were a few outliers. These outliers were clients with extremely high and low AUM values, which, after a few checks with the data governance team, she found were historical test case entries in the system. She made a point of removing these entries. She didn't want such outliers to heavily influence clustering. There would have been a chance that such a customer would not fit in most of the clusters and they might end up in a single cluster representing extreme values. Far worse was the scenario that they would be so different from the rest of the customers and from other outliers that the output may have a lot of clusters with individual records.

She also noticed that some of the data rows contained information about secondary customers. Even where it seemed to be a joint account, Vogue had put in a flag to say which of them was a primary customer. She was only keen on the primary customers as these were the people that Vogue had initially approached while they were prospects, or these were the people that they now interacted with to manage their affairs. None of these primary customers, according to the data governance policy of the company, were guardians or legal representatives of the account holder.

Vogue had not opened up its entire customer database in terms of sharing each and every detail they held about customers and their transactions. The variables that were shared were:

1. Gender
2. Age
3. Education
4. Occupation
5. Customer tenure
6. Country of citizenship
7. Country of birth

8. Risk appetite
9. Investment involvement
10. Complex product held
11. Investment potential
12. AUM
13. Net worth of secondary
14. Fund performance

With all these variables, there was a chance that some of them may be correlated. Correlated variables could heavily bias the cluster structures. Also, in many business scenarios, the number of variables available at the initial modeling stage far exceed the required or the manageable number of variables. The foremost criteria in variable selection should always be relevance to business goals. However, in segmenting credit card customers, let's assume that you have demographic, psychographic, and transactional-level details of customers' credit cards and their product relationship with various other bank departments. The total count of such variables could end up being in the hundreds in a typical data warehouse. Aren't all these three broad categories-demographic, psychographic, and transactional data-relevant? Yes, they are. However, some of the information could be of little additional value, as multiple variables could be pointing to the same conclusion. Variables such as a high credit rating, settled loan accounts, high disposable income, a large savings balance, and an occupation as a doctor may all point to the fact that the customer has a high probability of repaying all of the borrowed money. So, do we need all these variables? Think in terms of hundreds of such variables in a dataset. Shouldn't we save some of our computational resources and modeling time, and have a smaller list of variables to model? Should we be collecting so many data variables and putting effort into maintaining them in a database if they all point to the same factor? Clustering for large datasets requires high computational resources and hence it's best to reduce redundant variables. If the dataset is being specifically maintained for segmentation, then by using fewer variables we can also optimize data collection and storage. Even though 14 variables were shared for analysis, only 7 were considered fit to be considered for modeling. The reason for reducing the number of variables was a mix of data quality and a reluctance to accept insights that were generated using all variables. The final variables selected for analysis are mentioned in the `varclus` procedure in the following paragraph.

One of the ways to reduce the number of variables used is by running `Proc varclus` and looking at the cluster structure. `Proc varclus` is usually used in initial model building, and this is followed by running some other clustering procedures to get the final segmentation model. Let's run the `varclus` procedure for Vogue's dataset. The number of variables is just seven, and not the hundreds that a modeler could be faced with. It would be worthwhile to see whether `varclus` still adds value.

Here is an example of clustering via `Proc varclus`:

```
Proc varclus data=cluster_model;
var age aum risk_appetite fund_performance investment_potential
investment_involvement complex_product;
run;
```

After `varclus` execution, we can see that all the variables are initially put in a single cluster:

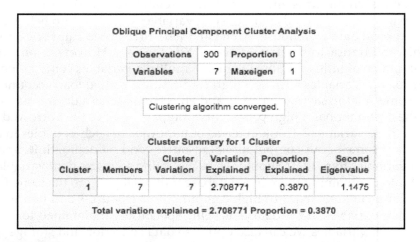

The clustering continues, and now we have a two-cluster solution with further details about the clusters:

Clustering algorithm converged.

Cluster Summary for 2 Clusters

Cluster	Members	Cluster Variation	Variation Explained	Proportion Explained	Second Eigenvalue
1	5	5	2.560532	0.5121	0.9845
2	2	2	1.126536	0.5633	0.8735

Total variation explained = 3.687068 Proportion = 0.5267

2 Clusters		R-squared with			
Cluster	Variable	Own Cluster	Next Closest	1-R**2 Ratio	Variable Label
Cluster 1	AUM	0.1048	0.0019	0.8970	AUM
	Fund_Performance	0.5926	0.0027	0.4085	Fund Performance
	Investment_Potential	0.7995	0.0159	0.2037	Investment Potential
	Investment_Involvement	0.6861	0.0056	0.3157	Investment Involvement
	Complex_Product	0.3776	0.0023	0.6239	Complex Product
Cluster 2	Age	0.5633	0.0224	0.4467	Age
	Risk_Appetite	0.5633	0.0810	0.4752	Risk Appetite

Standardized Scoring Coefficients

Cluster		1	2
Age	Age	0.000000	0.666212
AUM	AUM	0.126406	0.000000
Risk_Appetite	Risk Appetite	0.000000	-.666212
Fund_Performance	Fund Performance	0.300638	0.000000
Investment_Potential	Investment Potential	0.349211	0.000000
Investment_Involvement	Investment Involvement	0.323490	0.000000
Complex_Product	Complex Product	-.239975	0.000000

Figure 7.11: Varclus results

`Proc varclus` starts by assuming that all observations are in one cluster. It continues to split the observations until the second eigenvalue is greater than one. In our case, the clustering process stops after the creation of the second cluster. In the cluster summary for two clusters in *Figure 7.11*, we can see that we are left with two clusters. The first cluster contains five variables and the second cluster two variables. The total variation of 3.68 explained by the solution of two clusters is higher than the total variation of 2.7, which is explained in the one-cluster solution.

In the preceding table with the R squared values, if the variable has a low R square with its nearest cluster, the clusters are expected to be well separated. The last column contains the $(1-R^2_{own})/(1-R^2_{nearest})$ for each variable. Small values of the ratio indicate good clustering. However, the AUM variable in particular has a high value. In the Standardized Scoring Coefficients table, each variable is assigned to one cluster only, hence each row has only one non-zero value. The values can be both positive and negative:

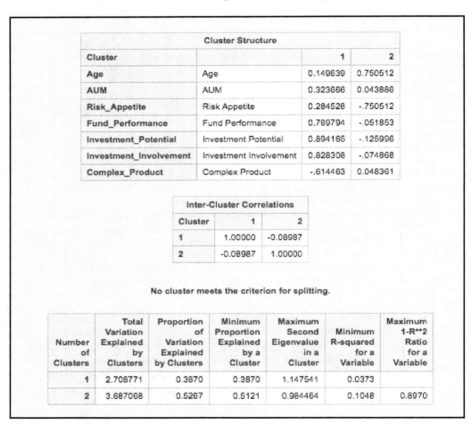

Figure 7.12: Varclus results

In *Figure 7.12*, we can see the structure of the cluster, the inter-cluster correlations, and the history of the clustering solution. The inter-cluster correlation in our business problem is quite low. The model says **no cluster meets the criterion for splitting**. As discussed earlier, this is due to the second eigenvalue being less than one after the creation of the second cluster:

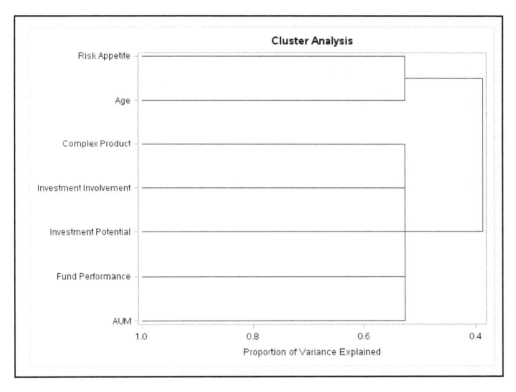

Figure 7.13: Varclus cluster chart

In *Figure 7.13*, we can see the cluster structure. The `varclus` procedure has performed a clustering oblique multiple-group component analysis. The cluster procedure, however, performs the hierarchical clustering of observations. `Proc varclus`, as discussed, is used primarily for variable reduction as it works well with variables that are correlated. Could both these methods produce different clustering solutions to our business problem? Let's try running a cluster procedure and see the differences. We will use the `ward` method as part of the procedure.

Here is clustering via `Proc cluster`:

```
Proc cluster data=cluster_model method=ward ccc pseudo out=tree
plots(MAXPOINTS=300);
    id custid;
    var age aum risk_appetite fund_performance investment_potential
investment_involvement   complex_product;
run;
```

In applying the `cluster` procedure, we have used the `ward` method. Most clustering methods are focused on distance metrics or measures of associations. The `ward` method instead tries to look at the clustering problem from an analysis of a variance problem. It starts with *n* number of clusters with each having size 1. It then aggregates and starts forming larger clusters with a higher number of constituents, and keeps on aggregating until reaching the stage of one large cluster containing all the observations. We have used the max points option in the code due to the high number of clusters being produced. If you look at the covariance matrix in *Figure 7.14*, you can see that, just like in the `varclus` procedure, the second eigenvalue is less than one. After this point, the eigenvalue continues to decline. The proportion of variance explained up to this point is 60.41%:

The CLUSTER Procedure
Ward's Minimum Variance Cluster Analysis

Eigenvalues of the Covariance Matrix

	Eigenvalue	Difference	Proportion	Cumulative
1	1.79942928	0.82292074	0.3916	0.3916
2	0.97650854	0.30676673	0.2125	0.6041
3	0.66974182	0.24944813	0.1458	0.7499
4	0.42029369	0.03629643	0.0915	0.8413
5	0.38399726	0.18238716	0.0836	0.9249
6	0.20161009	0.05812945	0.0439	0.9688
7	0.14348064		0.0312	1.0000

Root-Mean-Square Total-Sample Standard Deviation	0.810208

Root-Mean-Square Distance Between Observations	3.031522

The cluster history table gives us the cubic clustering criterion. At clusters 3 and 4, this goes into negative territory, thereby indicating the presence of potential outliers. Values between 0 and 2 tend to indicate potential clusters. Values greater than 2 or 3 generally indicate good clusters. At cluster 2, we have a value of 1.24. Remember, `varclus` suggested a two-cluster solution:

Number of Clusters	Clusters Joined		Freq	Semipartial R-Square	R-Square	Approximate Expected R-Square	Cubic Clustering Criterion	Pseudo F Statistic	Pseudo t-Squared	Tie
25	CL81	CL63	17	0.0059	.794	.754	7.53	44.3	18.2	
24	CL51	CL41	20	0.0059	.789	.749	7.21	44.7	8.8	
23	CL56	CL34	27	0.0059	.783	.744	6.34	45.3	10.0	
22	CL66	CL35	13	0.0064	.776	.739	6.06	45.9	5.5	
21	CL27	CL45	29	0.0065	.770	.733	5.83	46.6	7.5	
20	CL42	CL29	23	0.0066	.763	.727	5.64	47.5	7.9	
19	CL30	CL57	24	0.0066	.757	.721	5.51	48.5	6.4	
18	CL50	CL90	11	0.0069	.750	.714	5.39	49.7	9.8	
17	CL23	CL40	38	0.0078	.742	.707	5.20	50.8	10.3	
16	CL26	CL67	28	0.0088	.733	.700	4.95	52.0	17.6	
15	CL20	CL28	38	0.0091	.724	.691	4.74	53.4	9.2	
14	CL58	CL17	50	0.0103	.714	.682	4.47	54.8	12.4	
13	CL31	CL16	48	0.0112	.702	.673	4.20	56.4	15.1	
12	CL18	CL32	25	0.0114	.691	.662	4.05	58.5	10.4	
11	CL33	CL47	26	0.0115	.679	.650	4.05	61.3	14.2	
10	CL25	CL21	46	0.0131	.666	.636	4.04	64.4	14.2	
9	CL11	CL24	46	0.0136	.653	.621	4.21	68.4	12.2	
8	CL43	CL22	23	0.0153	.638	.604	4.48	73.4	12.7	
7	CL8	CL19	47	0.0300	.608	.583	3.18	75.6	19.4	
6	CL14	CL9	96	0.0304	.577	.558	2.44	80.3	25.3	
5	CL7	CL12	72	0.0404	.537	.527	1.13	85.5	20.7	
4	CL10	CL6	142	0.0579	.479	.486	-.66	90.6	41.2	
3	CL4	CL13	190	0.0750	.404	.418	-1.2	101	47.0	
2	CL5	CL15	110	0.0906	.313	.297	1.24	136	44.2	
1	CL3	CL2	300	0.3133	.000	.000	0.00		136	

Figure 7.14: Covariance matrix and partial cluster history

Let's look at the CCC graph in *Figure 7.15*. The graph shows a peak at cluster 2 and then the next at cluster 7. This correlates with the partial cluster history shown in *Figure 7.14*. While evaluating the CCC graph, we are on the lookout for spikes of positive values to determine the ideal cluster solution.

We also have the option of using the Pseudo F and the Pseudo T-Squared graphs in *Figure 7.15*. Relatively large values of Pseudo F are indicative of good clusters. This value is the highest at the start of the graph and the value of 136 is the highest, as also observed in *Figure 7.14*. To use Pseudo T-Squared, one should look at sudden and large decreases in value. Clearly, the steepest decrease in value is at cluster 2, with fairly large decreases at clusters 5 and 7 too.

One point that analysts should note is that while using `Proc cluster`, it is quite common for the code to produce the following message: **WARNING: Ties for minimum distance between clusters have been detected at n level(s) in the cluster history**. This happens as discrete data isn't usually as smooth as the textbook example data used. This warning can be ignored. However, there are ways in which the ties can be further explored and one solution is to club a few variables together to reduce the presence of ties. However, we shall not delve into this issue and will ignore the T values in the last column in *Figure 7.14*:

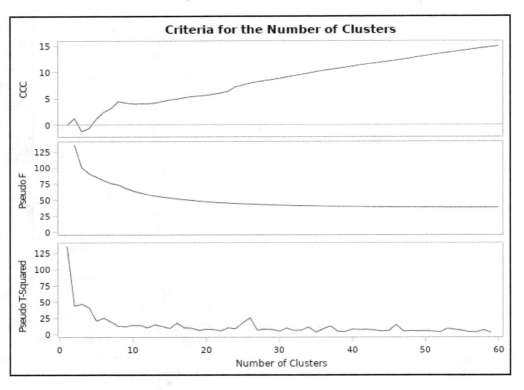

Figure 7.15: CCC, Pseduo F, and Pseduo T-Squared

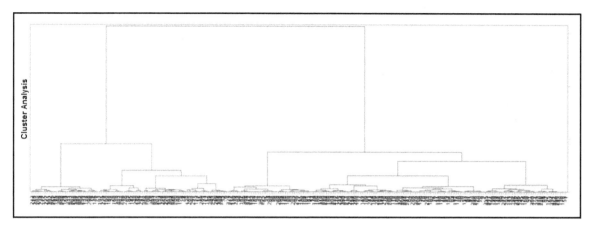

Figure 7.16: PROC cluster chart

We have reached the stage where both the `varclus` and `cluster` procedures are suggesting a two-cluster solution. However, does this meet the business objectives? Is clustering or modeling independent of feedback from the business? Will the hedge fund benefit by having a two-cluster solution?

In any business, a two-factor solution may be perceived as being a sort of binary outcome. Maybe all the good customers are in one cluster and all the bad or undesirable customers, or customer traits, are in the other cluster. This is an overly simplistic solution for most businesses. When Prof Cox looked at the two-cluster solution from an implementation perspective, she wasn't too happy. Clusters 3 and 4 don't make sense either, as they have a negative CCC. The Pseudo T-Squared suggests potentially good clusters at the 5 or 7 level. She felt that having seven clusters might be a bit too much for the business, as they will potentially have to deal with the fallout of having seven segments to deal with in terms of customized strategies. A cluster solution of five looked good to her from the statistical metric support and business implementation perspectives.

A modeler may face this sort of situation in a practical scenario rather than a textbook case. A textbook case will always pitch for a two-factor solution. But is the solution always so simple? Clustering at some level is a business decision that isn't based on a purely statistical basis. The overall aim of segmentation should be to find clusters of customers that have a statistical rationale, but also to segment the customers into a manageable number of clusters that help produce effective strategies. Prof Cox decided to go for the five-cluster solution and see what impact it had on the segments generated.

Unfortunately, the SAS University Edition on which the modeling has been done for the book doesn't support some visual features that help to effectively showcase the output of `Proc tree`. However, the full edition of SAS software produces a more visually appealing chart of the procedure. For our current consumption, only the tabular output has been shared in *Figure 7.17*. The procedure is going to help us to assign the cluster number to each of our customer IDs. This is an important step, as after this we can go ahead and try to understand the profiling of our cluster constituents.

This is a `Proc tree` five-cluster specification:

```
Proc tree data = tree out = cluster_output nclusters=5;
    Id custid;
    Copy age aum risk_appetite fund_performance investment_potential
        investment_involvement complex_product;
Run;

proc print data=cluster_output(drop=clusname);
run;
```

Obs	Custid	Age	AUM	Risk_Appetite	Fund_Performance	Investment_Potential	Investment_Involvement	Complex_Product	CLUSTER
1	11	2	4	2	2	3	2	0	1
2	16	2	4	2	2	3	2	0	1
3	9	1	1	1	1	1	1	1	2
4	22	1	1	1	1	1	1	1	2
5	3	2	4	2	2	3	3	0	1
6	27	2	4	2	2	3	3	0	1
7	8	3	2	3	3	3	3	0	3
8	32	3	2	3	3	3	3	0	3
9	12	1	2	3	1	2	1	1	4
10	41	1	2	3	1	2	1	1	4
11	21	1	3	2	1	1	1	1	5
12	51	1	3	2	1	1	1	1	5
13	1	1	3	1	1	1	1	1	5
14	53	1	3	1	1	1	1	1	5
15	34	1	1	3	1	1	1	1	4
16	54	1	1	3	1	1	1	1	4
17	31	1	2	2	1	1	1	1	4
18	55	1	2	2	1	1	1	1	4
19	28	1	1	2	1	1	1	1	4
20	58	1	1	2	1	1	1	1	4

Figure 7.17: Customer cluster allocation

Although there was a fair bit of confidence in going with the model generated up to now, there were a lot of other alternate models considered in the build phase. The models differed in the type of clustering used, the data standardization used, and the mix of variables used to build the models. Let's produce an alternative model using the following code:

```
/*Age and AUM have been dropped in the model*/
Proc varclus data=cluster_model;
    Var risk_appetite fund_performance investment_potential
investment_involvement    complex_product;
run;
```

The output in *Figure 7.18* shows that the model did not produce any splitting and suggested a single-cluster solution. This happened after two key variables were dropped from the modeling solution:

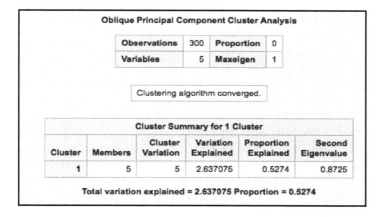

The chart reconfirms that we are left with a single cluster solution after the omission of two variables from the alternate model code:

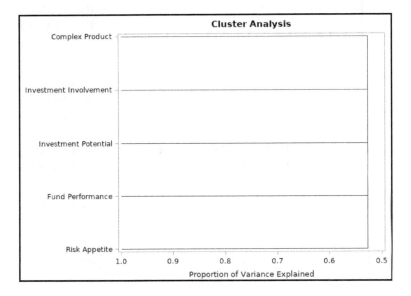

Figure 7.18: Alternate modeling attempt

Prof Cox gave the five clusters a name and recommended a strategic direction for Vogue to take regarding the clusters. As a modeler, the business expects that the model built is statistically robust. It can be validated and is documented with a high degree of governance during the build, approval, and implementation phases. However, modelers at times tend to forget how simple summaries of the model can help to create a greater understanding of the model and help trust the insights generated. The next few pages are dedicated to showcasing how Prof. Cox summarized the output from the model:

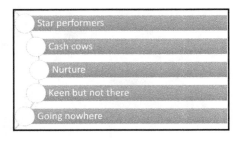

Figure 7.19: Segment profile as defined by the modeler

She further described the segments in *Figure 7.19* as:

- **Star performers**: These customers are the ideal age group. Probably the happiest Vogue customers in terms of returns on investment. They have a high level of AUM and there is a potential for further investment. They are medium risk takers and have no preference regarding simple or complex products. They are the smallest cluster of the five.

- **Cash cows**: They are split across the age groups. They behave like cash cows for Vogue as they have low-to-medium AUM, yet are large in number and help to sustain the business. They are involved in their decisions and aren't risk takers. 76% of them have experienced low returns with Vogue. However, due to their low risk-taking preferences, and in general, lack of inertia to move to competitors, they are thought to be good for the business in the long run. 18% of them have experienced medium returns and this percentage could be further increased in the years to come.

- **Nurture**: They are split across age the groups and have a medium-to-high-potential to invest. They have experienced a mixed level of fund performance. Their risk appetite is quite high and they don't tend to have complex products. The most promising feature of this segment is that they have low-to-mid-level AUM. Given their potential to invest, with a bit more focus this segment could become a more exciting segment for Vogue. After all, this is their second biggest segment.

- **Keen but not there**: A fairly big cluster of younger individuals with lower involvement, low fund performance, low potential to invest, and low-to-mid-AUM. These are high risk takers who tend to have complex products. They could also benefit from being nurtured, but they are probably not mature enough from a prospective client perspective. This is a segment that Vogue should continue to watch out for and be patient with.

- **Going nowhere**: This segment has young members. They have low involvement in investing and lower potential. The lower potential might stem from the fact that they already tend to have high AUM with Vogue. However, the predominantly low fund performance that they might be facing could be a factor in them expressing lower investment potential. Vogue needs to look at this segment and see if relationship managers need to focus less on these customers.

So, how did Prof Cox define and describe the segments? The output dataset produced as part of the proc tree code in *Figure 7.17* is where the cluster name is stored against each customer. However, the cluster name is a number and isn't a descriptive field describing the characteristics of the cluster/segment. Prof Cox had to produce some profiling tables from the output dataset. Let's look at them:

Age

Cluster	No of Customers		
	Young	Mid	Senior
1	14	22	2
2	36	36	24
3	30	18	24
4	42	6	
5	35	10	1

AUM

Cluster	No. of customers			
	Low	Med	Good	High
1		1	6	31
2	25	59	12	
3	30	33	9	
4	28	20		
5		1	35	10

Risk appetite

Cluster	No. of customers		
	Low	Med	High
1		32	6
2	70	25	1
3	13	6	53
4		11	37
5	13	24	9

Fund performance

| | No. of customers | | |
Cluster	Low	Med	High
1	1	8	29
2	73	18	5
3	20	13	39
4	39	6	3
5	33	12	1

Investment potential

| | No. of customers | | |
Cluster	Low	Med	High
1	1	2	35
2	84	12	
3	2	30	40
4	27	21	
5	42	4	

Investment involvement

Cluster	% of customers
1	13%
2	32%
3	24%
4	16%
5	15%

Complex Product

	No. of customers	
Cluster	No.	Yes
1	19	19
2	22	74
3	55	17
4	6	42
5	8	38

Cluster	% of customers
1	13%
2	32%
3	24%
4	16%
5	15%

Cluster summary

Cluster	Age	AUM	Risk appetite	Fund performance
1	Young to medium	High	Medium	High
2	Split across	Low to medium	Low	Low
3	Split across	Low to medium	High	Split across
4	Young	Low to medium	High	Low
5	Young	High	Split Across	Low

Cluster summary continued:

Cluster	Investment potential	Investment involvement	Complex product
1	High	Medium to high	No preference
2	Low	High	Yes
3	Medium to high	Medium to high	No
4	Low to medium	Low	Yes
5	Low	Low	Yes

Cluster	Segment
1	Star performers
2	Cash cows
3	Nurture
4	Keen but not there
5	Going nowhere

Figure 7.20: Segment allocation details

As you can see in *Figure 7.20*, we need to develop some profiling tables to understand the characteristics of our segment constituents. We can already see that the clusters differ between the mix of age groups, assets under management, and risk appetite. By adding profiling info using other variables for clustering, we can come up with descriptions of the segments. What Prof Cox has done is to go a step beyond and name the segments. Naming the segments is an easy way to remember the key characteristics of the segments. Some businesses prefer to name segments in a way that explains what each segment means to their strategy. There is no specific scientific way to describe and name a segment. The insights from profiling should make business sense, and the naming of segments should lead to the achievement of some business goals. Having named her segments and being ready with her proposed strategy for the segments, Prof Cox looked forward to sharing the modeling results with Vogue.

Summary

We have looked at two analysis methodologies in this chapter. MBA analysis and segmentation. Both use datasets related to time series, but they transform the data and don't consider the time element explicitly as part of the analysis. In the MBA analysis, we saw that sequence was a sort of proxy for time series. We generated insights by focusing on business problems that were the subject of modeling. MBA lacks the statistical depth and rigor that clustering has. However, neither are strictly statistically-driven analysis scenarios. With MBA, we showcased how it makes intuitive sense to evaluate the association between the products and services offered by a bank and leverage the information. In segmentation via clustering, we showcased how the number of clusters generated differed from the preferred statistical information available to us from two different methodologies. Yet, we decided to go for an approach that made business sense and could be supported by showcasing the analysis conducted.

Other Books You May Enjoy

If you enjoyed this book, you may be interested in these other books by Packt:

Big Data Analytics with SAS
David Pope

ISBN: 978-1-78829-090-6

- Configure a free version of SAS in order do hands-on exercises dealing with data management, analysis, and reporting.
- Understand the basic concepts of the SAS language which consists of the data step (for data preparation) and procedures (or PROCs) for analysis.
- Make use of the web browser based SAS Studio and iPython Jupyter Notebook interfaces for coding in the SAS, DS2, and FedSQL programming languages.
- Understand how the DS2 programming language plays an important role in Big Data preparation and analysis using SAS
- Integrate and work efficiently with Big Data platforms like Hadoop, SAP HANA, and cloud foundry based systems.

IBM SPSS Modeler Essentials
Jesus Salcedo, Keith McCormick

ISBN: 978-1-78829-111-8

- Understand the basics of data mining and familiarize yourself with Modeler's visual programming interface
- Import data into Modeler and learn how to properly declare metadata
- Obtain summary statistics and audit the quality of your data
- Prepare data for modeling by selecting and sorting cases, identifying and removing duplicates, combining data files, and modifying and creating fields
- Assess simple relationships using various statistical and graphing techniques
- Get an overview of the different types of models available in Modeler
- Build a decision tree model and assess its results
- Score new data and export predictions

Leave a review - let other readers know what you think

Please share your thoughts on this book with others by leaving a review on the site that you bought it from. If you purchased the book from Amazon, please leave us an honest review on this book's Amazon page. This is vital so that other potential readers can see and use your unbiased opinion to make purchasing decisions, we can understand what our customers think about our products, and our authors can see your feedback on the title that they have worked with Packt to create. It will only take a few minutes of your time, but is valuable to other potential customers, our authors, and Packt. Thank you!

Index

www.ingramcontent.com/pod-product-compliance
Lightning Source LLC
Chambersburg PA
CBHW080627060326
40690CB00021B/4839